NATIONAL
GEOGRAPHIC
TRAVELER

sicily

sicily

by Tim Jepson
photography by Tino Soriano

National Geographic
Washington, D.C.

CONTENTS

Pages 2–3: The Norman Castello di Venere and Torre Pepoli can be viewed from Erice.
Left: The sea at Aci Castello offers a bit of pure magic on Sicily's east coast.

TRAVELING WITH EYES OPEN

Alert travelers go with a purpose and leave with a benefit. If you travel responsibly, you can help support wildlife conservation, historic preservation, and cultural enrichment in the places you visit. You can enrich your own travel experience as well.

To be a geo-savvy traveler:

- Recognize that your presence has an impact on the places you visit.

- Spend your time and money in ways that sustain local character. (Besides, it's more interesting that way.)

- Value the destination's natural and cultural heritage.

- Respect the local customs and traditions.

- Express appreciation to local people about things you find interesting and unique to the place: its nature and scenery, music and food, historic villages and buildings.

- Vote with your wallet: Support the people who support the place, patronizing businesses that make an effort to celebrate and protect what's special there. Seek out local shops, restaurants, and inns. Use tour operators who love their home—who love taking care of it and showing it off. Avoid businesses that detract from the character of the place.

- Enrich yourself, taking home memories and stories to tell, knowing that you have contributed to the preservation and enhancement of the destination.

That is the type of travel now called geotourism, defined as "tourism that sustains or enhances the geographical character of a place—its environment, culture, aesthetics, heritage, and the well-being of its residents." To learn more, visit National Geographic's Center for Sustainable Destinations at *nationalgeographic.com/travel/sustainable.*

sicily

ABOUT THE AUTHOR & THE PHOTOGRAPHER

Tim Jepson has been a passionate and lifelong devotee of Italy. Since graduating from Oxford University, he has spent long periods of time living and traveling in the country and five years as a writer and journalist in Rome. Over the years he has written some 15 books on the country, as well as numerous articles for the *Daily Telegraph, Vogue, Condé Nast Traveller,* and other publications. He wrote *National Geographic Traveler: Italy* as well as *National Geographic Traveler: Naples & Southern Italy* among other guidebooks.

Now based in London, Jepson continues to visit Italy regularly, and, as a keen hiker and outdoor enthusiast, he takes a particular interest in the rural areas. He also revels in Italy's more sedentary pleasures—the food, wine, art, and culture.

Jepson has also worked on Italian programs for the BBC and commercial television, and his career has included spells in a slaughterhouse, on building sites, and as a musician playing piano and guitar in streets and bars across Europe.

Born and raised in Barcelona, Spain, **Tino Soriano** divides his work between photojournalism and travel photography. He has received a First Prize from the World Press Photo Foundation as well as awards from UNESCO, Fujifilm, and Fotopres.

In addition to Sicily, since 1988, Soriano has photographed in Spain (Catalonia, Andalucia, Galicia), France, Italy, Portugal, Scotland, and South Africa on assignments for National Geographic. His work has also appeared in *Geo, Merian, Der Spiegel, Paris Match, La Vanguardia,* and *El Pais* as well as many other major magazines around the world. He was involved in making three documentaries for the National Geographic Channel.

Soriano has also written several books, including *El Futuro Existe,* a story about children with cancer. He also regularly lectures, teaches workshops at the University of Barcelona, and serves as an expert on National Geographic Expeditions trips.

Charting Your Trip

Few places surpass Sicily, an island with all the great lures of Italy—the art, culture, food, wine, people, and landscapes—but with the many added attractions that come from a long and colorful history, and the unique social and cultural heritage of a Mediterranean land that has always stood magnificently apart from the European and Italian mainstream.

By the same token, the historical and other reasons that have set Sicily apart have also contributed to its present-day circumstances. Visitors often have to approach the island in a different way from the more cosmopolitan cities and regions of central and northern Italy. Life here is more traditional, the economy is weaker, people can be poorer, hotels less grand, travel slower. Sicily can be a little rough around the edges and, outside the main tourist sites, not necessarily equipped for visitors.

The Roman mosaics at the Villa Imperiale del Casale are a highlight of any visit.

How to Get Around

Railroads and public transit will take you only so far, and often at a gentle pace. To come to grips with the island and its many rural highlights requires a car (see Travelwise p. 160–161). Still, be prepared for slow going and distances to be greater than they appear on the map, especially in the interior, the south, and the Madonie and Nebrodi Mountains of the north. The exceptions are the north (A9–A20) and central (A19) highways. Consider which of the two major airports—Palermo or Catania (both served by airports throughout Europe)—are best as starting and finishing points. Note that navigation and parking in medieval towns or traffic-filled cities can be challenging.

Sicily is ringed with islands. This brings ferries into play (see Travelwise p. 160–161). Cars are often unnecessary on smaller islands (walking and biking are good options), and will make ferry crossings more expensive and time-consuming. Therefore, plan car-rental arrangements carefully, and ensure that you are able to pick up and drop off cars in different centers.

If You Have a Week

The logistical considerations associated with a visit to Sicily mean you should not try to see too much, and that you should plan so that you don't waste valuable time traveling from place to place. Consider your priorities: What do you most want to see—Sicily's Greek and Roman heritage in places like Agrigento, small baroque towns such as Noto, the mountainous redoubts of the Nebrodi and Madonie, set pieces such as Etna or Stromboli, or the beaches of Cefalù and the resort town of Taormina? These are the highlights, but it's tough to see them all in a week.

Palermo makes the best start for a general trip, while Catania is better placed for a tour that focuses more narrowly on Taormina, Etna, Syracuse, and the baroque towns of the southeast. Palermo is Sicily's capital, but on a short trip you don't need to spend more than a night here and—unless your hotel has parking—nor should you book a car until you want to leave the city. See the cathedral, La Martorana, and Palazzo dei Normanni, and walk the old center, taking in some of the churches and the Ballarò and Vucciria markets. If you are interested in archaeology and want some context for visits to the island's great Greek sites, head to the Museo Archeologico Regionale. Spend late afternoon on a trip to Monreale or the Catacombe dei Cappuccini.

From Palermo, drive directly on the good A29 highway to the great Greek temple at **Segesta** (47 miles/76 km) before continuing to overnight in the magical hill town of **Erice.** Drive south to **Agrigento,** unmissable for the Greek temples and museum in the Valle dei Templi. A drive from Erice to Agrigento should take in the coast and salt pans en route to **Marsala** and the archaeological site at **Selinunte.**

After a morning in the Valle dei Templi, drive to **Piazza Armerina** (59 miles/ 95 km) for the mosaics of the Roman Villa Imperiale del Casale. Continue to **Syracuse**—this would be a very long day from Agrigento—basing yourself in the pretty old quarter of Ortygia, probably for two nights, allowing time to explore its old streets before visiting the town's archaeological zone.

Next day drive north (about 65 miles/105 km), spending the best part of the day exploring **Etna** and concluding at **Taormina,** a good base for two nights. Alternatively, take a tour of Etna from Taormina, but in either case allow time to enjoy this sophisticated resort town. Taormina is well situated for flying out of nearby **Catania,** but if you have to fly out of Palermo, plot a scenic drive through

NOT TO BE MISSED:

Visitor Information

Start with the Italian State Tourist Office, or ENIT (*italia.it* or *italian tourism.com*). Other official sites are *visitpalermo.it, palermotourism.com* and *pti.regione.sicilia.it.* Use *turismo* and *ufficio informazioni* plus town name in searches on smaller areas. For museums, *www.museionline.it;* for parks and reserves, *parks.it;* for trains, *trenitalia.it.*

Essential Etiquette

Sicily is more conservative in most areas of life than northern and central Italy. Dress, especially for the older generation, is more modest. Follow this lead: In churches, legs and shoulders should be covered. Sicilians are also likely to be more formal and reserved. In rural areas, people may be relatively unaccustomed to visitors. English is less likely to be spoken.

Officialdom can move slowly—patience may be required in banks, stores, at hotel check-in, at car-rental desks, buying transit tickets, and so forth. Italians can also be assertive in lines—do not necessarily expect "fairness."

"Please" is *per favore; prego* means "you're welcome"; say *mi scusi* for "excuse me" or "I'm sorry," but *permesso* when you wish to pass somebody. Do not use the informal *ciao* as a greeting or farewell, but *buon giorno* (good day) or *buona sera* (good afternoon).

the mountains to **Cefalù** via the A20 (119 miles/180 km) or **Randazzo** and **Gangi.** A night in Cefalù allows time to wander the small old quarter and visit the town's Norman cathedral before the drive on the A9–A29 through Palermo to the airport (a total of 65 miles/105 km).

If You Have More Time

On a longer visit, spend additional time in the destinations mentioned above and add in a few more. Allow two days in **Palermo,** adding San Giovanni degli Eremiti to your itinerary and extending your walking tour to include the emerging Kalsa district, full of cafés and small galleries, and the Galleria Regionale di Sicilia south of the harbor. See both Monreale and the Catacombe dei Cappuccini. Then drive to **Segesta** (about 53 miles/85 km) and detour slightly north for the beaches near **Castellammare del Golfo** and the coastline around the **Riserva Naturale dello Zingaro,** which has hiking possibilities and a rich history tied to its tuna fishing industry.

Local Logistics

Sicily generally lags behind the rest of Italy in its infrastructure. On the ground, this may mean fewer ATMs, say, or slower trains and poor roads, especially in the hinterland. Most stores, banks, post offices, churches, visitor centers, and museums shut from about 1 p.m. to 5 p.m., especially in summer, before opening again until 7:30 p.m. or 8 p.m.

In bars, pay for what you want at the cash desk and then take your chit to the bar and place your order. Public restrooms (*il bagno*) are scarce and often in poor shape.

After **Erice,** if you have time for an overnight, visit one of the **Egadi Islands,** about 30 miles (48 km) west. **Levanzo** is the closest, **Marettimo** the most striking, with excellent hiking. Continue south, taking in **Mozia** (30 miles/48 km south of Erice) and **Selinunte** en route to **Agrigento** (70 miles/113 km south of Selinunte). After Agrigento, idle east, perhaps with time in **Enna** (50 miles/81 km from Agrigento), a hill town. After the mosaics at nearby **Piazza Armerina,** head south for about 90 miles (145 km) and allow two days to explore the baroque towns of **Noto, Ragusa,** and **Modica,** and the **Iblei** uplands. You might use **Syracuse** as a base before heading off for two days in or near **Taormina** (70 miles/ 113 km north of Syracuse), with at least a day to

In southeast Sicily, people unwind at a seaside café in Ortygia, Syracuse's charming island.

see and climb **Etna** (14 miles/23 km southwest of Taormina). The Circumetnea railroad offers a nice tour of the volcano's lower slopes.

Any longer tour should include a day or so in the **Nebrodi Mountains** (about 40 miles/60 km northwest of Etna), before you head roughly the same distance to the north coast at **Milazzo** to catch a ferry to the **Isole Eolie,** or Lipari Islands (2 hours to the main island of **Lipari,** 5 hours to **Stromboli;** hydrofoils make the trip in half the time). The standout experience: viewing the eruptions of Stromboli at night.

When to Visit

The best times to visit Sicily are mid-April to the end of May and mid-September to the end of October. The first of these is preferable, because this is late spring, when the countryside is at its best and temperatures in the cities are at their kindest. This period is also around Easter, when Sicily sees many well-attended colorful festivals and Holy Week processions.

Note, though, that mountain weather can still be quite cold and changeable. Mid-September to October may offer more rain-free days and more reliable, higher temperatures, but the landscapes will be baked brown, having been subjected to the high sun of July and August. This sun, and the extreme temperatures, make summer a bad time to visit.

History & Culture

The temple at Segesta dates from the fifth century B.C. Opposite: Life in Petralia Sottana and other hill towns has changed little over the centuries.

Sicily Today

One of the great enigmas, Sicily is an island of incomparable beauty and cultural wealth—yet it is also a world apart, separated from mainstream European life by a tumultuous history that has left a troubled present and the monuments of a glorious past. The result is a society rich in ambiguity and an island almost unmatched for the myriad pleasures of its art, architecture, food, wine, landscapes, and outdoor activities.

Sicily's location has long been its blessing and its curse. At one time, when the known world barely extended beyond the Mediterranean, it was at the crossroads of Africa and Europe, a conduit for trade and peoples—and a prize for all the covetous states that have risen and fallen in this region. The island was once a paradise

A wedding draws family together at the church of San Giorgio, Modica.

on Earth, a wealthy and fertile enclave of teeming seas, olive trees, citrus groves, vineyards, and rolling wheat fields. For three transcendent periods—under Greek, Arab, and Norman domination—the island was the cornerstone of the Mediterranean. Yet throughout its history, it was also ruled— usually badly—by foreigners.

Virtually all of Sicily's triumphs and present travails can be attributed to its invaders: Greeks, Romans, Vandals, Carthaginians, Arabs, Normans, French, British, Spanish, and the Italian state, the last as much an ineffectual impostor to many Sicilians as its predecessors.

The degree to which Sicily has been misruled, and the poverty, alienation, enforced self-sufficiency, and mistrust of authority it has engendered, goes a long way to explaining the complex nature of Sicilians. Stereotyping is always a dangerous game, but there is no doubt that Sicilians are a curious hybrid, a melting pot of an ancient race—itself split between the "Greek" east and "Arab" west—and the other peoples who invaded the island.

"Sicily is the schoolroom model of Italy for beginners, with every Italian quality and defect magnified, exasperated, and brightly colored."

The Sicilian character is a heady mix, at once brooding, suspicious, cynical, insular, fatalistic, and withdrawn, but also generous, sensuous, stoic, bright, calculating, curious, deeply cultured, and industrious. Sicilians have invariably been subjects not citizens, have felt oppressed rather than championed, and have cultivated a powerful sense of pride, vanity, and honor to confront the uncomfortable fact of their subjugation.

Misrule has engendered a mistrust of authority, and with it a tendency to eschew many of the more conventional structures of society. Loyalty is first and foremost to one's family, as in much of Italy, though as Luigi Barzini, author of *The Italians* (1964), has observed: "Sicily is the schoolroom model of Italy for beginners, with every Italian quality and defect magnified, exasperated, and brightly colored."

The reluctance to take on social and civic roles, and the perceived absence of a reliable and trustworthy central authority, are partial reasons for the existence of the Mafia (see pp. 52–53), still a presence in Sicily though not as dramatic as portrayed in the media. Certainly no casual visitor will feel its effect, and in the past decade there have been signs both of a weakening of organized crime and a change in the attitude of ordinary Sicilians and the Italian state—once passive at best and complicit at worse—to an organization that once held both in thrall.

Signs of change in Sicily's economy are more elusive. The desperate poverty of the past century, when millions of Sicilians emigrated, is mostly gone, but Sicily still has Italy's highest levels of unemployment and illiteracy; a per capita income half that of northern Italy; growing immigration from North Africa (see sidebar below); and, with a quarter of workers employed by the state, a bureaucracy and culture of *clientelismo* (patronage in return for political and other favors) that often stifle private initiative.

Tourism is now being championed as a panacea for Sicily's economic ills. What could be more tempting than Europe's finest mosaics at Piazza Armerina; the Greek remains of Syracuse, Agrigento, Segesta, and Selinunte; the lure of resorts like Taormina; the many glories of Palermo; the cathedrals of Monreale and Cefalù; the medieval beauty of Erice; the brooding majesty of Etna; and the charms of the Isole Eolie and other islands? Ironically, it could be Sicily's latest invaders—its visitors—who prove its ultimate salvation.

Island Front Line

Illegal immigration and refugees from North Africa are a contentious issue in Italy, especially in Sicily. Most migrants head for Lampedusa (see pp. 100–101), 156 miles (250 km) south of the Sicilian mainland but only 70 miles (113 km) from Tunisia in North Africa. Numbers total some 15,000 a year, plus 2,000 more that the United Nations estimates drown in the attempt. The population of Lampedusa is about 5,000.

Law changes in 2009 meant many migrants were detained on Lampedusa instead of being sent to the mainland. This in turn led to overcrowding and rioting by the immigrants in temporary centers, scenes that islanders felt threatened their tourism industry. Plans to expand and build more centers caused uproar on the island; its mayor, Dino de Rubis, echoed the islanders' determination that Lampedusa would not become a "prison island."

The Land

Sicily is the Mediterranean's largest island. Its breathtaking landscapes form a triangle (the ancients called Sicily Trinacria, or the Three Corners) measuring 9,926 square miles (25,709 sq km) just 1.8 miles (3 km) from the Italian mainland and 87 miles (140 km) from Africa. To the east, its shores are washed by the Ionian Sea, to the north by the Tyrrhenian, and to the south by the Mediterranean. About 62 percent of the island is hilly, with 24 percent classified as mountainous and the remaining 14 percent plain or lowland. The principal mountains, the Appennino Siculo, reach 6,491 feet (1,979 m) and parallel the north coast for about 125 miles (200 km). The three massifs—the Peloritani, Nebrodi, and Madonie—are a geologic continuation of the Apennines that form a spine on the Italian peninsula.

Western Sicily is more complex: a mixture of limestone outcrops, clay escarpments, and swaths of olives and vineyards stretched across the plains of Trapani and Marsala. In the east, the fertile agricultural plains of Catania give way to the Monti Iblei in the island's southeast corner, an enclave of tabletop uplands and steep-sided valleys.

The rolling interior is another landscape entirely: a region that the writer Giuseppe Tomasi di Lampedusa called "the real Sicily," a sort of petrified sea "aridly undulating to the horizon in hill after hill, comfortless and irrational . . . conceived apparently in a delirious moment of creation." The interior is where Sicily's acute lack of water is most apparent (the island has erratic rainfall and poorly managed water distribution, made worse by centuries of deforestation). There are few rivers; those in the north rush for a few days and then remain dry for much of the year. The most important rivers—the Dittaino, Simeto, and Gornalunga—drain and irrigate the plains around Catania in the east.

All of Sicily's natural features pale beside Mount Etna, a majestic geologic anomaly that is both the island's highest point (at about 10,900 feet/3,323 m) and Europe's most

Scopello, an inviting small village, sits on the rocky coastline above the Gulf of Castellammare.

active volcano. Its presence is due to Sicily's position astride major faults in the Earth's crust, making the island prone to occasionally catastrophic earthquakes. The same faults account for the Isole Eolie (Lipari Islands) off the north coast, where the island of Stromboli is a dramatic volcanic presence.

Parts of the coast have been spoiled by industry and pollution, around Gela and Augusta especially, but other areas remain delightful: the Zingaro reserve and Capo San Vito west of Palermo, for example, and the beaches of Noto Marina and Cala Bernardo (south of Syracuse), Porto Palo (near Selinunte), Cefalù and Marina di Modica, Cava d'Aliga, and Donnalucata.

Vegetation

Sicily's vegetation is as rich and varied as its landscapes. Mild winters, hot summers, fertile soils, varying altitude, and numerous habitats create a profusion of trees, plants, and flowers. Almond, peach, orange, and other citrus fruits flourish, providing creamy, scented blossoms in spring, along with the silvery green of olives, the red and white of oleander, the perfumed white stars of jasmine, and the bold blooms of bougainvillea.

Wheat on the plains lends its own palette, from the green of winter shoots to the dark ocher of the ripening crop. Introduced plants include cork (at Niscemi); manna ash (near Castelbuono); and papyrus, cultivated since Greek times on the Ciane River near Syracuse.

In the mountains, beech, pine, holm oak, chestnut, and other trees flourish in the woodlands, while the drier slopes below support prickly pears, cacti, palms, agaves, capers, and the classic plants of Mediterranean scrub (*maquis*) such as myrtle, euphorbia, and arbutus.

Etna has its own fecund vegetation—1,500 species in all—from the rare Etna ragwort to plants such as the silver-gray lichen, which manage to survive on still warm lava. And everywhere in the countryside in spring are spectacular swaths of wildflowers: poppies, orchids, irises, narcissi, and many, many more. ■

Food & Drink

Food in Sicily stands out, even in a country with as celebrated and varied a cuisine as Italy's. Numerous historical and geographic strands come together to create a culinary tradition that combines dishes from as far back as the ancient Greeks, Arabs, and Normans, and from as far afield as Spain, Greece, North Africa, and the Middle East. Added to the mix are Sicily's myriad natural ingredients, the bounty of a fertile land and teeming sea.

The ancient Greek city of Syracuse—once the culinary capital of the classical world—produced the West's first school of chefs and first recorded cookbook: Mithaecus' fifth-century B.C. *Lost Art of Cooking*. Many of Sicily's distinctive sweet-and-sour dishes, notably *caponata* (slow-cooked vegetables, olives, raisins, and pine nuts), may well date from Greek times.

Other dishes go back to the late eighth century and the arrival of the Arabs, who introduced innovative culinary and agricultural

Fishmongers at work in the noisy Vucciria (Voices) market in the *centro storico* district of Palermo

practices, as well as rice, citrus fruits, couscous, cane sugar, cinnamon, saffron—and ice cream and sorbets, made from the snow found year-round near the summit of Mount Etna. Later, Sicily's Spanish rulers would introduce tomatoes and chocolate from the New World.

The Arabs' sweet tooth accounted for many of Sicily's distinctive desserts and candies, notably *cassata* (sweetened ricotta cheese, sponge cake, candied fruit, and almond paste), which takes its name from the Arabic *quas-at,* the bowl in which it was made. They may also have had a hand in the cannoli, pastry shells filled with ricotta, chocolate, and candied fruit.

From the Arabs, too, came marzipan, used to make *pasta reale* and *frutta*

Martorana—marzipan shaped and painted to resemble various foods; and "virgins' breasts" *(minni di vergini)* or "chancellor's buttocks" *(fedde del cancellerie).* Frutta was made traditionally by nuns, in particular the nuns of Palermo's La Martorana convent, hence its name.

The Arabs were probably also responsible for one of Sicily's key pasta dishes, *pasta con le sarde* (with sardines, wild fennel, olive oil, raisins, saffron, and pine nuts). It is said the chefs with the Arabs' first invading army devised the dish simply by throwing together the ingredients that were at hand as the army marched through the countryside.

Available ingredients also accounted for the island's other pasta classic, *pasta alla Norma* (with sun-ripened tomatoes, salted ricotta, and eggplant), which may take its name from the fact that it was simply the basic, or "normal," pasta dish in eastern Sicily.

Whatever the derivation, Sicilian food remains wedded to simple ingredients and a peasant culinary tradition. Fish and seafood—notably sardines, clams *(vongole),* anchovies *(acciughe),* tuna *(tonno),* and swordfish *(pesce spada)*—are more common than and generally superior to meat. The exceptions are the lamb *(agnello)* and pork *(maiale)* from the Madonie, Nebrodi, and other mountain regions. From these same regions come superb cheeses, especially ricotta, *caciocavallo* (like a mature mozzarella), and pecorinos (hard sheep's milk cheeses).

Vegetables, particularly eggplant *(melanzane),* often take the place of meat in pasta and other dishes, which rely for zest on raisins, capers *(capperi),* wild fennel *(finocchio),* herbs, seeds, garlic, and other inexpensive gifts of field and forest. Beans, nuts, and pulses such as fava *(fave),* pistachios *(pistacchi),* almonds *(mandorle),* chickpeas *(ceci),* and lentils *(lenticchie)* are also common. Rice, less prevalent than it was, still appears in many excellent street and snack foods, notably as *arancini* (breaded and deep-fried rice balls with peas, ham, or meat ragout).

Innovative producers and new techniques have revolutionized Sicily's wine industry.

Wine

Archaeologists suggest that wine has been produced in Sicily since at least 1400 B.C., though it was the Normans who established viticulture as an important sector of the island's economy.

Sicily's climate and terrain are good, almost too good, for making wine, and the intense sun, long summers, and high and dependable yields meant that until recently the island produced quantity rather than quality where wine was concerned. Many wines were strong *vini da taglio,* literally "wines of cut," as they were produced in bulk and sent to "cut" with weaker wines of France and northern Italy to boost their color and alcoholic content.

There has been a dramatic change in Sicilian winemaking. Advanced techniques of viticulture and viniculture have been introduced, and the island, especially around Mount Etna, is now one of the world's most exciting wine destinations. It has been dubbed the "new California," and a measure of its success is the clamor by European and other wine companies to buy land and plant vineyards on Sicilian soil.

Italy's complicated and outmoded system of classifying wines is of little practical use when trying to assess quality. Best to ignore the ratings, therefore, and follow a particular producer or stick to restaurants' house wines *(vino della casa),* which are generally far better in Sicily than in much of rural Italy.

The reasons for Sicily's dramatic improvement are the same as elsewhere in Italy, namely that the land's natural advantages for wine-growing finally have been matched by innovative winemakers prepared to use modern techniques and native and foreign varietals.

Special account has also been taken of Sicily's often extreme conditions. Low, bush-trained grapevines that develop vast amounts of sugar under the Sicilian sun were replaced with wire-trained grapes farther from the heat-reflecting soil. Vines are pruned to improve quality; grapes are harvested early and at night (to prevent acidity levels dropping and to help them retain flavor); and pressed grapes are stored in cool vats to postpone fermentation.

Producers have not totally abandoned the old, however, and make a point of combining local traditional grape varieties with the international staples. With white wines, where the Sicilian wine revolution began, this has meant combining the age-old Grecanico, Catarratto, Inzolia, and Grillo grapes with Chardonnay, Sauvignon Blanc, and the occasional Viognier.

Good whites include Vigna di Gabbri and more basic Donnafugata from the big Tenuta di Donnafugata winery; the premium Colomba Platino, Bianco di Valguarnera, and lowlier Corvo

The Italian toast of *"cin cin"* derived from *"cent'ann"*—a wish of 100 years of health to your fellow drinkers. It is believed to have originated in Sicily.

—JUSTIN KAVANAGH
National Geographic Travel Books editor

Bianco from the Corvo label; and Inzolia, Tasca, and Nozze d'Oro from Regaleali. Among smaller estates, Cometa and Chardonnay from the Planeta winery near Noto are excellent, as are the wines of Rudini, Calabretta, Fondo Antico, and Racalmare di Morgante.

Sicilian reds are now overtaking the whites, but the basis of improvement has been the same: blending. Cabernet Sauvignon, Cabernet Franc, Syrah, Pinot Nero, and Merlot grapes are blended with traditional Sicilian varieties. The most notable of these is the Nero d'Avola, which makes deep-colored, fruity, and robust wines that are similar to

Syrahs. Good Nero d'Avola wines include Planeta's Santa Cecilia, the Duca Enrico of Duca di Salaparuta, and Fazio's Torre dei Venti.

Other reds of note with mixed grape composition include Donnafugata's Tancredi DOC Contessa Entellina and Mille e Una Notte Contessa Entellina; Spadafora's Don Pietro; the Terre d'Agula of Duca di Salaparuta; Planeta's Burdese and La Segreta Rosso; Morgante's Don Antonio; and Cusumano's Sagana, Noà, and Benuara.

The new wines should not obscure the virtues of some of Sicily's more established names such as the basic Bianco d'Alcamo and Cerasuolo di Vittoria. Marsala has acquired a bad name, but at its best from producers like Florio, Pellegrino, and Marco de Bartoli, it is a fine, dry, smooth sherry-like wine.

Even better are the dessert wines conjured from the volcanic soils of Pantelleria and the Lipari Islands. These are some of the best of their kind in Europe, in particular the delicate Moscato di Pantelleria, the richer Moscato Passito di Pantelleria, and the Lipari Islands' Malvasia di Lipari, especially the version from Salina.

EXPERIENCE: Sicily's Best Ice Cream

Sicily has raised ice cream to a delectable art form. Plan accordingly! Consider this roundup of *gelateria* just the tip of the ice cream iceberg.

ETNA
Vitale *(Piazza Antonio Longo 7, Nicolosi, tel 095 914 499)* gets especially high marks for the seasonal fruit flavors available in summertime.

NOTO
Vying for the title of Sicily's best ice cream are **Caffè Sicilia** *(Corso Vittorio Emanuele II 125, tel 0931 835 013, closed Mon.)*—try the lemon, and **Costanzo Corrado** *(Via Silvio Spaventa 9, tel 0931 835 243, closed Wed.)*—mandarin is a local favorite.

PALERMO
Ilardo *(Foro Italico Umberto I, tel 091 617 2118, closed weekdays in winter, anticagelateriailardo.it)* Just east of the Museo Internazionale delle Marionette, this is the city's oldest gelateria, founded in 1860.

RAGUSA
Gelati DiVini *(Piazza del Duomo 20, tel 0932 228 989, gelatidivini.it)* Specialties include pistachio and pine nut.

TAORMINA
Gelatomania *(Corso Umberto I 7, tel 0942 23900)* The melon ice cream has a deep, tart essence, but try *setteveli*—vanilla-seamed ribbons of chocolate that simulate the local seven-layer cake.

History of Sicily

The island's early history began gloriously, with several centuries of Greek domination, and flowered again under Arab and Norman dominion. For almost a thousand years, however, Sicily suffered grievously at the hands of less cultured and more rapacious foreign rulers. Only today, almost 150 years after Italian unification, are the effects of this long period of misrule being unraveled.

The first peoples to reach Sicily from mainland Italy are thought to have settled around 20,000 B.C., though the earliest known memorials to these Stone Age inhabitants are cave paintings from around 8700 B.C. Neolithic cultures are also known to have flourished around 4000–3000 B.C., especially on the Lipari Islands.

More coherent artifacts survive from around 1250 B.C., when the island was probably inhabited by three distinct groups: the Sikans (or Sicani), who dominated western Sicily, and were probably of Iberian (modern-day Spanish and Portuguese) origin; the Elymians (or Elimi), possibly of eastern Mediterranean origin, who settled in present-day Erice and Segesta; and the Sikels (or Siculi), a people from the Italian mainland who occupied eastern and central Sicily, and from whom the island took its name.

Sicily's proximity to Greece meant that all three peoples, and probably cultures before them, had strong trading and cultural links with the Greeks. It also meant that the more westerly peoples had ties with the Phoenicians from the eastern Mediterranean, who probably established trading outposts on Sicily's southern coast.

In time, the growing population of Greece, together with the Greeks' need to secure westerly trading routes—notably the Strait of Messina between Sicily and the Italian mainland—meant that the Greeks began to establish colonies on the island's eastern coast.

The first of these was Naxos around 735 B.C., followed a year later by Syracuse. Many more were quickly founded, the new colonists generally living side by side or assimilating with the Sikans, who, while resolute and civilized, lacked the Greeks' abilities as sailors and traders. The Greeks' relationship was less happy with the Phoenicians who, in 814 B.C., had established a trading base in North Africa called Carthage. In time, this city forged its own empire, and its people, the Carthaginians, traded and formed alliances with and against many of the Sicilian Greek colonies. The first great encounter with the Carthaginians ended with victory for the combined forces of Syracuse, Agrigento, and others at the Battle of Himera (480 B.C.). The ensuing peace allowed most Sicilian colonies to prosper—Syracuse in particular, which became so powerful that it aroused the envy of Athens, the most dominant of Greece's home cities.

Ancient Influence

The Phoenicians hailed from the Levant—modern-day Syria, Lebanon, and Israel. From about the 11th century B.C. they traded with the Greeks, who gave them the name "Phoenician," or Purple People, after one of their trading staples, a rare purple dye made from crushed shells. In time, the Phoenicians established trading posts in Sicily, notably at Motya (present-day Mozia), Panormos (Palermo), and Solus (Solunto). Among other things, they introduced the Phoenician alphabet, generally considered the basis for the Greek and Roman alphabets.

Angered by Syracuse's support for Sparta, another Greek colony, Athens dispatched a vast fleet against Syracuse in 415 B.C. The result was one of the great battles of the ancient world, and a victory for Syracuse that marked the end of the Athenian empire and, effectively, of Greece's golden age.

While Sicily prospered and Greece declined, a new power was emerging in central Italy. By the start of the third century B.C., Rome had already defeated most of the Greek colonies on the southern Italian mainland. It had also come into conflict with Carthage in the so-called First and Second Punic Wars (264–241 B.C. and 218–201 B.C.), during which Sicily was one of the main battlegrounds. When Syracuse sided with Carthage in the second war, it was besieged and captured by the Romans in 212 B.C., cementing a Roman hold on the island that would endure for some 600 years.

Sicily was one of Rome's first colonies, and one of its most important: Sicilian taxes and tributes are estimated to have covered a fifth of all of Rome's expenses in its early

The "Triumph of Rome Over Sicily" is the work of painter Jacopo Ripanda (circa 1508–1513).

years. The island became the empire's breadbasket, supplying grain and other resources. It also provided the conquering Romans with vast feudal estates, whose aristocracy of absentee landlords would be the curse of Sicily until the land reforms of the 1950s.

Such was the rapacity with which Rome exploited the island that when the Roman Empire crumbled in the fifth century A.D., the invading Goths and Vandals found so little of value that they left Sicily almost unscathed.

Much the same went for the Byzantines, the rulers of Constantinople (modern-day Istanbul), the capital of an eastern empire formed when Rome was divided in A.D. 286. The Byzantines' power outlived that of Rome, and saw them recapture parts of the old western empire, including Sicily, for some 300 years.

During the seventh century, Sicily came under the eye of a new invader, the Arabs of North Africa, who made their first incursions in 652. Little else happened until 827, when an inept Byzantine governor asked the Arabs for help to quell a revolt. A force of 10,000 Arabs, Berbers, and Spanish Muslims duly landed near Mazara in southwest Sicily. Within three years it had swept through the west of the island and taken Palermo.

From 878, when Syracuse fell, the Arabs effectively ruled Sicily. Their reign would be a golden age, the incomers promulgating new ideas in science, philosophy, learning, the arts, and agriculture. Irrigation was introduced, along with crops such as dates, citrus fruits, cotton, silk, sugar, flax, rice, nuts, and henna. Trade blossomed, and with it Palermo, whose wealth and dazzling court made it the Mediterranean's leading cultural and trading center.

In the tenth century, however, unrest in North Africa saw Palermo's role as the center of the Arab empire pass to Egypt. This, combined with the fact that the Arabs never established a powerful central authority in Sicily, left the island vulnerable to attack.

Sicilian Symbolism

The *trinacria*—a three-legged symbol with the head of Medusa—is something you'll see throughout the island, not least as part of the Sicilian flag. The three legs allude to the island's triangular shape, while the head of Medusa was used in classical antiquity to ward off evil. In mythology, the trinacria was worn on the aegis (collar or cape) of the goddess Athena, one of Sicily's pagan protectors.

The Normans, who originated in Scandinavia, settled in northern France in 911. Renowned fighters, they found work as papal and other mercenaries across Europe, but especially in the strife-torn lands of southern Italy. Here, the outstanding Norman fighters were a group of 12 brothers by the name of de Hautville. One of them, Roger (1031–1101), captured Palermo in 1072. By 1091, when Syracuse, the last Arab stronghold, was taken, he ruled the island and took the title of Count Roger, or Roger I.

The new ruler displayed great toleration of Sicily's mixed population as did his son and successor Roger II (1095–1154), who ruled from 1101. Sicily prospered again, bolstered by Roger's fusing of the best of Arab, Norman, and Byzantine traditions in art, architecture, administration, and agriculture. His court at Palermo became probably the wealthiest, and certainly the most cultured, of any in Europe.

The Norman system of rule, however, was a feudal one that relied on the king's supporters being rewarded with grants of land and titles, which created numerous semi-independent barons. Roger's less able son William I (1120–1166) would face several baronial rebellions, though it was the inability of William's son William II (1153–1189) to produce an heir that would have more far-reaching consequences.

In this early 20th-century lithograph, Frederick II holds court near Palermo in 1227.

In the absence of a natural successor, William II nominated as his heir his father's sister Constance (Constanza). She was married to Henry of Hohenstaufen (1165–1197), the son of the great Holy Roman (German) Emperor Frederick I, better known as Barbarossa. Thus Sicily's destiny became linked to that of the northern imperial powers.

Henry duly became Emperor Henry VI (and king of Sicily), but died soon after his coronation, leaving Constance as the regent for their three-year-old son, the future emperor Frederick II (1194–1250).

A man of prodigious talents, Frederick was a consummate statesman, commander, scholar, and legislator, known to contemporaries as Stupor Mundi, or the Wonder of the World. He reestablished Palermo as a court of European stature and rejuvenated Sicily as a whole, but when death removed his firm hand, his empire began to unravel.

His son Conrad IV (1228–1254) died within four years of assuming the throne, leaving Conrad's own son Conradin too young to assume power. Manfred (1232–1266), Frederick II's illegitimate son, then stepped into the breach. In a short time, much to papal horror, he soon controlled much of Italy.

The popes, nominal suzerains of Sicily and Italy, were forever in conflict with the empire, and ever anxious to deprive the Hohenstaufens of territory and influence. With the powerful Frederick II gone and helped by Manfred's illegitimacy (which weakened his claim), they saw their chance. Pope Urban IV, a Frenchman, awarded the title of King

Giuseppe Garibaldi began his successful military campaign to unite Italy on the west coast of Sicily in 1860.

of Sicily and Naples to Charles of Anjou, the ruthless younger brother of the French king Louis IX.

On its own the title might have meant little in practical terms, but the Anjou, or Angevins, had an army to back up their new claims. They defeated Manfred and the imperial Hohenstaufen forces in southern Italy in 1266. Manfred was killed during the battle, and his nephew and heir, 14-year-old Conradin, was beheaded by Charles in Naples in 1268.

The resulting unpopularity was compounded in Sicily by heavy taxes and a vicious campaign of revenge against former Hohenstaufen supporters. Sicilian nobles began to plot against Charles with an antipapal faction in Aragon (in present-day Spain), whose ruler, Peter III of Aragon (1239–1285), was married to Manfred's daughter, Constanza. This, in his eyes and those of most Sicilians, gave him a claim to Sicily and the Hohenstaufens' original domain.

As Charles's oppression continued, 1282 saw a popular revolt against the Angevins that precipitated the arrival of the Aragonese in Sicily. The Sicilian Vespers, as the revolt became known, allegedly was sparked on Easter Monday when a French (Angevin) soldier insulted a woman as the bell of Palermo's Santo Spirito church was calling her to vespers. The congregation reacted with fury, provoking a riot that quickly spread, eventually consuming all of Sicily in a frenzy of killing. Five months later, Philip of Aragon landed at Trapani in western Sicily. Within days he had been acclaimed king of Sicily in Palermo, though the Vespers war, waged mostly in Spain and at sea between Aragonese and Angevin forces based in Naples, would last another 21 years.

If the Spaniards were initially welcomed, their continued presence in Sicily for the next 578 years would ultimately bring death, chaos, stagnation, corruption, revolution, and a complex legacy that survives to this day. As Sicily turned to Spain, and the Ottoman Turks began to dominate the eastern Mediterranean, an island that had once been at the center of European affairs found itself consigned to the fringes. When Spain itself looked west to the riches of the New World after 1492, Sicily became even more marginalized.

Things started reasonably well. Peter of Aragon's son Frederick II (1296–1337) continued his father's strong, centralist government, but thereafter weaker Spanish rule saw the rise of the barons and civil war between Aragonese and lingering Angevin supporters. To take things in hand, Spain ruled Sicily directly after 1410, nominating a series of viceroys to control the island. After 1460 none of these would be of Sicilian origin. In the 300 years of vice-regal rule, only one Spanish monarch ever visited Sicily—Charles V, who made a fleeting call while returning to Spain from Tunisia in 1525.

Spanish rule and Sicily's isolation meant it was cut off from most of the great reforms and cultural movements of the Middle Ages. Not only did feudalism survive, it was reinforced as large estates were granted to Spanish nobles in return for military service. The Renaissance had virtually no impact on Sicily, and after the crowns of Aragon and Castile in Spain were united under Ferdinand and Isabella, the introduction in 1487 of the Inquisition (an oppressive Church court) saw intellectual and cultural life circumscribed. A conservative Church, a pillar of Sicilian society, fell in step with a conservative aristocracy. This, combined with widespread government corruption, meant prosperity for a few, and poverty and ignorance for many. The expulsion of the Jews from Sicily in 1492 is one example of the repressive tenor of the times.

Almost utter stagnation marked the 16th and 17th centuries in Sicily. This was compounded by natural disaster, notably a cataclysmic earthquake in 1693 and, in time, by the decline of Spain itself. This decline, and the extent to which Sicily had become a pawn to be bartered by the great powers, was underlined by the Treaty of Utrecht (1713) after the Wars of the Spanish Succession left Spain isolated. The victorious European powers awarded Sicily to the House of Savoy, rulers of Piedmont in northern Italy. They then traded it for Sardinia with the Austrians, who in turn, hardly caring for their distant possession, allowed the Spanish, this time under Charles of Bourbon (1716–1788), to capture the island in 1734. If the Aragonese had been bad, the Bourbons were even worse. Any and every means was devised to squeeze money from Sicily.

During the Napoleonic wars that followed the French Revolution in 1792, Sicily was the only part of Italy not conquered by Napoleon. Indeed, under its then ruler Ferdinand IV of Bourbon, Sicily supported Britain and its allies in their war against Napoleon, earning Britain's gratitude and support.

Noting Sicily's strategic importance, Britain assumed effective control of the island in 1811. Shocked at what it found, its envoys attempted reforms, only to lose interest when Napoleon was defeated. Ferdinand IV returned, and with him—and his successors—a cycle of repression, exploitation, and rebellion that continued until 1860, when the Risorgimento, or campaign to unify Italy, reached its climax.

Italy at the time was divided among the House of Savoy, which ruled much of the northwest; Austria, controlling the north and east; the French-backed papacy, whose domain extended across much of central Italy; and the Bourbons, who controlled Sicily and southern Italy.

> **During the Napoleonic wars that followed the French Revolution in 1792, Sicily was the only part of Italy not conquered by Napoleon.**

Skillful diplomacy on the part of the Savoys, who spearheaded the unification campaign, won them the backing of Britain and France, and the help of a French army, which dislodged the Austrians in 1859. A year later Giuseppe Garibaldi (1807–1882), a charismatic soldier frustrated by what he saw as the Savoys' slowness in advancing unification, raised a band of troops—the Mille, or Thousand—and decided to force the issue.

On May 11, 1860, Garibaldi landed at Marsala on Sicily's west coast. Four days later his small band defeated a Bourbon force of 15,000. By the end of July, Messina had been taken and Sicily was at last unequivocally free of Spanish rule for the first time since 1282. As Garibaldi moved up from the south, revolts and events elsewhere saw the new Kingdom of Italy proclaimed on March 14, 1861.

The distant, northern-based government soon proved as unable, and as reluctant, to address Sicily's ills as any previous Spanish administration. Unrest was quelled not only by repressive government action but also by gangs employed by landowners or their shadowy middlemen—a contributory factor in the growth of the Mafia, a term which began to be current in the 1860s. So desperate was the lot of most Sicilians that the only option was emigration. An estimated 1.5 million left for the Americas, Australia, and elsewhere between 1880 and 1914.

For 50 or 60 years after unification, Sicily simmered or slumbered, beaten, resentful, and impoverished, in the grip not only of political, social, and economic inertia but also the increasingly strong hold of the Mafia. After 1922, when Mussolini came to power in Italy, it would be the Fascists, ironically, who would come closest to defeating this criminal elite, thanks to the violent, illegal, and remarkably successful methods of Mussolini's infamous chief of police, Cesare Mori. Even more ironically, during World War II it would be the liberating British and Americans who would reestablish Mafia power.

In July 1943, Sicily's strategic position saw it chosen by the Allies as the obvious bridgehead for an attack on Europe's "soft underbelly." During Operation Husky, U.S. and British forces landed on the island's southeast coast, liberating Sicily after 38 days of tough fighting. Their progress on the ground was helped by "prominent citizens" provided by the only men in the United States with the appropriate contacts: Lucky Luciano and other Mafia dons. As the Allies marched on, they replaced Fascist officials in countless towns with these "influential" men.

After the war, Sicily despaired of the new Italian Republic and toyed briefly with separatism, not least under the infamous bandit Salvatore Giuliano (1922–1950), who was eventually conscripted by shadowy anti-Communist forces and died under mysterious circumstances. To placate the island, the Italian government awarded it semiautonomous status, with its own regional parliament. The old reactionary forces, however, often in collusion with a Mafia growing rich on the

To a New World

Sicily has known poverty for much of its history. Today, it is still one of the ten poorest regions in the European Union, with unemployment running officially at around 25 percent (and unofficially probably much higher). While more outsiders attempt to enter Sicily (see sidebar p. 16), more locals want to leave. This phenomenon is nothing new: The Sicilians' response to their impoverished lot has invariably been emigration. The first great wave came in the 1890s, prompted by economic recession across

Europe and the blight of phylloxera in the island's vineyards.

Between 1880 and 1914, an estimated 1.5 million left Sicily for the Americas, Australia, and elsewhere; 14,626, or 6 percent of the island's population, left in 1893 alone. More were to follow: 400,000, or 10 percent of the then population, left between 1951 and 1953, tempted largely by the lure of jobs in northern Italy and frustrated by lack of promised land reforms after World War II.

Palermo F.C. fans celebrate a success for their soccer team outside the city's Politeama Garibaldi, where drama unfolds beneath Rutelli's bronze statuary of Apollo in triumph.

postwar building boom, again stifled reform. Once more the Sicilians' only recourse was emigration; a million people left the island between 1951 and 1971 for the factories of Germany, Switzerland, and northern Italy. Certain land reforms were gradually pushed through, but centuries too late, because by the 1970s and 1980s the number of people working or dependent on the land was rapidly diminishing.

A gradual change in attitude toward the Mafia, both on the part of Sicilians and of central government, followed the shocking assassination in 1982 of General Della Chiesa, a tough chief of police, and the murders in 1992 of Giovanni Falcone and Paolo Borsellino, two respected Mafia investigators. Crackdowns appeared to have more bite and Sicilians lost some of their old fear.

At the same time, the Mafia question remains unresolved as do the evils of poverty and the curse of unemployment, crumbling infrastructure, and a political and bureaucratic system of often dubious reliability. In 2010, the imprisonment of Salvatore Cuffaro, former president of the Region of Sicily, underlined the ongoing problems. It is depressing to think that a place must remain a prisoner of its past, but in the case of Sicily, sadly, the deep-rooted historical problems engendered by centuries of exploitation and foreign misrule still run deep. Only belatedly, and very slowly, are they being resolved. ■

Art & Architecture

The three highest points of Sicilian art and architecture—the temples of the Greeks, evidence of the sublime decorative skills of the Arabs and Normans, and the majestic creations of the baroque—were forged by Sicily's extraordinary history and its long periods of isolation from the mainstream of Italian and other European artistic traditions.

Sicily's earliest known works of art are incised and painted figures created around 8700 B.C. in the Grotta Genovese, a cave on Levanzo in western Sicily. Some 5,000 years passed before the next body of coherent works was created, namely the incised pottery of the Stentinello, a Neolithic culture that was probably found in pockets across much of the island. The pottery motifs suggest the influence of traders and settlers from as far as Cyprus, Syria, Anatolia, Egypt, and North Africa. Such cross-cultural influences found their most obvious monuments in the art and architecture of the Greeks, whose earliest legacies were the sixth-century B.C. fortresses and fortifications of colonies such as Syracuse.

Sicily's Five Greatest Ancient Greek Sites

The legacy of ancient Greece is one of Sicily's special pleasures. Greek settlers crossed the Ionian Sea to forge colonies more than 2,700 years ago, and many well-preserved sites survive to this day. Topping the list:

- Segesta's temple and theater (see p. 72)
- Selinunte's temples (see p. 90)
- Agrigento's Valle dei Templi (see p. 93)
- Syracuse's Greek theater (see p. 114)
- Taormina's Greek theater (see p. 139)

Greek Temples & Theaters

Today, more Greek temples survive in Sicily than in Greece itself, with sublime examples at Segesta, Selinunte, and Agrigento—among them the largest and best preserved temples in the Hellenic world. Most temples in Sicily are Doric, the style of the Parthenon in Athens. A sober but majestic form that originated in the Peloponnese in southern Greece, it is distinguished by its monolithic and slightly fluted, tapered, and baseless columns, and by a relatively unadorned upper section. This lack of decoration, and of sculptural reliefs in particular, contrasts with the more ornate temples of mainland Greece and has yet to be properly explained. By the fifth century B.C., Sicily's temples showed a remarkable uniformity. They were usually peripteral (meaning they were surrounded by a line of columns) and hexastyle (meaning their front elevation contained six columns).

Similar uniformity was found in theaters—the Greeks' other major architectural legacy. Like temples, Greek theaters had a sacred as well as a cultural function. And, like temples, they often were situated in isolated or elevated locales—for striking impact.

Stone theaters, which were often carved from the surrounding rock, replaced wooden structures after the fourth century B.C. Sicily's most notable examples were the theaters

(continued on p. 34)

The color-drenched mosaics in the Cappella Palatina in Palermo fuse the best of Arab, Norman, and Byzantine artistic traditions.

Festivals

That Sicily is Italy magnified is clear in its countless festivals, where the many strands of the island's pagan and Christian traditions, its multifaceted history, its food, and the dramatic and visceral aspects of the Sicilian temperament find their most colorful expression.

Take Noto, a small town in Sicily's southeast corner, where events embracing all aspects of the island's festival traditions—religious, pagan, and cultural—occur alongside celebrations of the town's patron saint and protector. Then there is a festival with pagan roots, the Infiorata, celebrating spring when the streets are carpeted in vignettes of flowers. The after-dark La Notte di Giufa, is devoted to music and storytelling.

This is Noto, but it could well be almost anywhere in Sicily. Every community has its

Villagers in traditional dress participate in Randazzo's Festa Medievale.

saint—and the larger the town, the more lavish the festivities. In Palermo, for example, the U Fistinu festival dedicated to Santa Rosalia lasts for six days, but even the tiniest Sicilian hamlet enjoys at least a day's worth of festivities in honor of its patron.

Religious festivals peak on Good Friday when many towns stage processions and take part in celebrations that have not changed for centuries. Some of the most enthralling are in Trapani, Marsala, and Enna, where hooded penitents carry statues of the dead Christ and L'Addolorata (Our Lady of Sorrows).

Elsewhere, historical tradition is marked in

"Mosaics" of flowers fill the streets of Noto during the Festa dell'Infiorata.

Piazza Armerina, where the Palio dei Normanni celebrates the town's liberation by the Normans, while Gangi continues the pagan tradition of Sagra della Spiga, dedicated to the goddess Demeter (Ceres). Local products, always a source of pride and an excuse for feasting, feature in many small festivals.

EXPERIENCE:
La Festa della Madonna di Tindari

The Madonna Nera (Black Madonna) of Tindari, in the south of the island, is one of Sicily's most venerated statues. Visitors can easily join the annual pilgrimage procession (santuariotindari .it) to her sanctuary on the evening of September 7 or participate in the festivities the following day, which include a street fair, fireworks, and a special Mass that involves choirs from across the island.

at Taormina, Syracuse, Tindari, and Segesta. Like temples, their design was almost uniform and consisted of the cavea, a semicircular series of tiered ledges; the orchestra, a circular area for the chorus and actors; and the proscenium, for scenery and storage.

Piecemeal changes to these theaters were one of the very few legacies left by the Romans in Sicily. Their lack of interest in the island is reflected in an absence of major temples, baths, or other monuments. Although they laid the foundations of Sicily's road network, the Romans' only other significant memorial is the Villa Imperiale del Casale (see pp. 102–105). While this is an isolated example of Roman art, it is also an exceptional one and features the finest collection of Roman mosaics in Europe. Other art from the period of the late Roman Empire is scant: a few traces of wall frescoes in the catacombs at Syracuse, the earliest example of Christian art on the island.

Sicily's Stunning Norman Treasures

Arab domination of Sicily was followed in the 11th century by the Normans, French conquerors who left a legacy of art and architecture. In Palermo, don't miss the church of La Martorana (see p. 46), San Cataldo (see p. 46), and the Cappella Palatina (see p. 50); in Monreale, the cathedral (see p. 64); in Cefalù, the cathedral (see p. 154).

Arab Influence

Also lacking are any major monuments to Sicily's next invaders, the Arabs, though their considerable artistic and architectural acumen survives in the influence they would have on the Normans and their successors. The Arabs introduced mosques, gardens, and palaces, as well as the skills and imagination required for their fine decorative conceits: the use of colored ceramics and the introduction of the horseshoe arch, intricate designs, carved and painted wooden ceilings, and delicate honeycombs of stalactite plasterwork (muqarnas).

While the Normans were supremely tolerant of their Muslim subjects, most Arab buildings were appropriated and altered, the result being the distinctive Arab-Norman hybrid that represents Sicily's second great artistic flowering. To the Arabs' decorative skills the Normans added their own Romanesque forms, notably the rounded arches and carved capitals and cloisters copied from France's great Burgundian and Provençal churches. In embracing Greek- and Byzantine-influenced mosaics, the Normans also added a third element to what would be a remarkably coherent composite style.

The results of this hybrid were not only some of Sicily's finest medieval buildings but also some of the most exquisite buildings of any era anywhere. Most of them are religious rather than secular, the most notable being Palermo's Cappella Palatina and the cathedrals of Cefalù and Monreale, places where decorative elaboration—and mosaics above all—reached its apotheosis.

The political instability that followed the Normans' demise proved anathema to art and architecture. As a result, Sicily largely failed to register the impact of the Gothic art then being forged in the developing city-states of central and northern Italy.

The exceptions were in Syracuse, Catania, and Enna, where Gothic forms were introduced when the towns' castles were refortified in the middle of the 13th century. The Gothic new wave also made mild ripples in Palermo, where the so-called Chiaramonte style fused classic Gothic mullioned windows with Arab-Norman decorative features to create a widespread local Gothic idiom.

Syracuse's Greek theater, among the largest in the ancient world, remains impressive.

15th- & 16th-Century Style

By the middle of the 15th century, the consolidation of Aragonese (Spanish) rule in Sicily further stifled the development of the flamboyant Gothic style then reaching its zenith in northern Italy. Instead, the island's ruling Spanish viceroys and their architects naturally looked to Spain, where a more sober Gothic style was prevalent—a form that today can be seen in both the main doorway of Palermo's cathedral and the Palazzo Corvaia in Taormina. The key Sicilian exponent of the style was Matteo Carnelivari (active in the late 15th century), a native of Noto who was responsible for Palermo's Abatellis and Ajutamicristo palaces.

The same Spanish bias, together with Sicily's increased isolation from the Italian mainstream, also accounts for the almost total absence of any great artists of the caliber emerging in Florence and elsewhere in the mid-15th century. This bias and underlying stagnation continued for the next hundred years, a period that embraces the height of the Italian Renaissance, an artistic reawakening that passed Sicily by almost completely. That it did not leave the island entirely untouched was basically due to a single artist. Antonello da Messina (1430–1479), born in the northeast of the island, is the only Sicilian painter in the first rank of Renaissance artists. Even so, Antonello had to leave Sicily to forge his career, probably learning his craft in the workshops of Naples and Venice, where he would have come into contact with Flemish painters and Italian artists such as Giovanni Bellini and Piero della Francesca.

> **Antonello da Messina (1430–1479), born in the northeast of the island, is the only Sicilian painter in the first rank of Renaissance artists.**

From the Flemish he acquired a consummate skill in the handling of oil paint, then a relatively new and exacting medium. Just four of his typically understated and subtly colored paintings survive in Sicily: one each in galleries in Messina, Cefalù, and Syracuse, and his masterpiece, the "Annunciation" (1476), in Palermo's Galleria Regionale di Sicilia.

In Renaissance sculpture, the story was similarly limited, with only two artists making an impact on the greater Italian stage. The first was Francesco Laurana (1430–1502), a Dalmatian artist who spent five years in Sicily (1466–1471), during which time he worked on the Cappella Mastrantonio in Palermo's church of San Francesco d'Assisi and completed his celebrated bust of Eleanor of Aragon (now in Palermo's Galleria Regionale di Sicilia). The second was Domenico Gagini (circa 1430–1492), a sculptor from Lombardy in northern Italy who founded a dynasty of sculptors that included his son, Antonello, born in Palermo in 1478. Gagini's descendants continued to thrive in Sicily until the mid-17th century.

Baroque & Beyond

If the Renaissance eluded Sicily, the period of the baroque during the 17th and 18th centuries marked the island's third period of artistic transcendence. One reason was the ornate and theatrical nature of baroque style, which suited the Sicilians' love for the decorative, a passion that dates back to the Arab period. With this dramatic architectural style came the Sicilians' natural flair for utilizing color, gilding, and other effects.

Another reason was that the baroque found favor in Spain, and thus Sicily, which was still under Spanish rule. Yet another was the catastrophic 1669 earthquake that

Palermo's church of Sant'Ippolito sports the ornate decoration of the baroque style.

destroyed swaths of southeast Sicily, opening the way for the creation of new or nearly new towns such as Noto, Ragusa, and Scicli, where architects could give full rein to their baroque ambitions.

The greatest of such architects, Messina-born Filippo Juvarra (1676/8–1736), abandoned his native Sicily in 1700, achieving fame in Rome, Madrid, and Turin. Of those that remained, nearly all were priests, and nearly all trained in Rome, then the epicenter of Italian baroque. Their training notwithstanding, most added a peculiarly Sicilian twist to their work, giving lie (as with the Normans' reworking of Arab and Byzantine idioms) to the notion that Sicilian art only copied or recycled the imported styles of its many foreign rulers.

Scholars still debate the precise influences and intricacies of Sicilian baroque. But briefly put, whereas baroque elsewhere in Italy reveled in geometry and the complex interplay of light and shadow, Sicilian baroque was more exuberant and concerned with detail and fantastical decoration. Some of its earliest proponents were Paolo Amato (1633–1714), responsible for Palermo's San Salvatore, the first Sicilian church built on a curvilinear plan, and Giacomo Amato (1643–1732), who built numerous palaces and churches in his native Palermo. Better known were Giovanni Battista Vaccarini (1702–1770), who redesigned 18th-century Catania virtually single-handedly, and Rosario Gagliardi (circa 1700–1770), the most important of the architects who created the "new" towns of the southeast corner after the 1669 earthquake.

> **Many of the episodes in Homer's Greek epic *The Odyssey* take place in Sicily, and the island was the setting for Plato's book *The Republic*.**

Sicilian painting and sculpture in their purest forms may have been negligible during the baroque period, but the work of the craftspeople responsible for the decoration of palaces and churches was second to none. The island's greatest decorative artist was Giacomo Serpotta (1656–1732), whose extraordinary work in stucco (plaster) graces the oratories of Santa Cita, San Domenico, and San Lorenzo in Palermo. Thereafter, the art and architecture rarely touched the heights, with the exception of brief visits from mainland artists such as Caravaggio (1573–1610) in 1609, and the flowerings of the neoclassical and Liberty, or art nouveau, styles in the 19th and early 20th centuries.

More recently, the energetic expressionistic paintings of Renato Guttuso (1912–1987), born in Bagheria just east of Palermo, have achieved fame in Italy and beyond, as have the bronzes and other works of Catania-born sculptor Emilio Greco (1913–1995). Palermo, with a superb new home for its civic collection, is increasingly a center for contemporary art (see sidebar p. 57).

Literature

Sicily's early literary glory was borrowed or reflected. Many of the episodes in Homer's Greek epic *The Odyssey* take place in Sicily, and the island was the setting for Plato's book *The Republic.* The Greek writer and philosopher used the island to represent a utopian state.

Later, the wealth of patrons in the island's Greek colonies lured other Greek writers, notably poets such as Pindar (circa 522–438 B.C.) and the playwright Aeschylus (525–456 B.C.), both of whom worked in Syracuse. Homegrown talent included Syracuse-born Theocritus (circa 300–260 B.C.), who is credited with inventing pastoral poetry.

In medieval times, a pure form of Sicilian, stripped of its colloquial idioms, became one of Europe's foremost literary languages. The genre reached its zenith under Emperor Frederick II in the 13th century, when his court played host to exponents of the Sicilian School of Poetry. The school's poets included Giacomo da Lentini (circa 1210–1260), who is often credited with inventing the sonnet form, and who, with his contemporaries, looked to the Provençal troubadour tradition for the style and content of his tales of courtly love. While this tradition would fade, Sicilian literature, even today, has never lost its taste for dialect and the vernacular.

Nor in its greatest writers has it flinched from confronting the travails and complexity of life in Sicily. This has naturally required a strong sense of realism, an approach pioneered in the 19th century by the poems of Mario Rapisardi (1844–1912) and the theoretical writings of Luigi Capuana (1839–1915).

Realism also formed the cornerstone of the writings of Giovanni Verga (1830–1922), the first major Sicilian writer to make a lasting impact on the greater international stage. In novels such as *I Malavoglia* (1881), he explored what he saw as the real Sicily, portraying the lives of ordinary Sicilians in a characteristically somber prose style.

It was realism that also influenced the early work of Sicily's best known writer, Luigi Pirandello (1867–1936), whose plays and experiments with form and content won him

Best known for his plays, Luigi Pirandello, the 1934 Noble Prize winner in literature, strikes a pose aboard the S.S. *Conte Di Savoia* on October 5, 1935.

EXPERIENCE: Literary Walks & Italian Lessons

Il Gattopardo (The Leopard) is not just one of the great works of Sicilian literature; it is among the greatest 20th-century European novels. Join one of half a dozen literary walks around **Palermo** and you'll experience not just an insight into the novel's author, Giuseppe Tomasi di Lampedusa, and his links with the city, but you'll also visit and learn about all sorts of hidden corners around old Palermo.

Or you can walk around the city's port while listening to extracts from the works of 18th- and 19th-century visitors.

Two-day literary tours to other landmarks in Sicily associated with the author are also available and include food and accommodations. Special Italian-language courses can also be arranged (with 24 hours' class time over eight days), where the emphasis is on learning Italian in a literary context. For further information on walks and tours, contact **Parco Culturale del Gattopardo** (*tel 091 625 4011 or 327 684 4052, parcotomasi.it*).

the Nobel Prize in literature in 1934. His play *Six Characters in Search of an Author* (1921) explored the theme of isolation and the role of individuals in societies or situations alien to them.

Pirandello's body of work was in contrast to the single, lyrical masterpiece of Giuseppe Tomasi di Lampedusa (1896–1957), an aristocrat whose posthumously published novel *Il Gattopardo (The Leopard)* is a magnificent study of the profound social changes in Sicily in the mid-19th century. Today, Lampedusa is one of only a few Sicilian writers whose works are available in translation. This honor is shared by Elio Vittorini (1908–1966), a staunch anti-Fascist best known for *Conversation in Sicily* (1937), a deceptively simple novel that follows an emigrant returning to Sicily and his encounters with other travelers and everyday Sicilians.

Vittorini continued Sicilian literature's affinity for realism and the use of Sicilian as part of literary language. So, too, did the widely translated Leonardo Sciascia (1921–1989), who, in novels such as *The Day of the Owl* (1961), used the conventions of crime fiction to explore the complexities of the Mafia and Sicilian life. Similar political and social issues were also the concern of the poet Salvatore Quasimodo (1901–1968), awarded the Nobel Prize in literature in 1959.

The principal traits of Sicilian literature continue to flourish in the work of Andrea Camilleri (born 1925), whose Inspector Montalbano crime novels—popular in Italy and abroad—are not only highly realistic but they also use Sicilian expressions and dialect to powerful and original purpose.

Cinema

Sicily is a filmmaker's dream: The island's complex and often contradictory nature makes it ripe for interpretation and cinematic exploration. The people, similarly, are both generous and hospitable, but also proud, passionate, and inscrutable. The ravishing countryside and historic towns and villages provide locations galore. And in the Mafia lies a subject that, for good or bad, is tailor-made for the big screen. No wonder that the island has attracted some of the world's finest directors.

Many of the best early films set in or inspired by Sicily were based on the island's great literary works. The Italian director Luchino Visconti, for example, used Giovanni Verga's masterpiece *I Malavoglia* as the inspiration for his 1948 movie *La Terra Trema (The Ground Trembles),* the tale of an impoverished fishing community near Catania. The same director looked to another literary masterpiece, *Il Gattopardo,* by Giuseppe Tomasi di Lampedusa for his eponymous 1963 epic starring Burt Lancaster, Alain Delon, and Claudia Cardinale.

Landscape was part of the inspiration for Roberto Rossellini in *Stromboli: Terra di Dio (Stromboli: Land of God).* The 1950 movie stars Rossellini's real-life lover, Ingrid Bergman, as a Lithuanian refugee involved in a torrid affair with a native fisherman amid the harsh volcanic landscapes of Stromboli, one of Sicily's Isole Eolie. The same islands feature as settings in the Taviani brothers' visually stunning *Kaos* (1984), based on several often mournful and bittersweet stories by Luigi Pirandello.

A more poetic view of the Isole Eolie appears in Michael Radford's touching 1994 movie *Il Postino (The Postman),* set on Salina in the 1950s. Massimo Troisi plays a postman hired to deliver mail to the exiled Chilean poet, Pablo Neruda, who guides him to a love of poetry (which gets him the girl) and a greater political awareness (which results in his death). The film garnered several Oscar nominations and was hugely popular abroad, echoing the success of Giuseppe Tornatore's *Cinema Paradiso* (1988), a wonderfully nostalgic,

Director Giuseppe Tornatore is best known for his autobiographical film *Cinema Paradiso* (1988).

comic, and exuberant look at the arrival of the talkies in Sicily.

Films about crime and the Mafia in Sicily had an early pedigree, notably *Salvatore Giuliano* (1961) by the great Italian director Francesco Rosi, one of several Italian filmmakers to adapt the subtle, crime-based novels of Leonardo Sciascia for the big screen. The 1976 movie *Cadaveri Eccellenti (Excellent Corpses)* is one of the most accomplished of these adaptations.

Over time, though, Mafia films became a debased cinematic staple in Italy, portraying a dramatic but biased view of Sicily. It took an Italian-American director to redefine the genre—Francis Ford Coppola, whose *The Godfather* trilogy (1972–1990) was set partly in Sicily.

Recently, Italian films have followed his more intelligent lead, notably Tullio Giordana's *I Cento Passi (The Hundred Steps),* the story of a journalist who was murdered by the Mafia, which won the best screenplay award at the 2000 Venice Film Festival. ■

Sicily's fascinating, colorful capital—where the country's plethora of artistic, cultural, and historic strands come together

Palermo

Detailed stonework adds life to the exterior of the cathedral in Palermo.

Palermo

Big, battered, and bustling, Palermo is not a city for all tastes; its traffic, poverty, and decaying sense of baroque grandeur don't always sit well with the fainthearted. At the same time, it is one of Italy's most vibrant and atmospheric cities, a sultry, sensuous place of ancient origin that still bears the stamp of its Arab, Norman, and Spanish rulers. Monuments to past glories rise amid the modern tenements and cramped backstreets, fighting for space in a city whose Arab bazaars, flourishing port, seedy dives, and teeming thoroughfares offer a dramatic contrast between past and present.

Palermo's stupendous location has long been its unquestionable lure. The city is geographically blessed with a natural harbor, a ring of encircling mountains, and, between, the sweeping amphitheater of the Conca d'Oro, or Golden Shell. Once a fertile hinterland of palms, citrus groves, and vineyards, the Conca d'Oro now is virtually lost under the apartment blocks of the 720,000 or so people who call the modern city home.

The area's earliest inhabitants were probably the prehistoric dwellers whose engravings adorn caves on Monte Pellegrino, the 1,988-foot-high (606 m) mountain to the north of town. From about the eighth century B.C., the city was a port and trading post for the Phoenicians and Carthaginians, peoples of North African origin. The latter prevailed until the city fell to the Romans in 254 B.C.

A golden age began under the Arabs from 831 to 1072 and continued into the 12th century with the Normans—who originated in Scandinavia and moved into northern France—under whom Palermo became the most cultured, cosmopolitan, and prosperous city in Europe.

The Normans bequeathed Palermo its greatest monuments—the cathedral at Monreale and the Cappella Palatina in the Palazzo dei Normanni. But the flavor of Arab rule is apparent in the labyrinthine streets, busy markets—notably Vucciria—the love of flamboyant decoration, and the city's exotic and colorful air. But also compelling is the mark of later epochs. In the end, the accretion of the centuries adds up to one of Palermo's defining and most alluring qualities.

Extravagant baroque and Renaissance churches, for example, are found at every turn—notably La Martorana, San Giuseppe dei Teatini, and the oratories of San Domenico and Santa Cita. Then there are the city's monumental museums, the equal of anything in Italy, such as the Galleria Regionale di Sicilia and Museo Archeologico Regionale, which showcase the centuries' art and artifacts.

Yet for all the splendor and grace there is no doubt that Sicily's capital city is a damaged metropolis. Traffic is a nightmare, noise cacophonous, poverty endemic, and grim modern building—the enduring legacy of corrupt

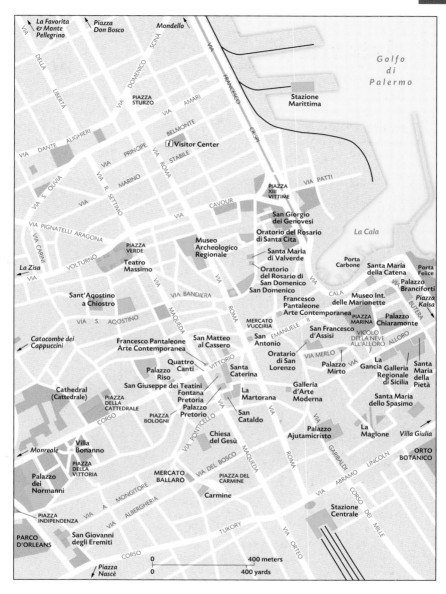

La Favorita & Monte Pellegrino
Piazza Don Bosco
Mondello

VIA DELLA LIBERTA
VIA DOMENICO SCINA
VIA FRANCESCO CRISPI

Golfo di Palermo

PIAZZA STURZO
VIA AMARI
BELMONTE
VIA PRINCIPE STABILE

Stazione Marittima

VIA DANTE ALIGHIERI
VIA S. OLIVIA
VIA R. SETTIMO
VIA MARINO
VIA ROMA

i Visitor Center

PIAZZA XIII VITTIME
VIA PATTI
VIA CAVOUR

La Cala

VIA PIGNATELLI ARAGONA
VIA CARINI
VOLTURNO

PIAZZA VERDE

Museo Archeologico Regionale

San Giorgio dei Genovesi
Oratorio del Rosario di Santa Cita
Santa Maria di Valverde

Porta Carbone
Santa Maria della Catena
Porta Felice

La Zisa
VIA

Teatro Massimo

Oratorio del Rosario di San Domenico
San Domenico

Palazzo Branciforti
Piazza Kalsa

Sant'Agostino a Chiostro

VIA BANDIERA
VIA MAQUEDA
VIA ROMA

Francesco Pantaleone Arte Contemporanea

CALA
Museo Int. delle Marionette

Palazzo Chiaramonte

VIA S. AGOSTINO

MERCATO VUCCIRIA

PIAZZA MARINA

Catacombe dei Cappuccini

Francesco Pantaleone Arte Contemporanea

San Matteo al Cassero

San Antonio
VIA EMANUELE II

San Francesco d'Assisi

VICOLO DELLA NEVE ALL'ALLORO
ALLORO

Quattro Canti
Palazzo Riso
San Giuseppe dei Teatini

VITTORIO
Santa Caterina

Oratorio di San Lorenzo
VIA MERLO

Palazzo Mirto
La Gancia

Galleria Regionale di Sicilia

Santa Maria della Pietà

Cathedral (Cattedrale)
PIAZZA DELLA CATTEDRALE

Fontana Pretoria
Palazzo Pretorio
PIAZZA BOLOGNI

La Martorana

Galleria d'Arte Moderna

Santa Maria dello Spasimo

CORSO
VIA PONTICELLO
VIA MAQUEDA

San Cataldo

Monreale

Villa Bonanno
PIAZZA DELLA VITTORIA

Chiesa del Gesù

Palazzo Ajutamicristo

La Magione
Villa Giulia

VIA GARIBALDI
LINCOLN

ORTO BOTANICO

Palazzo dei Normanni

VIA A. MONGITORE
ALBERGHERIA

MERCATO BALLARO
PIAZZA DEL CARMINE
VIA DEL BOSCO

VIA ABRAMO
CORSO DEI MILLE

PIAZZA INDIPENDENZA

Carmine

Stazione Centrale

PARCO D'ORLEANS

San Giovanni degli Eremiti

TUKORY
CORSO

VIA ORTEO

Piazza Nascè

0 400 meters
0 400 yards

local government and Mafia malfeasance—a terrible blight.

And yet the city of Palermo is not irreparably damaged or a lost cause. In the past few years honest administrators have begun to turn the city around, directing considerable sums from the central government as well as the European Union to the restoration of Palermo's historic center.

Chances are good that decadent decay will always be one of Palermo's defining charms, but at least now there is the certainty that this decay will remain picturesque rather than terminal. ■

Around the Quattro Canti

The Quattro Canti has not always been at Palermo's heart. The center of the ancient and Arab-Norman city was bounded by two small rivers and focused on an area to the west of the crossing, near the site of the present cathedral. Its main thoroughfare was the Cassaro. As the city grew and the rivers became silted, the Cassaro—now the western half of Corso Vittorio Emanuele II—was extended eastward. Via Maqueda, the famous old street that crosses the Corso at the Quattro Canti, was laid out in 1600.

Corso Vittorio Emanuele II and the streets around the 400-year-old area known as Quattro Canti make up the bustling hub of historic Palermo.

History & Legacy

The **Quattro Canti** itself was created between 1608 and 1620. Initially it took the name Piazza Vigliena, after the duke of Vigliena, the Spanish viceroy who commissioned the crossing and its four **baroque palaces.**

Each palace's facade is divided into three sections, and each section boasts a central statue and one of three orders of classical columns: Doric, Ionic, or Corinthian. The fountains and statues on each of the lowest registers symbolize the four seasons; the central statues represent the four Spanish kings of Sicily (see p. 26); and the upper statues portray the four patron saints (Christina, Ninfa, Oliva, and Agatha) of the old city quadrants defined by the

Quattro Canti—the Kalsa (southeast), Amalfitania (northeast), Sincaldi (northwest), and Albergheria (southwest).

Once this was a natural meeting place, but the intense traffic now means that pedestrian respite is best enjoyed on **Piazza Pretoria** immediately to the south. Here, the most eye-catching feature is the **Fontana Pretoria** (1554–55), a magnificent central fountain that lends the square its colloquial name, the Piazza della Vergogna, or Piazza of Shame, after the uninhibited nudity of its male and female figures. Local nuns, it is claimed, were so outraged by the work that they broke off the noses of the male statues, only modesty preventing them from removing the more obvious male protuberances. The fountain is the work of a Florentine, Camillo Camilliani (active 1550–1586), and was commissioned by the city's then Spanish viceroy, Don Pedro of Toledo, for his Tuscan villa. The viceroy's son eventually sold the statue to Palermo, where it was reassembled to mostly lascivious approval in 1573.

The fine buildings around the square add to the fountain's considerable theatrical effect, notably the flank and dome of the sumptuously decorated but rarely open Dominican church of **Santa Caterina** (1566–1596; *tel 338 451 2011, closed p.m. daily Nov.–March, Sun. p.m. April–Oct., $*) and the **Palazzo Pretorio** (*tel 091 740 1111*), also known as the Palazzo delle Aquile, after the eagles (*aquile*) that adorn its exterior. Begun in 1463 and much

remodeled since, the palace has long served as the seat of the city's council and is still the Municipio, or City Hall. The facade contains a statue (1661) of St. Rosalia (1132–1166), a niece of the Norman king William I. She became Palermo's patron saint after a procession of her bones, found in 1624, was believed to have saved the city from a plague epidemic. The facade's plaques commemorate a variety of events, including visits from Pope John II and Giuseppe Garibaldi, one of the leading lights of the campaign to unify Italy in the mid-19th century.

INSIDER TIP:

You won't be allowed to enter the Norman-era Cappella Palatina [see p. 50] if you have bare shoulders or are wearing a short skirt, shorts, or low-cut top.

—TIM JEPSON
National Geographic author

Across Via Maqueda from the piazza you'll find **San Giuseppe dei Teatini** (*tel 091 331 239*), *closed noon–5:30 p.m. Mon.–Sat. & 1:15 p.m.–6 p.m. Sun.*), a plain-faced church built between 1612 and 1645 with a lavish baroque interior. Just north of the square, on the Corso, is the more modest and only intermittently open **San Matteo al Cassero** (*tel 335 749 0960, closed Sun. & 1:30 p.m.– 4 p.m. daily*), another beautiful mid-17th-century church with

Palermo

- ⓐ Map p. 43 & inside back cover

Visitor information

- ✉ Via Principe Belmonte 92
- ☎ 091 585 172
- 🕐 Closed Sun., & 2 p.m.–2:30 p.m.

provincia.palermo.it

Visitor information Airport office

- ☎ 091 591 698
- 🕐 Closed Sun.

Quattro Canti

- ⓐ Map p. 43
- ✉ Via Maqueda & Corso Vittorio Emanuele II

links to the Miseremini, an order devoted to the hearing of Masses for souls suffering in purgatory.

Of note are the churches on Piazza Bellini adjoining Piazza Pretoria to the south: **San Cataldo** and **La Martorana** *(tel 091 616 1692,. closed p.m. daily except Wed. & Fri., 3 p.m.–6 p.m.),* the city's most compelling church after the cathedral. Begun in 1143, the glorious Martorana is also known as Santa Maria dell'Ammiraglio, or St. Mary of the Admiral, after its Syrian founder, Georgios Antiochenos, who later became Norman king Roger II's "commander of the ocean," or *amir al-bahr* in Arabic, from which English derives the word "admiral." The church's more common name comes from a nearby convent founded in 1146 by Eloisa de Marturanu, whose nuns were presented with the church in 1433. The same nuns invented Sicily's celebrated *frutta Martorana,* and *pasta reale*—marzipan cakes and candies shaped to resemble fruit.

Sadly, the nuns were less inspired when it came to their inherited church; their many alterations destroyed much of the original building and its decoration. Left untouched, however, were the magnificent mid-12th-century dome mosaics, the side vaults, and the left and right apses. By the door on the west end, on both sides of the steps, look for mosaic panels in baroque frames: One depicts Antiochenos presenting the church to the Virgin; the other shows Roger II (labeled Rogerios Rex) being crowned by Christ. The latter is the only known portrait of the king in Sicily.

Next door to the south, **San Cataldo** *(tel 091 348728, itimed .org, closed 12:30 p.m.–3 p.m. daily, guided tours only, $),* with its bulbous domes, lacks its neighbor's mosaics but is still a captivating Norman building. It was founded by Maio di Bari, William I's chancellor, but left largely undecorated

The 12th-century embellishments in La Martorana are some of the oldest and most magnificent in Palermo.

on his death in 1160. The interior columns are from an older structure, and the marble pavement survives from the original church.

Walk south from San Cataldo on Via Maqueda, and Via Ponticello leads to Piazza Professa, containing the **Chiesa del Gesù** (tel 091 332 213 or 334 187 9038, closed Sun. p.m., daily noon–4:30 p.m., and p.m. daily in Aug.). Built between 1564 and 1636, it was the first church founded by the Jesuits on their arrival in Sicily. Their masterpiece on the island, it shows the Jesuits' typical love of decorative excess, a trait designed to awe potential doubters after the advent of Protestantism with a show of sheer grandeur.

INSIDER TIP:

Tiny, spotless, tucked-away I Cuochini [Via Ruggero Settimo 68] is the place to go for deftly deep-fried savory pastries at exquisitely low prices.

—ROS BELFORD
National Geographic Traveler
magazine writer

Ballarò Market & Nearby

Just beyond San Cataldo, Via Ponticello continues to Piazza Ballarò, the northern limit of the **Mercato Ballarò,** a superb general market (closed Sun.) that infiltrates the streets and alleys to the south as far as Piazza del Carmine. This is the fringe of the **Albergheria district,** one of

EXPERIENCE:
Fuel Up on Great Coffee

Enjoying a cup of coffee is a staple Italian experience. To do so in Palermo, in the company of the locals, head north of the city center to the unassuming **Bar Alba** (Piazza Don Bosco 7c, tel 091 309 016, closed Mon. in winter), said to sell Sicily's best coffee. More central is **Caffè Letterario** (Vicolo della Neva all'Alloro 2–5, tel 091 616 0796, closed Tues.), just off Piazza Marina and close to the Galleria Regionale di Sicilia (see pp. 56–57). It's one of the city's great historic cafés, favored by literary and artistic types over the years. Also noteworthy is the historic **Spinnato** (Via Principe di Belmonte 107–115, close to the visitor center in the north of the city, tel 091 749 5104), near the Palazzo dei Normanni (see pp. 49–51). The chic minimalist bar in the new **Palazzo Riso** contemporary art museum (Corso Vittorio Emanuele II 365, tel 091 587 717) serves espresso, cappuccino, and flavored coffees.

Palermo's poorest quarters, an area that has never really recovered from bomb damage suffered in 1943. Its tiny streets, moribund palaces, and ancient tenements are wonderfully atmospheric.

The soaring, tile-covered dome of **Chiesa del Carmine** (Piazza del Carmine, tel 091 651 2018, closed from 12:30 or 1:30 p.m. daily) strikes an incongruously grand note amid the market's picturesque squalor. Inside, the highlights are two extravagantly decorated altars in the transepts.

From the church, retrace your steps, heading toward **Piazza Bologni,** a large baroque square off the corso that leaves you well placed to visit the cathedral and Palazzo dei Normanni. ■

The Western City

Palermo's western quarter was the heart of the ancient city, its high ground the site of the fortresses and palaces of Sicily's rulers for almost three millennia. The area's principal sights are the cathedral, built over a former mosque, and the majestic Palazzo dei Normanni, whose tiny Cappella Palatina is the city's most compelling Norman monument.

Then and now: Moorish motifs of Palermo's 12th-century cathedral share the scene with street art.

Palermo's **cathedral,** had it not been tampered with over the centuries, would rank as one of Italy's foremost churches. Built on the site of a Byzantine church and later ninth-century mosque, it was founded in 1185 by Walter of the Mill, Palermo's English archbishop. William had been sent to Sicily by King Henry II to tutor William II, in anticipation of the future Norman king's marriage to Joan Plantagenet, the English sister of King Richard I, better known as Richard the Lion-Hearted.

Once in Sicily, the tutor insinuated himself into Sicilian politics, gaining the office of archbishop, in the words of one contemporary historian, "less by election than by violent intrusion." His foundation of the cathedral was in response to his former pupil's foundation of Monreale (see pp. 64–67), the great cathedral located just outside Palermo and designed at least in part to undermine the archbishop's influence.

It is unlikely that the church would have matched Monreale, but enough survives of the original to suggest that its mosaics (these were removed in the 15th century) and decorative stonework would have been of the first rank. That they are not is mostly the fault of Ferdinando Fuga, an 18th-century architect commissioned to "improve" the cathedral with a baroque and neoclassic makeover. Fuga ripped out the wooden ceiling, tore down several walls, and whitewashed much of the interior. Perhaps his worst crime was the addition of the anomalous dome (1781–1801).

On the exterior, only the wonderful Islamic-inspired stonework at the church's eastern end hints as to what might have been, along with the Catalan Gothic **main porch** on the south side *(Piazza della Cattedrale),* begun around 1426. This is noted for the fine portal and doors (1426–1432),

the early painted decoration (1296) above the three main arches, and a column on the left beneath the porch inscribed with a passage from the Koran, evidently a surviving fragment of the earlier mosque.

The **chapel** in the cathedral's southwest corner contains six Norman and Aragonese **royal tombs,** including that of the Norman king Roger II (died 1154; rear left), removed, against his wishes, from the cathedral at Cefalù; that of his daughter, Constance (died 1198; rear right); and the grave of Frederick II (died 1250; left front), the great emperor and king of Sicily. Also buried here is Constance of Aragon (died 1222; far right), Frederick's wife, whose crown was removed from her tomb and is one of the exhibitions in the cathedral's fascinating little **treasury,** entered at the top of the south (right) aisle. Equally interesting is the **crypt,** entered from the north transept, where among 23 numbered tombs is the sarcophagus (No. 16) containing the remains of Walter of the Mill, the church's founder.

Palazzo dei Normanni

West of the cathedral, the Palazzo dei Normanni, or Palace of the Normans, occupies the highest point in the old city, a position that probably has contained either the castle or royal palace of Sicily's rulers since Phoenician times. Even today, the present building on the site is the seat of the Assemblea Regionale Siciliana, the Sicilian regional parliament, housed here since 1947. The area's

Cathedral

🅰 Map p. 43

✉ Piazza della Cattedrale, off Corso Vittorio Emanuele II; also entrance on via Incoronazione

☎ 091 334 373

🕐 Church: closed Sun. 1:30 p.m.– 4:30 p.m. year-round; p.m. Mon.–Sat., Nov.–Feb.

💲 Treasury & crypt: $

cattedrale.palermo.it

Palazzo dei Normanni & Cappella Palatina

🗺 Map p. 43

✉ Palazzo dei Normanni, Piazza Indipendenza

☎ 091 626 2833

🕐 Palazzo apartments & chapel closed Tues.–Thurs., Sun. p.m. Chapel closed Sun.

💲 $$ (includes Sala di Re Ruggero)

first documented fortress was an Arab castle, abandoned by the ruling emir for reasons of security in 938, when the royal residence was moved to the Kalsa district to the southeast. The castle was later reoccupied and enlarged by the Normans, when it became the seat of the most splendid European court of its day.

Much has been added since, notably the long facade (1616), a legacy of Spanish rule, and little of the Arab-Norman building now exists. The principal exceptions are the **Torre Pisana** at the northern end, the only survivor of four original towers, and the **Cappella Palatina,** an exquisite fusion of Arab, Norman, Byzantine, and Sicilian art and architecture. Be prepared to stand in line at this popular site during busy periods.

The Cappella was begun as a private chapel by Roger II in 1130 and was largely completed by about 1140. Once it would have stood alone, but over the years it has been enveloped by the burgeoning palace. Inside, the chapel is split into two, with a lower nave

divided into three aisles by ten granite columns, and the raised chancel and apses at the eastern end. The latter area contains the older mosaics, the chief glory of the chapel's extraordinary decorative scheme. Probably the work of Byzantine artists, these panels (circa 1140–1150) cover the apse and cupola, with the dominant image the apse figure of Christ Pantocrator (see photo p. 31). The later nave mosaics (circa 1150–1170) portray scenes from the Book of Genesis on the south wall. The aisles show episodes from the lives of Sts. Peter and Paul.

This Islamic influence is more marked in the grand wooden ceiling, carved from Lebanese cedar and decorated by Arab craftspeople with scenes from an idealized daily life. Roman and Norman artists left their mark in the 12th-century Cosmati stone floor, marble walls, and majestic pulpit. (The Cosmati were Roman masons who gave their name to a style of decorative stone inlay.) The same artists made a greater impact in the large candlestick,

Christian & Muslim: A Unique Mix

The **Cappella Palatina** is a Christian building, but it embraces Byzantine (Eastern Orthodox) and Arabic–Muslim style elements. This is partly because of the huge influence of Sicily's recent Arab rulers on the island's art and partly because Roger II, who commissioned the chapel in the 12th century, was a cosmopolitan ruler. There are many who argue, however, that the chapel's Islamic elements were a sign of Roger's secret Muslim identity.

The Arab influence is chiefly seen in the marble inlays of the walls and the extraordinary carving of the ceiling, a dense, intricate wooden honeycomb known as *muqarnas.* The chapel is the only original Christian building in the world with such decoration. At the same time, various of the chapel's mosaic panels depict episodes from the Crusades, celebrating episodes in which Christian armies were victorious against their Muslim counterparts.

a spiraling sculpture with more than a hundred figures topped by Christ holding the Gospels. A figure in the garb of a bishop kneels below, and two ranks of birds (vultures and storks) support three figures symbolizing the three ages of humankind.

Elsewhere in the palace, only a limited area is open to the public, notably the **Sala di Re Ruggero** (or the Salon of King Roger), which generally can be seen on a 30-minute guided tour. Part of the former Royal Apartments, this echoes much of the Cappella Palatina, particularly in its mosaics (1140), which portray hunting scenes in typical Sicilian countryside, and symbolic animals: the lion, suggesting royalty and strength, and the peacock, whose supposedly incorruptible flesh made it a symbol of immortality.

San Giovanni degli Eremiti

The picturesque red domes of this deconsecrated church (1132–1148) make it one of the city's most distinctive landmarks. Situated south of the Palazzo dei Normanni, it is Palermo's most romantic Norman monument, not so much because of its austere interior but because of its Moorish domes, its beautiful cloisters, and the little garden—a scented pocket of green calm full of palms, bougainvillea, jasmine, and orange trees.

The church itself was built on the orders of Roger II, and almost certainly stands on the site of an earlier mosque, part of which probably survives in the shape of

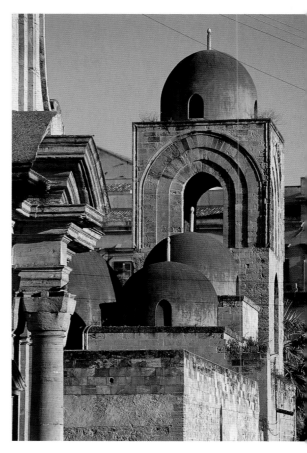

The distinctive domes of San Giovanni degli Eremiti reveal the work of Arab-influenced architects.

the simple hall just to the right of the church.

If the gardens here whet your appetite for bucolic escape, then make your way to the **Villa Bonanno.** This larger oasis is located just to the northeast of the church. Entered from Piazza della Vittoria, the sizable public park is a perfect place to relax and watch the Palermitans as they come out to play. ■

San Giovanni degli Eremiti

🔼 Map p. 43

✉ Via dei Benedettini 16–20

☎ 091 651 5019

🕐 Closed Mon. & Sun. p.m.

💲 $$

The Mafia

Everyone has heard of the Mafia. The word first appeared in Italian around 1860. By 1866, it was used by Sicily's British consul, who reported to his superiors that "maffie-elected juntas share the earnings of the workmen, keep up intercourse with outcasts and take malefactors under their wing and protection." The word "mafia" has ancient origins, likely linked to the Arab word *mu'afàh,* meaning protection, skill, beauty, ability, and safety.

In Catania, police pose with the goods—the work of an infamous Cosa Nostra weapons maker.

The organizational roots are more elusive. Many scholars believe the seeds were sown as early as the 12th century, when secret societies were created to resist the imposition of rule by the Holy Roman Empire. Others point to the Bourbons, who used ex-brigands to police the remote Sicilian interior, a system that quickly led to the brigands taking bribes in exchange for turning a blind eye to the activities of their former criminal colleagues. Many also cite the rise of the so-called *gabellotti,* middlemen who acted as rent collectors or mediators between peasants and landowners and quickly grew rich by intimidating the former and acting as agents for the latter. United by similar aims, the gabellotti became a separate class, bound by distinct codes of honor and behavior.

The centuries-old gulf between Sicilians and agents of authority was fostered by Sicily's long succession of exploitative foreign rulers. Nowhere was the breach more keenly felt than by landless peasants forced to work on the island's *latifundia,* vast feudal estates owned by absentee landlords. The system went back to Roman times and survived until well after World War II. Where conventional justice and authority were either lacking or despised, it was only a matter of time before the gap was filled by all manner of local arbitrators—the so-called *amici* (friends) or *uomini d'onore* (men of honor).

The traveler Patrick Brydone, writing in *A Tour through Sicily and Malta,* summarized the situation in 1773: "These *banditti,*" he wrote, "are the most respectable of the island, and have the highest and most romantic notions of what they call their point of honour...with respect to one another, and to every person to whom they have once professed it, they have ever maintained the most unshaken fidelity. The magistrates have often been obliged to protect them, and even pay them court, as they are known to be extremely determined and desperate; and so extremely vindictive, that they will certainly put any person to death who has ever given them just cause of provocation."

The World War II Connection

What many people do not know is that Italy once came within a whisker of overturning this state of affairs. Under Mussolini, the legendary police chief Cesare Mori used brutal and entirely illegal measures to combat the Mafia, and, but for World War II, might have crushed it.

Ironically, it was the intervention of the Americans that foiled the venture. In preparing for the invasion of Sicily in 1943, the Allies had only one source of intelligence and logistical support—the Mafia—with whom it forged links by exploiting the contacts of Italian-American gangsters such as Lucky Luciano.

Once the Allies had taken Sicily, they reinforced Mafia power by drafting its often highly placed members onto the new Allied Military Government—of 66 Sicilian towns, 62 were entrusted to men with criminal connections.

Power was further consolidated in Italy's postwar boom, when fortunes were made in construction. Two Mafia-connected officials took control of the Office of Public Works in 1956; until 1963, some 80 percent of building permits were awarded to just five men. Money was then laundered into legitimate businesses or funneled into cigarette smuggling and drugs.

Addio Pizzo

Casual visitors will not be aware of the Mafia's activities in Sicily, but many local businesses cannot help but take account of the organization's presence. The Addio Pizzo, or "Goodbye Pizzo," movement *(addiopizzo.org),* set up in 2004, states that some 80 percent of the island's businesses pay some form of protection money—for which the slang term is *pizzo*—producing an estimated "income" for the Mafia of $1.5 billion annually. Businesses in the movement are fighting back and attempting to end the practice.

Two so-called Mafia wars in the 1970s resulted in the deaths of hundreds of *mafiosi,* as well as many innocent victims, but the 1980s saw a sea change, beginning with the defection of Tommaso Buscetta, a leading clan member who turned informant. This was followed by the prosecution of criminals by magistrates Giovanni Falcone and Paolo Borsellino—both murdered in 1992.

The Future?

Recent arrests of major bosses include Bernardo Provenzano in 2006 and Guido Spina in 2014. Despite these and other successes, however, the Mafia's dismemberment remains highly unlikely largely because its tentacles are now so tightly entwined in Italy's legitimate economy: Not for nothing do the Italians refer to the Mafia as *la piovra*—the octopus.

The Eastern City

The eastern quarter of Palermo from the Quattro Canti to the harbor embraces the Kalsa, the old Arab and medieval heart of the city. Badly damaged by Allied bombing in 1943, it is a traditionally poor area, but one that is undergoing belated restoration. The Eastern City includes many palaces, churches, and the Galleria Regionale di Sicilia, the city's foremost art museum.

The Museo Internazionale delle Marionette holds one of the world's largest collections of puppets, including this knight.

A Casual Walking Tour

Start at the Quattro Canti and walk east along Corso Vittorio Emanuele II to Via Roma, a relatively modern street. Just beyond, Via Paternostro leads to **San Francesco d'Assisi** *(Via del Parlamento, tel 091 582 370, closed noon–4 p.m., Sat. p.m. & Sun. during services & sometimes Sat. p.m.),* a 13th-century church much altered over the centuries. Outside, the main Gothic portal and pretty rose window are the key features, while inside the highlight of the stripped-back interior is the Cappella Mastrantonio, the fourth chapel on the south (left) side. Its lovely carved arch (1468), the work of Francesco Laurana (1430–1502), was the first major Renaissance work in Sicily.

Also noteworthy are the eight statues in the nave by Giacomo Serpotta (1656–1732), who was responsible for the outstanding stucco work of the **Oratorio di San Lorenzo** *(tel 091 611 8168, enter at Via dell'Immacolatella 5, 10 a.m.–8 p.m. daily, $),* next to the church on the left. The artist's masterpiece, the decoration depicts events from the lives of St. Laurence (Lorenzo) and St. Francis of Assisi.

Via Merlo leads from Piazza San Francesco to the 17th-century **Palazzo Mirto** on the right *(Via Merlo 2, tel 091 616 7541, may close*

INSIDER TIP:

For generous portions of great food, head to Bar Touring [*Via Alcide De Gasperi 237*], right near the botanic gardens [see p. 57].

—MICHAEL COON
Culinary Institute of America
travel director

Sun. p.m., $), the seat of the Lanzi-Filangeri family until it was donated to the city in 1982. The interior offers a good idea of how a princely family residence of the period might have looked, with a series of well-preserved rooms.

Via Merlo opens out beyond the palace onto the large **Piazza Marina,** part of the old port before it silted up. Most activity centers on the central Giardino Garibaldi and its magnificent banyan trees. The area was once close to two prisons, including one run by the Spanish Inquisition, and was the scene of burnings and other public executions.

Palazzo Chiaramonte dominates the piazza's eastern flank, built in 1307 for the Chiaramonte, Palermo's most flamboyant 14th-century family. The building was later appropriated by Palermo's Spanish viceroys and handed to the Inquisition. After 1782, when the Inquisition was abolished in Sicily, it served as the city's law courts. Today, it is used for exhibitions. Note the lower windows, whose decoration is so distinctive that the name Chiaramonte is

given to the style, which is used in many buildings around the city.

Not far from the palace is one of Palermo's most charming museums, the **Museo Internazionale delle Marionette** (*Piazza Antonio Pasqualino 5, tel 091 328 060, closed Sun. & 1 p.m.–2:30 p.m. Mon.–Sat., museomarionettepalermo .it, $$*). Devoted entirely to puppets, its fabulous 3,000-strong collection showcases marionettes from throughout Sicily, where puppet theaters were an important cultural phenomenon for centuries before their decline in the 1960s. Today, something of a revival of the old plays and courtly characters has taken place. Along with performances, the museum devotes considerable space to puppets from around the world.

Tears of an Art Thief

The theft of a Caravaggio masterpiece Nativity painting from Palermo's Oratorio di San Lorenzo in 1969—the painting was hacked from its frame—is a crime that remains unsolved. In the 1980s, however, a Mafia boss, Francesco Marino Mannoia, confessed to the robbery during his trial, but claimed the painting was damaged beyond repair, and that upon seeing the ravaged work, the man who had commissioned the heist burst into tears.

North of the museum and Piazza Marina is La Cala, the remains of the old Arab and Norman port, which once extended much farther into the heart of the city. On its south side, on the corso, stands **Santa Maria della Catena** (*Piazza delle Dogane, tel 091 321 529, $*), an elegantly

Guests dine alfresco at the Antica Foccaceria on Piazza San Francesco in the heart of old Palermo.

restored 16th-century church whose name—St. Mary of the Chains—probably derives from the chain *(catena)* that was once stretched nightly across the harbor from here.

To the east, at the end of the corso, is the modern **waterfront,** entered via the Porta Felice (1582) gateway. In its day, this was one of Italy's great promenades, but the current area, cut through by the busy Foro Italico-Umberto I, though still a popular meeting place, is an unattractive affair.

Palaces, Paintings, & Places of Worship

Backtrack through the Porta Felice, passing the **Passeggiata delle Cattive,** or Walkway of the Mean-Spirited, on the south (left) side of the corso. One of the last fragments of the old Arab wall that once enclosed the Kalsa, it takes its name from the old women who used to look disapprovingly on the antics of couples promenading below.

Just beyond, turn left off the corso on Via Butera, passing by the impressive 17th-century Palazzo Branciforti on the left and, alongside it, the site of the Trinacria, Palermo's smartest hotel between 1844 and 1911. Soon after comes Via Butera's intersection with Via Alloro, traditionally the Kalsa's main street, though its once fine palaces have suffered greatly from years of neglect.

One that hasn't is the Palazzo Abatellis (1484–1495), home to the **Galleria Regionale di Sicilia** *(Via Alloro 4, tel 091 623 0011, closed Sun.–Mon., $$$),* Palermo's foremost gallery of paintings and sculpture. The pictorial highlight is the "Triumph of Death" (circa

1449), by an unknown (possibly Flemish or central Italian) painter. Many later artists, including Pablo Picasso, were inspired by the work. Other highlights include Francesco Laurana's 15th-century bust of Eleanor of Aragon and the paintings that trace the history of Sicilian art from Byzantine times. Here are several works by Antonello da Messina, Sicily's foremost Renaissance painter, and in particular his "Annunciation" (1476), considered his masterpiece.

Before leaving the vicinity of the gallery, look at the churches immediately to its east and west on Via Alloro, both with fine facades and rich interiors: the 17th-century **Santa Maria della Pietà** (enter on Via Torremuzza, tel 091 616 5266, closed Sun. & daily noon–4 p.m.) is on the left as you face the gallery and 15th-century **La Gancia** (tel 091 616 5221, closed p.m. daily) is on the right.

Turn left off Via Alloro beyond La Gancia, and Via Vetriera leads to Piazza dello Spasimo, named after the nearby **Santa Maria dello Spasimo** (1509), a rare piece of Sicilian Gothic architecture (tel 091 617 1658, closed Tues. a.m. & 11 a.m.–4:30 p.m. daily). The church's name probably derives from the first spasm of pain endured by Mary when she saw Christ on the Cross. Now deconsecrated, the building serves as an important cultural center, and has become a symbol of the restoration under way in the Kalsa.

Further evidence of this restoration can be seen in the blossoming **Villa Giulia** (Via Abramo Lincoln) to the south, once a park

(created in 1778) in which no self-respecting Palermitan would venture by day, never mind night. Next door is Palermo's delightful botanical garden, the **Orto Botanico** (Via Abramo Lincoln 2b, tel 091 623 8241, ortobotanico.unipa .it, $$), first opened in 1795.

If you turn right on Via dello Spasimo, you'll see the isolated **La Magione** (Piazza Magione), a sensitively restored Arab-Norman Romanesque church founded in 1151. From the church, Via Magione leads west to Palazzo Ajutamicristo (1490) and Via Garibaldi, named after the eponymous Italian revolutionary who led his troops up this very street in 1860 during the campaign to unify Italy. ■

Contemporary Art

Impressive new galleries of contemporary art symbolize the renaissance of Palermo's historic center. Experience the regeneration firsthand by visiting **Francesco Pantaleone Arte Contemporanea** (Corso Vittorio Emanuele II 303, tel 091 332 482, fpac.it, closed Mon.) at the heart of the city, and the **Palazzo Riso** (Corso Vittorio Emanuele II 365, tel 091 587 717, palazzoriso .it, closed Mon., $$), elegantly occupying a 17th-century palace and devoted to work by Sicilian painters and international artists working on the island.

The city also has a striking new home for its civic collection of 19th-, 20th-, and 21st-century art, the **Galleria d'Arte Moderna,** in the beautifully restored Sant'Anna palace complex (Complesso Monumentale di Sant'Anna, Via Sant'Anna 21, tel 091 843 1605, galleriadartemoderna palermo.it, closed Mon., $$). Book a guided tour if you want to learn more about the art on display.

A Walk Around the Northern City

Northern Palermo hinges around two districts: the Capo, one of the most impoverished and battered parts of the old center, and the Vucciria, an area centered around a superb market. The latter lies close to the city's main historical museum and two oratories that contain some of Palermo's finest baroque decoration.

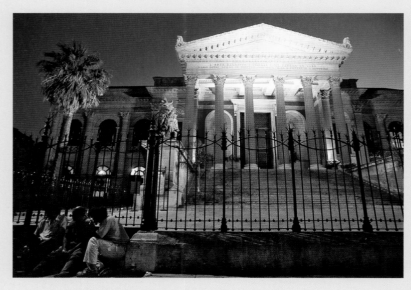

The restored 19th-century Teatro Massimo has become a symbol of Palermo's recent cultural rebirth.

Start a tour of the northern city by walking east from the Quattro Canti on Corso Vittorio Emanuele II. After two blocks, on the left stands the little church of **San Matteo al Cassero** ➊ *(closed Sun.)*, whose interior features a glorious frescoed ceiling and 17th-century statues by Giacomo Serpotta, a foretaste of the superb works you will see later in the walk by this master of stucco (plaster) decoration.

A left turn up Via Roma leads past the church of **San Antonio** ➋, rebuilt after an earthquake of 1823, which commands the highest point in the eastern quarter of the old city. Steps alongside the church, and streets to the north and the south, lead to the **Mercato Vucciria** ➌, Palermo's wonderfully lively main market *(closed Sun. & daily p.m.).* Less a feast for the senses

NOT TO BE MISSED:

Vucciria • The oratories of San Domenico and Santa Cita • Museo Archeologico Regionale

than an assault on them, the narrow streets here are crammed with stalls selling everything from cascades of brains, tripe, swordfish, and live octopus (among many other foodstuffs) to fake designer bags, contraband cigarettes, and bargain-priced household goods such as porcelain pasta bowls and espresso cups.

At the market's northern limit, just off Via Roma, stands the church of **San Domenico** ➍

(*Piazza San Domenico, tel 091 589 172, domenicani-palermo.it, closed p.m. daily*). It was rebuilt in its present form in 1640, only the cloisters surviving from the 14th-century original. Inside are the tombs of numerous illustrious Palermitans, but here the interest is found not in the main church but in the tiny oratory to its rear—the 16th-century **Oratorio del Rosario di San Domenico** ❺ (*Via dei Bambinai 2, tel 091 609 0308, closed Sun. & p.m. daily, $; see sidebar p. 60*).

The interior of the oratory is filled with some of Palermo's finest baroque decoration, namely the extraordinary stucco work of Giacomo Serpotta, who was born in the city in 1656 and devoted most of his life to working

in a medium with little of the versatility, tradition, or potential for artistic glory of paint or marble. This oratory was his last work (1720) and one of his most joyful and vivacious. The cream of Palermo's high-society ladies provided the models for the many allegorical figures. Gracing the main altar is a painting by Anthony Van Dyck, the "Madonna With St. Dominic and the Patron Saints of Palermo" (1628), completed in Genoa after a plague epidemic forced the artist to flee Palermo.

Continue north on Via dei Bambinai, passing on the left **Santa Maria di Valverde** ❻ (*tel 091 332 779, closed Sun. & p.m. daily, $$*), another 17th-century church with a majestic baroque interior. A few steps beyond stands

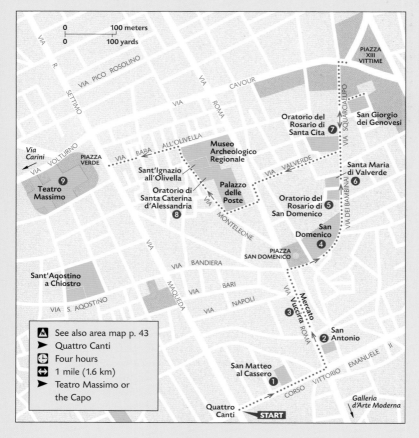

0	100 meters
0	100 yards

PIAZZA XIII VITTIME

VIA R. SETTIMO

VIA PICO ROSOLINO

VIA CAVOUR

VIA ROMA

VIA SQUARCIALUPO

Oratorio del Rosario di Santa Cita ❼

San Giorgio dei Genovesi

Via Carini

VIA VOLTURNO

PIAZZA VERDE

VIA BARA

ALL'OLIVELLA

Museo Archeologico Regionale

VIA VALVERDE

Santa Maria di Valverde ❻

Teatro Massimo ❾

Sant'Ignazio all'Olivella

Oratorio di Santa Caterina d'Alessandria ❽

Palazzo delle Poste

VIA DEI BAMBINAI

Oratorio del Rosario di San Domenico ❺

VIA MONTELEONE

San Domenico ❹

VIA

PIAZZA SAN DOMENICO

Sant'Agostino a Chiostro

VIA BANDIERA

VIA MAQUEDA

VIA BARI

VIA NAPOLI

VIA S. AGOSTINO

Mercato Vucciria

VIA ROMA

San Antonio ❷ ❸

San Matteo al Cassero ❶

CORSO VITTORIO EMANUELE II

Galleria d'Arte Moderna

Quattro Canti

START

🅰 See also area map p. 43
▶ Quattro Canti
🕓 Four hours
↔ 1 mile (1.6 km)
▶ Teatro Massimo or the Capo

Package Deal

A single ticket, the Tesori della Loggia (*tel 091 785 3181, ilgeniodipalermo.com, $$*) gets you into five sights in northern Palermo: **San Giorgio dei Genovesi, Santa Maria di Valverde,** the **Chiesa di Santa Cita,** the **Oratorio del Rosario di San Domenico,** and the **Oratorio del Rosario di Santa Cita** (*all closed Sun. & p.m. daily Nov.–March, closed Sat. p.m. April–Oct.*). Tickets can be purchased online or at the Oratorio del Rosario di Santa Cita (see below).

Santa Cita, or Zita, rebuilt between 1586 and 1603, but badly damaged by bombs in 1943. Here, as in San Domenico, the main attraction is not the main church but its oratory, the **Oratorio del Rosario di Santa Cita** ❼ (*Via Squarcialupo, tel 091 785 3181, closed Sat. p.m. & Sun. April–Oct., Sun & after 3 p.m. daily Nov.–March, $$*), usually entered through the church.

Here, too, the lure is the work of Serpotta, who between 1686 and 1718 created another mesmerizing swirl of stucco angels, miscellaneous figures, and numerous cherubs (for which Palermo's street children provided the models). The centerpiece at the rear of the nave is a depiction of the Battle of Lepanto (1571), in which a Christian fleet defeated the Ottomans (Turks). During the battle the victorious fleet looked for protection to the Madonna of the Rosary, hence the stucco reliefs elsewhere in the oratory portraying 15 Mysteries of the Rosary. The south (right) wall depicts the so-called Sorrowful Mysteries—including Calvary, the Thorn of Crowns, and Christ's Flagellation—and the left wall the Joyful Mysteries, notably the Resurrection, Ascension, and Assumption of the Virgin.

To the north and east of Santa Cita is an area badly damaged in 1943, a forlorn district best avoided except for a brief few steps down Via Squarcialupo to visit **San Giorgio dei Genovesi** (1581), a now deconsecrated church built for Palermo's Genovese merchants, and **Piazza XIII**

Vittime beyond, a square with monuments to the 13 nationalists shot by the Bourbons in 1860 on the eve of Italian unification. Also here is a shrine (1989) to victims of the Mafia.

Walk back to Santa Cita and turn right (west) down Via Valverde to emerge on Via Roma in front of the city's colossal post office, a brutal Fascist-era monolith (1933). Walk behind it on little Via Monteleone past the **Oratorio di Santa Caterina d'Alessandria** ❽ on the right at No. 50 (*Piazza Olivella I, tel 091 872 8047, irregular hours, $*), which has stuccos (1719–1726) by Giacomo Serpotta's son and apprentice, Procopio.

Also visit the church next door, **Sant'Ignazio all'Olivella** (*tel 091 586 867, closed Sun. p.m., 11 a.m.–5 p.m. rest of week*), an opulent baroque affair built in 1598 on the reputed birthplace of Santa Rosalia, Palermo's principal patron saint.

Alongside the church is the northern quarter's main highlight, the **Museo Archeologico Regionale** (*Piazza Olivella-Via Bara all'Olivella 24, tel 091 611 6805, closed p.m., Sat. & Sun., $$*). Devoted to the history and archaeology of western Sicily, this museum's only Sicilian rival is the museum in Syracuse, which performs a similar role for the eastern part of the island. Most eras of Sicily's long past are covered, with wonderful displays of Neolithic, Phoenician, Greek, Roman, Arab, Norman, and other artifacts. The highlights are the metopes, or sculpted reliefs, from the temples at Selinunte (see pp. 90–92); 12,000 votive offerings to Demeter Malophoros from the same site; a fine collection of Greek ceramics; and seven Roman bronzes, including a celebrated third-century B.C. bronze ram.

Round off your tour of the northern city by following Via Bara all'Olivella west from the museum to see the **Teatro Massimo** ❾ (1875–1897), Europe's third largest opera house.

Finally, if time and spirits allow, venture southwest into the heart of the **Capo,** Palermo's least developed and, most would agree, least savory popular neighborhood—in particular the **market** in and around Via Carini—but be prepared for a very poor and largely shabby area.

Catacombe dei Cappuccini

Long after other memories of your visit to Sicily have faded, chances are that you will recall the Convento dei Cappuccini with a sort of grisly fascination. In one of Italy's most bizarre and macabre sights, the corpses of some 8,000 people are preserved in period dress and in various states of bodily decay.

Little in the entrance to the Capuchin convent on Palermo's outskirts suggests what is to come. A long, whitewashed corridor curves underground as a faint, unearthly smell of damp and decay assaults the nostrils. Then comes a scene from somewhere between a horror film and a canvas by Hieronymous Bosch. Row after row of lolling heads, faces twisted in grimaces, frozen screams, and skeletal smiles gaze down from cobwebbed corridors. Men, women, and children, dressed as they were on the day of death, or in clothes they chose for the afterlife, stand shackled to the walls. Skulls and splintered bones break through stretched and shrunken yellow skin. Time has been kind to a few. Some are simply theatrical; others, in slippers and top hats, almost comical. Many, hooded and funereal, are the Grim Reaper incarnate.

This bizarre catalog of death is unique. Other catacombs have their ossuaries, vast repositories of bones and skulls, but only here has the effort been made to immortalize corruptible flesh. At first, the dubious honor of cheating death was reserved for the convent's Capuchin monks. The first was placed here in about 1599. In time, however, rich patrons of the monastery came to share

Dressed as in life, preserved corpses of monks, priests, and others interred in the Capuchin catacombs present a hard-to-forget macabre window on the past.

the perverse privilege. Eventually, anyone with sufficient funds could buy a place. Business was brisk until outlawed in 1881.

Various methods were used to preserve bodies. During plague epidemics, corpses were preserved in baths of arsenic or covered in a protective coating. Upon others,

Convento dei Cappuccini

- Map p. 43
- Via Pindemonte-Piazza Cappuccini
- ☎ 091 652 4156
- $ $
- Closed noon–3 p.m., plus Sun. p.m. Nov.–March

catacombepalermo.it

doctors performed crude surgery to leave only skin, hair, and nails. The most common method was simple desiccation, bodies being left in special terra-cotta urns or placed in closed cells in the area's dry tufaceous subsoil. After eight months of burial or drying, corpses were pickled in vinegar, baked in the sun, and then sent to join the bodies already in the catacombs. Once, all the corpses were fitted with glass eyes, but U.S. troops carried them off as souvenirs in 1944.

The collection is divided into sections: men, women, priests, and so-called professionals, the last rewarded with a coffin, albeit one that is open or has windows cut into its sides. Whether as a reward or perverse prudery, virgins are also segregated, as are cardinals and archbishops, distinguished by the faded glory of threadbare vestments. In fact, it's the clothes and other memento mori that are most poignant: bones pushing through kid gloves, fine silks and satins crumbled almost to powder, and the fading Sunday best of some inmates, the peasant burlap of others.

The family groups are particularly moving. In one corner, a small group stands under an Old Testament quote from Job: "I said to putrefaction and the vermin: You are my mother and father." Nothing, however, is as affecting as the corpse of two-year-old Rosalia Lombardo, who died in 1920, but whose auburn hair and honeyed skin are almost perfectly preserved. Her embalmer, a local doctor, took the secret of his successful (and illegal) techniques to the grave. ■

Stuck in time: Visitors at the Convento dei Cappuccini view rows and rows of corpses that have been segregated by gender, social rank, and profession.

EXPERIENCE: Palermo's Street Food—Step Right Up

Eating in a restaurant is one thing, but you'll have a far more authentic Palermitan food experience by sampling some of the city's celebrated street fare. Mix with the jostling crowds in the Vucciria market and join a line at one of the various *friggitorie,* or fried-food stands, savoring the tempting smells wafting on the air and the boisterous banter that flies between customers and vendors.

Order *frittula* (pieces of fried meat served on waxed paper) or hearty *panelle* (chick-pea fritters) crammed into a warm bread roll (*malfadina*) at the **Vucciria market** (see p. 58). Or, if your stomach and sense of adventure are stronger, how about *pane con la milza—pani cà meusa* in the local dialect (calf's spleen sandwiches)— or *stigghiola* (grilled goat or sheep's intestines)? Another common dish is *babbaluci* (baby snails marinated in olive oil and served with garlic and parsley).

Wash down the snacks with a drink at **Taverna Azzurra** (*Via Domenico Scinà*), a traditional tavern in the Vucciria market that is always busy and fun.

Other places to sample food on the street include **Friggitoria Chiluzzo** (*Piazza Kalsa*), where you shelter under a simple canopy, drink beer from the bottle, and eat bread and panelle from waxed paper. Or head for **Franco 'U Vastiddaru** (*corner of Piazza Marina & Corso Vittorio Emanuele II—near the Palazzo Chiaramonte*), and tuck into *crocchè* (potato croquettes with anchovy and cheese) and pani cà meusa, eaten off plastic plates with plastic knives and forks.

In business since the days of Moorish occupation, the Ballarò market still has the feel of a millennium-old Arab suq.

Down by the port, watch out for **Pani Cà Meusa** (*Via Cala 62*), the place for calf's spleen sandwiches (all that's served here).

Elsewhere, experience another extremely common local specialty, *sfinciuni* (a type of spicy pizza), whose dialect name may be a corruption of the Greek *sponghía* (*spugna* in Italian, sponge in English), after the food's appearance. It's made with dozens of slightly different recipes but usually involves a dough that features beer and olive oil, plus tomatoes, onions—sometimes anchovies—and oregano and *caciocavallo* (a large Sicilian cheese made primarily from the milk of cows). Once the dish was made only at Christmas or to celebrate an engagement; now it is available year-round from stands at the **Vucciria, Ballarò, Del Capo,** and **Borgo Vecchio** markets, and in many *focaccerie* (old-style sandwich bars) such as **Antica Focacceria San Francesco** (*Via Alessandro Paternostro 58, tel 091 320 264*), **Focacceria Basile** (*Via Bara all'Olivella 76, Piazza Nascé 5*), **Cibus** (*Via Emerico Amari 64, tel 091 323 062*), and **Pizzeria Astoria** (*Via della Libertà 64*).

Monreale

One of Europe's supreme cathedrals, Monreale stands as a monument to the greatest traditions of Arab, Norman, and Byzantine art and architecture. Sadly, it has the misfortune to be stranded in a town almost subsumed by the seething suburbs of present-day Palermo. Brave the surroundings, however, because the church, and its mosaics in particular, constitute Sicily's single greatest treasure.

Monreale cathedral represents the pinnacle of Arab-Norman-Byzantine art and architecture.

Monreale was built on the whim of Norman monarch William II (1153–1189). The king's royal predecessors had all endowed or created magnificent religious foundations in Sicily. William was determined to do the same. The impulse to build the church, he claimed, was the result of a dream-vision he'd had in 1174 in which the Madonna revealed the location of a great treasure hidden by his father, William I (1120–1166). The treasure was hidden on Monte Reale, or the Royal Mountain, a hunting estate in the hills above Palermo. It was to be used, the vision instructed, to build a magnificent church.

Monreale's Roots

In truth, the motives for creating so magnificent a building were as much political as religious. In Walter of the Mill, Palermo's powerful English archbishop,

William had a significant political foe. The autocratic archbishop had vast lay as well as religious powers, and the support of much of the nobility. The king, by contrast, was more kindly disposed toward the papacy, an institution for which the independently minded nobles had little sympathy.

The creation of Monreale would have two advantages: First, an awe-inspiring building would underline William's worldly power—and undermine the prestige of Archbishop Walter. Second, in turning over the completed church to the Benedictines, William was able to create a new archbishopric to challenge that of Palermo, for the abbot of a religious order thus endowed automatically became archbishop.

Walter's response was to begin work on his own pet project—the enlargement of Palermo's cathedral—though he could scarcely match the colossal financial outlay of William. As for his response to the new archbishopric, there was little to be done, especially as Pope Alexander III gave Monreale his special blessing, further undermining Archbishop Walter's authority.

Building Monreale

Exactly where William found the resources necessary to build so sumptuous a church is one of Monreale's many mysteries. Unlike projects of a similar scale—the cathedral in Orvieto, Italy, for example, which took 350 years to complete—the Sicilian cathedral took a little over 10 years from vision to consecration. Such speed

must have required prodigious numbers of laborers and craftspeople, not to mention considerable sums for precious marble and other materials—the mosaics alone utilized 4,885 pounds (2,200 kg) of the highest quality gold.

The effects of so rapid a creation were significant. That the project was so personal to William meant that Monreale's political influence survived only as long as the king, who died just four years after the cathedral's completion. More significantly, it meant that the building achieved an architectural and decorative

INSIDER TIP:

During the Sacred Music Week in November, concerts by performers from all over the world take place in the famous cathedral.

—SHEILA BUCKMASTER
National Geographic Traveler
magazine editor at large

unity that would have been compromised by a longer gestation. Thus in Orvieto, and most other major medieval building projects, the changing architectural taste over several decades or centuries was often reflected in a medley of Romanesque, Gothic, and other building styles.

In Monreale the result was not only Europe's finest Norman building and its most impressive synthesis of Arab and European

Monreale

🅰 Map p. 43

✉ Piazza Guglielmo II

☎ 091 640 4501

💲 Cathedral: $, Tower & Treasury: $, Cloisters: $$

🕐 Cathedral: closed Sun. 10 a.m.–2:30/ 3:30 p.m. & possibly 12:45 p.m.– 2:30/3:30 p.m. daily Nov.– March Cloisters: closed Mon. Ticket office closes 1:30 p.m.– 2:30 p.m. daily but Cloisters remain open to those already in the complex.

monrealeduomo.it

cattedralemonreale .it

Pertinent Practicalities

Monreale lies in the hills 6 miles (10 km) southwest of Palermo on the SS186 road, and can be seen as a half-day excursion from the city or a stop en route to **Segesta** (see pp. 72–73) or **Erice** (see pp. 76–79). Numerous companies offer organized bus tours to the town, but it's just as easy—and less expensive—to visit independently. A cab is the simplest way to go, but note that it can be difficult to find a cab in Monreale for the return trip. If you come by car, park in one of the lower lots in town and take the stairs to the center. You can also get there by public transit from Palermo. The 389 bus (*www.aziendasicilianatrasporti.it, $*) departs every 25 to 60 minutes from Piazza Indipendenza (take AMAT, *amat.it*, bus 109 from the railroad station), which is just west of the Palazzo dei Normanni in the city center. Journey time is between 30 and 45 minutes, depending on traffic.

styles but also the world's most extensive array of medieval Christian mosaic work.

Little on the cathedral's exterior, however, suggests the splendor within. The two towers on the west end facing Piazza Guglielmo II (William II Square) frame a banal porch added in the 18th century, lifted by the fine portal and superb **bronze door** (1186). The latter is the work of Bonanno da Pisa, the architect largely responsible for the Leaning Tower of Pisa. The door's 46 panels depict scenes from the Old and New Testaments, their earthy, Romanesque simplicity in marked contrast to the more intricate Byzantine-influenced panels of the door (1179) by Barisano da Trani on the left (north) side of the cathedral

on Piazza Vittorio Emanuele II. Inside, the building is a marvel, shimmering with gold leaf, paintings, richly colored marble, and a staggering array of mosaics. If you have seen Palermo's Cappella Palatina (see pp. 50–51), founded by William's grandfather Roger II, both its interior and decoration are similar, though on a massively grander scale. The arches of the nave, the main central body of the church, are carried on 18 slender columns, all made from granite except for one, which is of *cipollino* (onion) marble, probably designed to symbolize the office of archbishop. The columns clearly come from some earlier pagan temple or temples, though from where scholars are unsure, for the stone is of northern European origin.

The **mosaics,** one of Europe's great artistic glories, surpass even those of Ravenna (on Italy's east coast) and the Basilica of St. Mark in Venice. Covering an area of 64,000 square feet (5,950 sq m), the cycle was probably completed around 1182 by a combination of Greek, Byzantine, and Sicilian craftsmen. Some of the mosaics, notably those that line the nave and walls, are probably later works, dating from after William's death. These panels have a greater naturalism and sense of movement, suggesting that they are the work of Venetian artists sent south on the orders of the papacy.

The nave mosaics depict episodes from the Old and New Testaments, starting with the Creation in the upper tier at the nave's far end on the right (south) side and moving clockwise around the church. Mosaics in the crossing and transepts portray scenes from the Nativity and Christ's Passion, while the central apse's centerpiece is the majestic half figure of Christ Pantocrator, hovering above the traditional hierarchy of Madonna, angels, and named saints.

Tombs, Treasury, & Views

The right (south) transept contains the tombs of William I and William II, while across the church in the opposite transept are the tombs of Margaret, Roger, and Henry, the wife and sons of William I. To their right is an inscription marking the presence in 1270 of the French St. Louis, whose body was laid in the cathedral en route to France after his death in Tunis during the Crusades. His heart is buried here.

Close to the tombs is the entrance to the cathedral **treasury,** home to numerous precious reliquaries, though your time is better spent climbing the 180 steps to the roof for superlative views of the cathedral, the cloisters, Palermo, and the town of Monreale. The entrance is in the lower right (southwest) corner of the church. The climb should whet your appetite for a closer look at the **cloisters,** a sight that alone is worth a visit to Monreale. They are entered outside the cathedral from Piazza Guglielmo II.

The cloisters, part of the old Benedictine abbey attached to the cathedral, represent another pinnacle of Arab-Norman art, their myriad arches borne by 228 paired columns and capitals, very few of which are alike. Most of the fabulous 12th-century Romanesque capitals—the work of Burgundian and Provençal masons—display a bewildering range of styles, mixing religious, pagan, classical, mythical, and other iconography.

Be sure to visit the monastery **gardens,** usually entered from the southeast corner of Piazza Guglielmo II. They are lovely, with some fine old plants, including several magnificent banyan trees. ■

Children play around a statue of William II, Monreale's Norman founder, who is portrayed presenting his cathedral to God.

More Places to Visit in Palermo

The sandy beach at Mondello sits sheltered by the craggy slopes of Monte Pellegrino.

La Favorita

This large park, created in 1799 at the foot of Monte Pellegrino (see below), is best visited in daytime to see the **Museo Etnografico Siciliano Pitrè** *(Viale Duca degli Abruzzi 1, tel 091 740 4893, closed for restoration)*. Sicily's largest ethnographical museum is an essential for anyone interested in folk traditions. Among the many aspects and objects of traditional Sicilian life shown here are the beautifully painted carts for which rural Sicily was once famous.

La Zisa

The best of the surviving Arab-Norman secular buildings, **La Zisa** *(Piazza Zisa 1, tel 091 652 0269, closed p.m. Sun. & Mon., $)* is one of the Norman palaces built on the city's outskirts. The 12th-century palace has been beautifully restored, and the gardens screen the encroaching modern world. To the north is the **Villa Whitaker Malfitano** *(Via Dante 167, tel 091 682 0522, www.fondazionewhitaker .it, closed daily p.m. & Sun., $$)*, built in 1887 by an English wine merchant. It is full of exquisite furniture and fittings, and the large park and garden contain rare trees and shrubs.

Mondello

Palermo's seaside resort, with its 1.25-mile (2 km) sandy beach, lies 7 miles (11 km) northwest of city center between Monte Pellegrino and the headland at Capo Gallo. In summer many people come for the waterfront trattorias, where the morning's catch of fish and seafood is laid out for inspection. For quieter resorts, continue west around the headland to the Golfo di Carini and the towns of Sferracavallo, Isola delle Femmine, and Terrasini.
🚌 Bus: 806 & 833 from Piazza Politeama or Via della Libertà

Monte Pellegrino

Rising 1,988 feet (606 m) northwest of Palermo, this rocky redoubt is a popular destination for hikers and picnickers. Take the panoramic Via Pietro Bonanno to the **Santuario di Santa Rosalia** *(tel 091 540 326)*, an unexceptional 17th-century sanctuary built over the cave in which were discovered the bones presumed to belong to St. Rosalia. A road and steep trails continue beyond here to the mountain's summit, a fine viewpoint just 9 miles (14 km) from Palermo's Via della Libertà.

Great cultural and scenic variety, with ruggedly pretty islands, coastal gems, and ancient towns—all south and west of Palermo

Western Sicily

Tins of tuna from the island of Favignana, where fishing has been an economic mainstay for centuries.

Western Sicily

Where eastern Sicily looks historically to ancient Greece, the island's seafaring western region leans to Africa—and to the age-old cultures of the Arabs and Carthaginians. Although often marginalized and wracked by poverty, this part of the island retains several glorious medieval villages, some resplendent ruins, and a handful of Sicily's most beautiful islands and maritime landscapes.

The farther south you travel in Italy, the poorer and harsher life becomes. Western Sicily, the country's most peripheral region, graphically underscores that point. Only recently, with the opening of the A29 autostrada, has this insular

and rather indefinable area become more integrated with Sicily, never mind Italy.

Parts of the region have a reputation as a Mafia heartland, and though times are changing, the names of villages in Palermo's

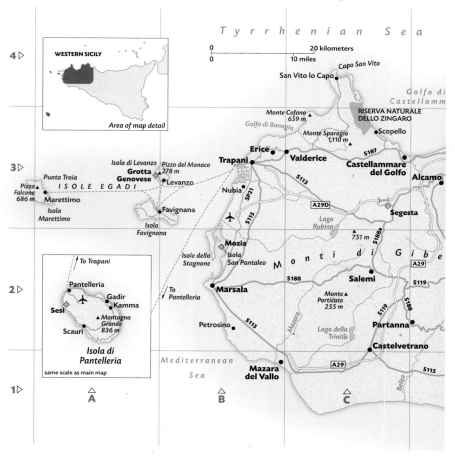

hinterland such as Prizzi and Corleone have the most sinister resonance of any on the island.

Casual visitors, though, will find little or no evidence of Mafia activity. On the contrary, they will find a region of complex history and wonderfully varied attractions.

On the west coast, the provincial capital, Trapani, is closer to Tunisia than it is to the Italian mainland, which lends the area's landscape and manners a distinctly African hue. Elsewhere, there are straggling whitewashed villages (the names of which can be traced to Arabic roots), a summer light of shimmering intensity, and festivals and traditions—notably

NOT TO BE MISSED:

Admiring the beautifully sited Tempio di Segesta 72–73

Hiking the stunning coast of the Riserva Naturale dello Zingaro 74–75

Taking the cable car to Erice 76–79

A boat trip to Levanzo and a swim in an isolated bay 80

Exploring Marettimo's interior 81

Visiting Marsala's dessert wine producers—and sampling 86

Learning about sea salt in Mozia 86

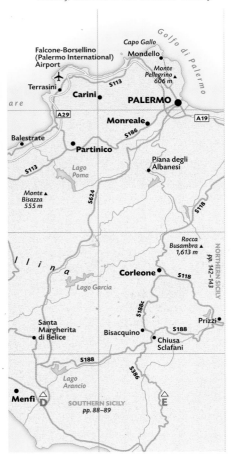

the *mattanza,* the ancient, ritual springtime slaughter of bluefin tuna—in which distant cultures still resonate.

The area reflects its African links with Carthaginian settlements such as Mozia and the Arab towns of Marsala and Mazara del Vallo. But it also embraces ancient peoples of more mysterious origin, notably the shadowy Elymians (Elimi), responsible for the temple at Segesta—Sicily's most romantic ruin—and the sacred citadel of Erice, now the island's finest medieval village, but once the Mediterranean's most important temple to the goddess of love.

Further variety is apparent in the region's many landscapes, from the olive groves, vineyards, and fertile plains of the interior to the salt marshes of Trapani, the beaches of San Vito lo Capo, and the peerless coastline of the Riserva Naturale dello Zingaro, Sicily's first protected nature reserve. Equally stunning landscapes can be found on the rugged and mountainous island of Marettimo, one of the Isole Egadi (Egadi Islands), and on strange, volcanic Pantelleria, a chic island stranded halfway to Africa.

Food and wine across the region are also excellent, with superb fish, seafood, and Arab-influenced dishes such as couscous, as well as celebrated wines, including Marsala and the rare dessert wines of Pantelleria. ∎

Segesta

Segesta is Sicily's most captivating Greek temple, not because it is the largest or best pre-served—though its appearance is one of the most perfect and harmonious imaginable—but because of its locale, rising in glorious isolation in the middle of beautiful pastoral countryside.

Dramatic lighting casts a seductive glow on Segesta's glorious—yet unfinished—ancient temple.

**Tempio di
Segesta**

- Map p. 70 C3
- 1.25 miles
  (2 km)
  E of A29D
  (Segesta exit)
- 0924 952 356
- Open 9 a.m.–
  one hour before
  sunset
- $$

The ancient city of Egesta was the principal city of the Elymians, or Elimi, who also founded and settled Erice (see pp. 76–79). Some schol-ars believe this mysterious people originated in Spain or Liguria on Italy's west coast; others claim they came from Anatolia. The Elymians themselves, according to later Greek historians, claimed to be refugees from the Fall of Troy.

The site at Egesta was probably settled in the 12th century B.C., but was rapidly hellenized after the Greeks arrived in Sicily. From about 580 B.C. it was in almost constant dispute with the Greek colony of Selinus, or Selinunte (see pp. 90–92). It looked to Ath-ens as an ally in 426 B.C., famously deceiving the Athenian ambas-sadors sent here as to the extent of its wealth, but suffered when the Athenians were defeated by Syracuse in 420 B.C. It rose again under Carthaginian protection, only to massacre its Carthaginian garrison during the First Punic War (264–241 B.C.) between Rome and Carthage. Thereafter it became the first Sicilian city to declare its allegiance to the

Visit Segesta, standing in the solitude of the valley, at night, when it is illuminated and the very few visitors look like ghostly figures.

—TINO SORIANO
National Geographic photographer

burgeoning Roman Empire, under which its name was changed to Segesta. The subsequent history is sketchy. Nor is much known about the Doric **temple,** its air of mystery only adding to the appeal.

The Temple

Framed by mountains, the 36-column monolith sits on a low hill, close to the ravine into which troops from Syracuse are said to have catapulted 8,000 of the colony's inhabitants after their victory here in 307 B.C. Open countryside dotted with *bagli,* or traditional fortified farms, stretches all around. Early morning and evening visits are magical.

The unfinished temple probably dates from around 426 B.C. to 416 B.C. One theory is that the temple was part of the deception designed to lure the Athenians into an alliance; built quickly and cheaply, it was left undone once allegiance had been won. No writings survive to reveal the true story.

There is a parking lot, ticket office, and bar at the entrance. A ticket also gives you access to the **theater,** the only other major survivor of ancient Egesta, located 1.2 miles (2 km) away. The road to the theater is closed to cars, but in summer a shuttle bus runs every 30 minutes; tickets are sold at the bar.

The Theater

Views from the road and theater are superb. The area is being excavated, with remains of buildings from a range of eras being unearthed. The theater probably dates from the mid-third century B.C., when the city was coming under Roman rule. It has seating room for 3,200 spectators. Concerts and plays are staged here throughout the summer. ■

Behold the Wagons of Many Colors

Beautifully painted traditional farm carts are some of Sicily's most striking examples of folk art. They can be glimpsed all across Sicily, but especially in villages inland from Palermo and in the west of the island.

The wagons, no longer used in a working context—they're too valuable—are often paraded during village festivals, pulled by horses or donkeys decked out in highly decorative harnesses. The wagons' painted scenes usually represent religious stories or tales of knights and chivalry.

There's a museum devoted to the wagons in Terrasina (about 50 miles/80 km northeast of Segesta), the **Museo del Carretto Siciliano** *(Palazzo d'Aumale, Lungomare Peppino Impastato, tel 091 881 0989, closed p.m. Sun.–Mon., $$).* The tradition of decorating work vehicles continues in the painted, motorized three-wheel pickups known as *api* (bees), after the low buzz of their engines, named in contrast to the whine of the Italian motor scooter known as a Vespa (Italian for wasp).

Riserva Naturale dello Zingaro

Much of Sicily's once outstanding coastline has been lost to industry, roads, and developers, making the glorious Zingaro Nature Reserve all the more remarkable. It preserves a pristine pocket of beaches, coves, cliffs, and mountains filled with a rich variety of flora, fauna, and hiking trails.

Ruins of former tuna fisheries dot the coastline in and around the Zingaro reserve.

The Zingaro reserve was Sicily's first protected area, created in 1981 after a demonstration by environmentalists opposing a coastal road planned between Scopello and San Vito lo Capo. For years, it is claimed, the Mafia used the coast's coves and beaches for smuggling drugs and other contraband. (The whispered implication is that the reserve was possible only with tacit Mafia sanction.) Whatever its history, the reserve was the catalyst for more than 25 protected areas in Sicily.

The Zingaro covers an area of 4,076 acres (1,650 ha), with the most popular access from the coast road that ends just beyond **Scopello.** (The less busy entrance is at the end of the road from **San Vito lo Capo** in the north.) Scopello and San Vito are worth visits—San Vito in particular, a small resort with fine beaches and a large bay.

The reserve has a parking lot and a visitor information center (*tel 0924 35 093, variable hours Sept.–May*) located near the Scopello entrance.

Most local visitors come here for the beaches, making this a popular destination on summer weekends, but plenty of good

INSIDER TIP:

Look out for the gongilo [*Chalcides ocellatus*, or ocellated skink] a snake-like lizard with a small head, cylindrical body, and four feet.

—PETER GWIN
National Geographic
magazine writer

hiking trails allow you to escape the sunbathers. Because cars are banned and most visitors don't walk beyond the first beach **(Punta della Capreria)**, successive beaches at **Cala della Disa, Berretta, Marinella,** and **Torre dell'Uzzo** are also usually quieter.

Exploring the Area

Spring (April–early June) is the best time for hiking and enjoying the flora and fauna. Some 670 species of plants, trees, and shrubs flourish here, including the dwarf fan palm, Europe's only indigenous palm. The craft of weaving baskets from the palm fronds has been practiced for centuries. In the past, local people exploited trees such as olive, carob, and manna ash, the last for its nutritious sugary sap, and utilized the thick, plumed grass (known locally as *disa*) as string or to shape pasta (around its woody stems).

The area's rugged shoreline, rocks, caves, and thick vegetation provide cover for a wide variety of birds, present in ever greater numbers since the creation of the reserve (39 species have been recorded). Especially notable are

rare raptors, including peregrine falcons, Bonelli's eagles, and griffon vultures, with Europe's smallest seabird, the storm-petrel.

There are hiking trails to suit all abilities, and though the map available from the visitors kiosk or via download is poor, the trails are fairly self-evident, especially the coastal path (allow four hours). A loop follows this path in one direction, returning by a more strenuous inland route via Borgo Cusenza, Contrada Sughero, and Pizzo del Corvo, a round-trip of 10 miles (16 km), with a change in altitude of 2,000 feet (604 m) (allow five hours). Take food and water on this and other hikes (none is available in the reserve), and bear in mind that there is little by way of shade along the trails. ■

Riserva Naturale dello Zingaro

⚐ Map p. 70 C3

Visitor information

✉ Via Segesta 197, Castellammare del Golfo

☎ 0924 35 108 or toll-free in Italy 800 116 616

$ $$

turismo.trapani.it

EXPERIENCE:
Diving Into History

The sea off the Zingaro reserve is as pristine as the interior landscapes. You can experience wonderful snorkeling and diving here, with the opportunity to visit underwater caves, explore the wreck of the *Capua* (a merchant ship carrying arms to Africa, sunk in 1943), and a special "underwater museum" itinerary that includes dives to various subterranean sites full of vases and other artifacts lost from ships as far back as the second century B.C.

Contact the Cetaria Diving Center in Scopello (*Via Marco Polo 3, tel 0924 541 177, cetaria.it*) and choose from 11 guided dives (equipment rental is available), or join one of the diving center's highly recommended boat excursions (4.5 hours) for snorkeling, swimming in quiet coves, and admiring the Zingaro's wonderful coastal terrain.

Erice

Erice is easily Sicily's most atmospheric village, a magnificent mountaintop settlement that seems more Tuscan than Sicilian, more pagan than Christian. It has a mythical and sacred foundation, stupendous views as far as Tunisia and Etna, and narrow medieval streets that are a sheer pleasure to explore.

The Castello di Venere offers a view over the mist-shrouded village of Erice.

Erice

🗺 Map p. 70 B3

Visitor information

✉ Pro Loco,
  Via Castello
  di Venere

☎ 393 271 7255

🕐 Closed Sat.–Sun.
  & p.m. daily,
  extended hours
  in summer
  sometimes

prolocoerice.it

A holy place since time immemorial, Erice was home to one of the most significant cults and divinities of the classical age. Even today, its cobbled streets have a feeling of mystery, especially in winter, when mist swirls and the wind chills. The Italian writer Carlo Levi (1902–1975), author of *Christ Stopped at Eboli* (1945), compared it to Assisi, another town of centuries-old sanctity. Erice, he wrote, is "the Assisi of the south, full of churches, convents, silent streets, and of the extraordinary accumulation of mythological memories."

Erice, however, has far older roots than Assisi. One reason is its position, a virtually impregnable aerie 2,463 feet (751 m) above Sicily's west coast—precisely the sort of site that would have suggested itself both as a stronghold and the potential seat of a cult and temple. The cult in question was that of the goddess of love and fertility—Astarte to the Phoenicians, Aphrodite to the Greeks, and Venus to the Romans—and her temple at Erice, ancient Eryx, was revered across the classical and western Mediterranean world.

It was mentioned by the Greek writer Virgil in *The Aeneid*. Another myth has Hercules (or Heracles) taking the city on his return to Greece. Yet another has Erice as the place in which Daedalus landed.

Some of the site's earliest residents were the Elymians, a mysterious 15th- to 8th-century B.C. people who also settled Segesta (see pp. 72–73). They probably introduced the fertility cult that would be adopted and adapted by subsequent Phoenician, Carthaginian, Greek, and Roman invaders. All revered the goddess and contributed to the famously rich treasury of her temple—a temple so sacrosanct that it remained undesecrated by invaders over several centuries.

The cult reached its zenith under the Romans, who built temples to the goddess in Rome itself, but even much later invaders appropriated its sacred nature.

The Modern Town

Erice is one of those happy places that clings to its charm in the face of mass tourism. The local population is in decline, but in summer its streets are as full of visitors and second-home owners as any Tuscan or Umbrian hill town. None of these factors reduces its appeal, however, but winter, fall, or early spring remain the ideal times to appreciate the village at its strange and otherworldly best.

If you come off-season, however, pick a clear day, for some of Erice's most memorable sights are its views. These unfold as you approach by car from Valderice or take the cable car Funivia di Erice *(tel 0923 569 306, funiviaerice.it, closed Mon. a.m., $$)* from Trapani. The vistas extend over the Egadi Islands to the west and the headlands of Monte Cofano and Capo San Vito to the northeast.

INSIDER TIP:

The historic complex of Erice, among the most memorable sites in Sicily, is a photographer's dream when the wind brings in the fog. In the presence of this veil it becomes intensely mysterious.

—TINO SORIANO
National Geographic photographer

Leave your car in the parking lot outside Porta Trapani (also near the cable car station), the main southwest entrance to town, and be sure to bring comfortable shoes for the cobbles and climbs, and a sweater (or more substantial warm clothing in winter) for the breezes and evening chill.

Erice has few specific sights, but any walk around the village is entrancing, wending through the ancient labyrinth and negotiating alleys *(vanelle)* so narrow they

INSIDER TIP:

Buy a combination ticket [$$] to see the attractions in five of Erice's finest churches. They're available from any participating church, including the Duomo and San Martino.

—TIM JEPSON
National Geographic author

often are wide enough for one. The facades of the houses may look forbidding, but they conceal secret courtyards or boast delicate balconies and other baroque or medieval details. Much of their stone has been used and reused, and many buildings contain the fragmentary ghosts of Elymian and Carthaginian walls or Roman and Greek temples.

Start a tour at **Porta Trapani,** the town's 14th-century gateway,

which has Norman roots and is built over Elymian fortifications. From here Via Vittorio Emanuele II climbs toward Piazza Umberto I, the main square. En route it passes Erice's main church, the 14th-century **Chiesa Madre,** known as Santa Maria dell'Assunta. Its detached bell tower predates the main church and was built in about 1315 as an Aragonese watchtower. The church's lovely porch (1426) is Gothic, unusual in predominantly baroque Sicily, but the "Gothic" interior is actually a pastiche, completed in 1852.

Cultural Highlights

Piazza Umberto I has a spread of outdoor café tables and is home to the Municipio, or town hall (on the left, or west, side), which contains the small **Museo Cordici** (*tel 346 577 3550, closed Nov.–March, joint ticket with Castello, $*). This museum features minor archaeological finds, miscellaneous paintings and sculptures from

---

EXPERIENCE: Try Italy's Tastiest Pastries

Pastries and candies are among the glories of Sicily, so a *pasticceria* (pastry store) that by general consent sells the best sweet treats on the island has to be worth a visit. Anyone who has read Mary Taylor Simeti's book *Bitter Almonds* will be familiar with the pasticceria owned by **Maria Grammatico** (*Via Vittorio Emanuele II 14, tel 0923 869 390, mariagrammatico.it, closed in Jan.*).

Maria's father died when she was just 11 years old, and when her mother was pregnant with a sixth child, Maria and a sister were sent to live in the cloistered

San Carlo orphanage in Erice, where they learned the art of pastry making from the orphanage's nuns.

At 22 Maria left and established the business that has been a place of culinary pilgrimage ever since.

Tuck into staple Sicilian classics such as cannoli, filled with ricotta cheese; *cassata,* made with almonds, vanilla, candied fruit, and buttermilk curd; *cuscinetti,* small fried pastries; or *buccellati,* small, hard cookies. In March and April, buy the delightful little almond-lemon lambs, baked especially for Erice's Easter celebrations.

various eras, and a fine relief of the "Annunciation" (1525) by Sicilian sculptor Antonello Gagini.

Among the collection are coins bearing doves, Erice's ancient symbol—white doves having been sacred to Venus. Hundreds of the birds were released from the temple once a year toward the goddess's sister temple, Sicca Veneria, in present-day El Kef, Tunisia. Doves were supposed to accompany the goddess when she moved south for the winter, her return to Sicily signifying the advent of spring. The doves were released in mid-August, and it can be no coincidence that the feast day of Erice's Christian patroness, Our Lady of Custonaci, is August 16.

Other places worth seeing include **Piazza San Domenico** and its pretty church, and the village's pastry shops, Erice being famous for its *dolci ericini* (sweet almond and marzipan cakes and candies). Once these tasty delights were the preserve of local novice nuns, but the convent in question closed in 1975. The pastry shop of Maria Grammatico (see sidebar p. 78) is now the place to indulge.

Other local craft products include *frazzate,* bright cotton rugs made by local women and available for sale in outlets around the village.

Erice's best views can be had from the **Giardino del Balio** (1870), communal gardens in the village's southeast corner. From here a ramp leads past the privately owned Torre Pepoli, a Norman keep, to the **Castello di**

The **Chiesa Madre** is one of ten major churches in Erice.

Venere, a crag-top 12th-century castle built over the remains of the once great temple to Venus (Venere). Whether it fell into ruin or the Norman ruler Roger I hastened its demise in the 11th century, eager to erase its pagan associations, is unknown. ■

Isole Egadi

The Isole Egadi—Favignana, Levanzo, and Marettimo—are the islands closest to Sicily, and the easiest to access. Only Favignana offers significant facilities for travelers, leaving its two beautiful but disparate neighbors largely unvisited and unspoiled.

The island's barren western shore is stark but beautiful.

Favignana is the largest and most populated Egadi island, covering 8 square miles (20.7 sq km). It lies 10 miles (17 km) from Trapani, the port of embarkation for all three islands. Formerly, its economy rested on tuna and tufa, a soft, easily worked stone that was exported across the region.

Old tuna canneries are the first thing you see as you sail into Favignana town, the island's main settlement. Next is the faded **Palazzo Florio** (1876), built by the Marsala Florio wine dynasty, which bought the Egadi Islands from the Genoese Pallavicini family, who had acquired them from the Spanish in 1637 in lieu of a business debt.

Favignana has relatively little to see or do save for some good beaches and swimming, notably at **Cala Burrone, Cala Azzurra, Cala Rossa, Cala Rotonda,** and **Cala Grande.** Bikes are easily rented, and many fishermen offer boat trips around the island.

Top Sites

Levanzo is much smaller than Favignana (at just 2 square miles/5.2 sq km), but its austere, rocky landscape has more in the way of isolated island charm. Although it is bisected by just one road and has only one tiny community, it offers numerous coastal and inland trails, including one leading to **Pizzo del Monaco**

On the popular island of Favignana, the Costanza Bakery [Via Roma 31] sells what may be the best bread in Sicily. Try the *filone*, a yeast bread studded with anise, sesame, and fennel seeds.

—ROS BELFORD
National Geographic Traveler
magazine writer

(912 feet/278 m), the island's highest point, and boasts plenty of little bays and pebble beaches for swimming and snorkeling.

Many visitors come here for the **Grotta Genovese,** a cave with some of Italy's most important cave paintings, dating back between 6,000 and 10,000 years. These can be seen only as part of a two-hour tour by Land Rover or boat; reservations are essential *(tel 0923 924 032 or 339 741 8899, $$$$),* or you can walk for two hours and pay at the entrance to the cave *($$)*—but you still must book ahead.

While Levanzo has a couple of hotels, magical **Marettimo** (4 square miles/10.4 sq km) has just a handful of sleepy trattorias and a few rooms for rent in local houses Reservations are needed in summer; at other times you may be met by locals offering rooms. The 300 or so residents are mostly fishing families, some of whom offer boat trips around the island's grand coastline.

On Marettimo, however, the mountains and breathtakingly

beautiful interior are the main attraction. The island was long the haunt of pirates, which discouraged settlement; today, its near pristine state is protected by a nature reserve. The relatively luxuriant vegetation, with some 515 species of plants, provides cover for thousands of migrating and nesting birds.

Forest rangers care for much of the island, with the result that many paths are marked and maintained. Hiking is, therefore, possible (see sidebar below), with recommended trails to the **Case Romane** (old Roman earthworks), **Cala Sarde** and **Cala Nera,** the summit of **Pizzo Falcone** (2,251 feet/686 m), and **Punta Troia.** Rough maps of the island can usually be obtained from local cafés and the ferry ticket office in Marettimo town. ∎

Isole Egadi

- ⬛ Map p. 70 A3

Visitor information

- ✉ Piazza Matrice 68, Favignana
- ☎ 0923 921 647
- 🕐 Closed Sun. except June–Sept. & 12:30 p.m.–4 p.m. daily

welcometoegadi.it

egadi.com

www.egadiweb.it

favignana.com

trapani-sicilia.it

marettimoresidence.it

GETTING THERE
Several companies operate daily ferries and hydrofoils from Trapani to all three islands or from Marsala and Marettimo. For information, contact the visitor center or go to *siremar.it* and *usticalines.it.*

EXPERIENCE:
Marettimo by Foot

Gentle hikes in the Egadi Islands are possible on Levanto and Favignana, but the best walks in the archipelago are on Marettimo. Numerous trails thread into the majestic mountainous interior; many start in Marettimo town. From here to Pizzo Falcone, a superb viewpoint, takes three hours. Or follow the trail along the east cost from the town to the ruined castle at Punta Troia, on the island's northern tip, a hike of about two hours. Many inns and B&Bs on the island offer accompanied treks. One to try is La Terrazza (Via Guglielmo Pepe 24, tel 092 392 3252, bedandbreakfastmarettimo.it), which can also arrange boat and bird-watching trips.

La Mattanza

La mattanza is a centuries-old collective hunt that involves the slaughter of many hundreds of tuna as they swim south to spawn in the waters around Sicily. Once intrinsic to a traditional way of life and the economic mainstay of many communities, the mattanza now survives only off Favignana, where it is in danger of becoming a cruel spectacle played out for tourists.

Fishermen haul in tuna for the traditional killing of the fish—a ritual known as *la mattanza.*

Tuna live for much of the year in the Atlantic, but at the beginning of spring, they start their migration through the Mediterranean toward their warm-water spawning grounds off the coast of Sicily. Since Phoenician times, and possibly the Bronze Age, fishermen have waited for them, though it took the arrival of the Arabs in the ninth century to educate the Sicilians in fishing for creatures that can weigh as much as 1,300 pounds (600 kg). The Arabs, for example, taught the islanders that tuna rarely take bait before spawning, and they

introduced them to the technique of drift netting, the method at the heart of the mattanza.

Around May, when the local *favinio* (wind that brings flowers) begins to blow, tuna begin to run in the channels near Favignana. Teams of fishermen set out in traditional flatboats with nets as much as 10 miles (16 km) long, preparing a series of corridors and holding pens that force the tuna into a closed *camera della morte,* or chamber of death. When a hundred or so fish are trapped, the head fisherman orders the 60-strong crew to haul the 100-foot-deep

EXPERIENCE: Getting Below the Surface in Western Sicily

La mattanza is increasingly a dubious spectacle played out largely for tourists, and the tuna and other marine life of the region can be much better appreciated by joining a diving or snorkeling trip. Much of the sea around the islands is protected by marine reserves *(parks.it, ampisoleegadi .it)*, especially the waters around Marettimo. Divers can explore the region with Fabio Tedone of the **Marettimo Diving Center** *(Via Cuore di Gesù 5, Isola di Marettimo, tel 333 190 2720, marettimo divingcenter.it)*. You can book seven-day trips, with two dives daily, or arrange for single dives and day trips. Nondiving companions can join and snorkel, swim, or simply spend time on deck. The boat moors in delightful coves. Trips to the waters around the other Egadi Islands can also be arranged.

(30 m) net to the surface. This is done to the rhythmic chant of ancient songs, the *cialoma,* or *scialome,* that date from Arab times or earlier. As the frenzied mass of fish rises to the surface, the tuna are clubbed, speared, and hooked until the sea froths with a bloody foam. (The word "mattanza" suggests slaughter, a description that any spectator, and there are many, would not refute.)

Cultural significance aside, there is a considerable element of cruelty in the ritual. Tuna tend to dive when panicked; many are already stunned or severely injured through collision as they are dragged to the surface in their *sarabanda della morte,* or dance of death. This dance may take 15 minutes and death is usually slow, though some fish die quickly from heart attacks or too much oxygen.

This cruelty might be more tolerable were fishing the economic mainstay it once was, but these days only one of Sicily's 50 former tuna stations is still working. In Favignana's heyday, 150,000 tons (136,078 mt) of tuna might have been caught and processed; today, it's between 1,000 and 1,500 tons (907 and 1,360 mt). The mattanza barely survives, with maybe one or two held between May and June. Contact the local visitor center for information.

A turn for the worse: Migrating tuna swim into a drift net.

Pantelleria

Pantelleria is the largest and most westerly of Sicily's offshore islands, a fascinating outpost with a rich history, dramatic coastline, fertile volcanic interior, and the sort of isolated and bohemian charm that has begun to attract such high-profile visitors as Sting, Madonna, and Giorgio Armani.

Fishermen harvest crayfish along the rocky coast of Pantelleria, Sicily's biggest island.

Pantelleria
🅜 Map p. 70 A2
Visitor information
✉ Pro Loco,
Lungomare
Borsellino
☎ 0923 911 838
prolocopantelleria.it

Pantelleria owes its prosperity to its volcanic soils. These attracted Neolithic visitors, who built rock tombs, or *sesi,* unique to the island. It also benefited from being just 52 miles (84 km) from Tunisia, tempting African traders such as the Phoenicians, who called it Hiranin, or the "place of birds," after the many species that still use it for migration.

To the Greeks it was Kossyra (the "small one"), though its present name derives from the Arabic *bint er-rhia,* or "daughter of the winds." During a 400-year occupation, the Arabs introduced palms, cotton, vegetables, and citrus fruits, as well as the walled gardens designed to protect against the wind.

Later, Mussolini described the island as an "unsinkable aircraft carrier," a strategic merit that prompted the Allies to bomb it for a month before its capture on

EXPERIENCE: Hear Pantelleria Whisper

The last eruption on Pantelleria was in 1835, and though the old crater, Montagna Grande, is thought to be extinct, the island still hisses and steams from 24 minor craters (cuddie) and from blowholes (mofete). Hike to the crater, part of an evocative, protected park reserve (parks.it/riserva.pantelleria). Take a towel so you can sample the best of the mofete, the Stufe (Ovens) de Khazeri, which you pass as you climb from the village of **Siba.** The stufe form a natural sauna in a dark cave, where the heat is such that few visitors last more than ten minutes. Elsewhere, explore the hot springs that boil into the sea at **Sataria;** the thermal pools at **Gadir;** or the lovely **Specchio di Venere** (Venus's Mirror), a volcanic lake in an old crater that is constantly warmed from below.

June 11, 1943. The rebuilt main town and harbor are a depressing prelude to what otherwise is a wonderful island.

Visitors are not here to lounge on beaches; there are none, though the water is sublime and coves, cliffs, and inlets abound. Instead, they come to hike, birdwatch, snorkel, dive (the diving is world-class), cruise the majestic coastline, soak in natural hot pools, and enjoy excellent food and wine. Small farms sell wine, oil, figs, capers, and more.

Getting Around

At 32 square miles (83 sq km), Pantelleria is not so large that you need a car, though cars, bikes, and scooters can be rented. Buses run to most points, and there are hiking trails, not least the one to **Montagna Grande** (2,742 feet/836 m), the island's crater and highest point. May, June, September, and October are best for a visit; the water is warm and you can enjoy the birds and flowers without crowds and heat.

The best of the megalithic sesi are off the coastal road just southwest of Pantelleria town, 1.8 miles (3 km) beyond Mursia (Villaggio Neolithico). Once, the island probably had some 500 of these elliptical burial mounds, but their stones have been pilfered, mostly to build the island's dammusi (vaulted dwellings), whose angular stone blocks match those of the 27 surviving sesi.

The west coast hamlets of Scauri, Nikà, and the southern coast are good for views, hot springs, and caves, notably at **Bagno Asciutto, Grotta di Sataria, Favara Grande,** and **Grotta di Nikà.** The island's loveliest settlement is **Gadir** on the northeast coast (Giorgio Armani has a villa nearby), connected by a scenic inland road to Tracino. Nearby **Kamma** and the ghost village of **Mueggen** (accessible by a walking trail) are also captivating.

Other good inland destinations are the **Specchio di Venere,** a hot-water lake; and the **Valle di Monastero** and **Valle della Ghirlanda**—pretty, verdant valleys for hiking. **Sibà,** on Montagna Grande's west slope, is a fine, crumbling village with some of the island's oldest dammusi. ■

GETTING THERE:
By air: 40-minute flights from Trapani Meridiana, tel 0789 52 682, within Italy, meridiana.it. In summer, flights from Rome, Venice, Bologna, and Milan on Alitalia, alitalia.com
By car ferry: Daily service (5 hours) from Trapani. Siremar, tel 091 749 3315, siremar.it.
By hydrofoil: Daily, (2.5 hours) service from Trapani or Mazara del Vallo (near Agrigento); three weekly, one hour 45 minutes. Ustica Lines, tel 0923 873 813, usticalines.it.

More Places to Visit in Western Sicily

From Trapani to Marsala, the coastal road is lined with otherworldly salt pans.

Castellammare del Golfo

Get a taste of a Sicilian resort: families on the beach, a long break for lunch, promenades in the evening cool, dinner under the stars—at Castellammare del Golfo. There's also a small castle and historical museum. Eat seafood straight off the boat at the tiny Del Golfo restaurant. *touristworldservice.it* Map p. 70 C3 **Visitor information** ✉ Via Medici 61 153 ☎ 0924 32 227

Marsala

The mostly modern town of Marsala, long synonymous with the wine of the same name, has several producers, whose sites can be visited by appointment, including **Florio** *(Via Vincenzo Florio 1, tel 0923 781 111, duca.it)*, **Pellegrino** *(Via del Fante 39, tel 0923 719 911, carlopellegrino.it)*, and **Rallo** *(Via Vincenzo Florio 2, tel 0923 721 633, cantinerallo .it)*. Also worth seeing are the **cathedral**; the small **Museo degli Arazzi** *(Via Giuseppe Garraffa 57, tel 0923 711 327, closed 1 p.m.–4 p.m. & Sun., $)*; and the **Museo Archeologico Baglio Anselmi** *(Lungomare Boeo 20, tel 0923 952 535, closed Mon., $)*, with its rare Carthaginian ship (241 B.C.). Map p. 70 B2 **Visitor information** Via XI Maggio 100 ☎ 0923 714 097 🕐 Closed Sun. p.m. & daily 1:30 p.m.–3 p.m.

Mazara del Vallo

Once one of the Arabs' most important Sicilian outposts, this town has a lovely palm-lined waterfront, booming fishing industry (see the day's catch unloaded and sold in the market on **Piazza dello Scalo),** and a delightful old center; some streets have a decided North African air. **Piazza della Repubblica** offers a fine ensemble of baroque and other buildings, as does the **Piazza Plebiscito,** home to the **Museo del Satiro danzante** *(tel 0923 808 111, closed Sun. p.m., $$)*. Above the dock stands **San Nicolò Regale** (1124), an outstanding Norman church. *prolocomazara.it* Map p. 70 B1 **Visitor information** ✉ Pro Loco, Via XX Settembre ☎ 0923 944 610

Mozia

Mozia, or Motya, is Sicily's only surviving Carthaginian site. Founded by the Phoenicians in the eighth century B.C., it became a major trade center. Razed in 397 B.C., it was rediscovered after 1913 by James Whitaker, a Marsala wine magnate and amateur archaeologist. A foundation in his name owns and manages the island *(tel 091 682 0522)*. Adding appeal to the site *($$)*, with its fine small **Museo Whitaker** *(tel 0923 712 598, closed after 3 p.m. Nov.–March, $$$)*, is its location on the **Isola San Pantaleo,** an island in the **Isole dello Stagnone**—a lagoon, salt flats, and nature reserve between Trapani and Marsala. From the minor SP21 road, where you get the ferry to the island, you'll see old windmills and salt pans. Visit the **Saline Ettore e Infersa** *(tel 0923 733 003, salineettoreeinfersa.com, open daily May–Sept.; by appt. only Nov.–March, $)* a mainland museum devoted to the salt industry, housed in the 300-year-old home of a local salt worker. *trapaniwelcome.it, turismo.trapani.it* Map p. 70 B2 **Visitor information** Casina delle Palme, Via Regina Elena, Trapani ☎ 0923 29 000 🕐 Closed Sun. & daily 1:30 p.m.–3:30 p.m.

A largely quiet corner with two major sights: Agrigento's Greek temples and the Roman mosaics at the Villa Imperiale del Casale

Southern Sicily

Villa Imperiale del Casale's Roman mosaics are almost perfectly preserved.

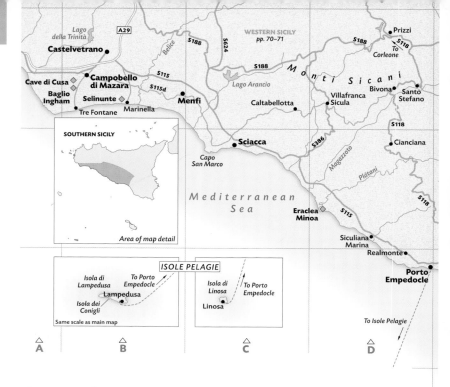

Southern Sicily

Southern Sicily is the most enigmatic region of an enigmatic island, its miles of lonely coast and empty beaches, classical ruins, and insular fishing villages backed by wheat-rich plains that rise to mostly deserted mountains. While major attractions are few, those that are here—notably the temples of Agrigento and mosaics of the Villa Imperiale del Casale—rank among Europe's finest Greek and Roman sites.

The often dry, sparsely populated coast that looks to Africa may be less verdant than much of Sicily, but its hills and plains are rich, fertile agricultural land—the lure that in the sixth century B.C. first tempted ancient Greek settlers.

Today, most of the great cities they forged are gone, including Eraclea Minoa, now visited as much for its magnificent beach as its partially excavated ruins. Others have been brought to light or retain monuments to their past, notably Selinunte, which has the remains of eight major temples and an acropolis spread across a large, pastorally pretty site. Even grander is Agrigento, still a large, modern town but best known for one of Italy's great classical sites and the finest

Greek remains outside Greece—the Valle dei Templi, or Valley of the Temples, a series of sublime temples and other remains, with one of Sicily's foremost archaeological museums.

But much of modern, concrete Agrigento and its surroundings is unattractive, something to remember on this coast, where towns such as Gela and Porto Empedocle leave much to be desired. Portions of the coast remain unsullied, however, with some fine beaches, especially around the vibrant little town and resort of Sciacca, a great favorite with Sicilian families.

When it comes to getting around, there are none of the autostrade of Sicily's other coasts; just the old, slow S115 road, with no-nonsense

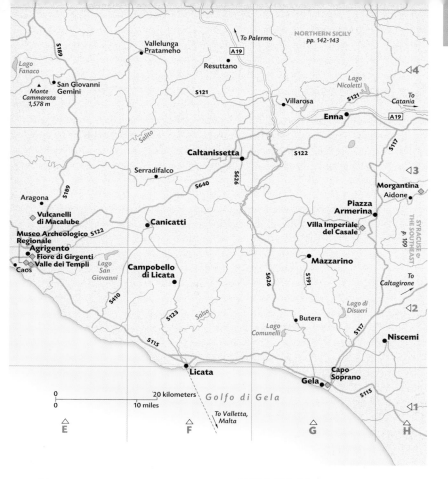

fishing towns such as Licata, stretches of empty, beach, and the occasional industrial blight.

Inland, a monument from another era matches the coast's ancient ruins: the extraordinarily well preserved Villa Imperiale del Casale, which contains Europe's finest Roman mosaics. The villa is fairly easily approached via Enna or Catania, but its rather isolated position hints at the dilemmas of planning an itinerary in a region that has little of interest outside its main centers. Inland routes through the mountains are slow but also rewarding in their way, with slumbering (occasionally shabby) hill villages and sweeping panoramas. Finally are the islands—the Isole Pelagie (Pelagie Islands), popular among divers and snorkelers, and Linosa and Lampedusa, the last increasingly troubled given illegal immigration from North Africa. ■

NOT TO BE MISSED:

The ancient temples and acropolis at Selinunte **90–92**

Exploring the Greek temples and museum in Agrigento's Valle dei Templi **93–99**

Visiting Agrigento's hinterland when the almond trees are in blossom **97**

A boat trip around Lampedusa and time on its black-sand beaches **100–101**

The vast array of exquisite Roman mosaics at the Villa Imperiale del Casale **102–105**

Selinunte

While some archaeological sites in Sicily are compromised by their modern surroundings, Selinunte rivals Segesta for the beauty and unsullied romance of its setting. Edged by the sea to the south, its eight ruined temples and ancient acropolis occupy a lovely pastoral setting scattered with wildflowers, aromatic herbs, and the wild celery (*selinon* in Greek) that gave the colony its name.

The ruins of one of Selinunte's eight Greek temples greet the sun.

Ancient Selinus probably was founded in 651 B.C. by settlers from Megara Hyblaea (a colony north of Syracuse), attracted by the area's fertile floodplain. The colony prospered for 200 years, but in time attracted the covetous Segesta, whose own territories were close by.

In 409 B.C., after Selinunte sided with Syracuse against Carthage, a North African power, the Segestans allied themselves with the Carthaginians, unleashing a force of more than 100,000 on the unsuspecting city. Selinunte fell in nine days, with 16,000 of its inhabitants butchered and 5,000 sold into slavery.

The colony was never quite the same, and though it staggered on for another 150 years, it eventually was abandoned. In later years, only a Byzantine and tenth-century Arab settlement took temporary root among the ruins. The near total destruction of the city, however, is not believed to have been entirely the result of Segesta's assault, but a consequence of countless earthquakes. The site was rediscovered in the 16th century. Excavations began in the 1820s under two Englishmen, Samuel Angel and William Harris. Organized excavations began in the 1950s and continue to this day.

The Ruins

There are three groups of ruins: a trio of temples on the Collina Orientale, or East Hill; five temples of the ancient Acropoli (central citadel); and the sacred area of the Santuario della Malophoros. The eight temples have been designated by letters—archaeologists do not know to which gods they were dedicated.

The **Collina Orientale** is entered through landscaped earthworks at the site entrance and parking lot. Adjoining **Temples E** (480–460 B.C.) and **F** (560–540 B.C.) are the best preserved, but it is the ruins of the third, **Temple G**—just a single column remains standing—that most capture the imagination. This was Sicily's second largest temple, after the Tempio di Zeus Olimpico in Agrigento (see p. 98), 17 columns long and 8 wide (a design matched only by the Parthenon in Athens), and measuring 373 feet by 178 feet (110 m by 50 m). Each column, 53 feet (16 m) high and 12 feet (3.5 m) in diameter, is made of several 100-ton (90,718 kg) stone drums.

From the Collina Orientale it is a ten-minute walk or short drive west on the Strada dei Templi to the **Acropoli.** Along the way you pass the colony's old silted-up harbor. The Acropoli would have held many of the main civic and religious buildings, along with one or two houses belonging to the town's most prominent citizens. The colossal walls were built in 306 B.C.—too late to withstand the onslaught of the Carthaginians—while the early sixth-century B.C. **Temple C** is the site's earliest and its best preserved monument. The fine frieze panels in Palermo's Museo Archeologico Regionale (see p. 60) came from this temple.

INSIDER TIP:

If you have mobility challenges, rent a small electric cart at Selinunte's main site entrance. It's a smart way to get around the ruins.

—TIM JEPSON
National Geographic author

A ten-minute walk west brings you to the **Santuario della Malophoros** (575 B.C.), a sanctuary centered on a large sacrificial altar and devoted to the goddess Demeter Malophoros (the Bearer of Pomegranates). The environs are covered in an unexcavated necropolis that stretches several miles to the west. Also unexcavated is the ancient city proper, which extended north of the Acropoli.

Selinunte

🅰 Map p. 88 B4

Visitor information

✉ Entrance north of Marinella off Via Caboto (S115d)

☎ 0924 46 251 Ticket office: 0924 46 277

🕐 Open Mon.–Sat. 9 a.m.–one hour before sunset. Closed Sun. p.m.

💲 $$

selinunte.net

After seeing the site, visit the sandy **beach** that runs west from the adjacent, rather shabby, village-resort of **Marinella.** Follow the path from the site's second parking lot. Even if you don't wish to swim, you could have lunch at a trattoria on Via Marco Polo above the beach. Alternatively, consider a picnic in the shady valley between the Acropoli and Collina Orientale; tables are available.

Cave di Cusa

If Selinunte is lovely, then the Cave di Cusa—the quarry from which the city's stone was mined—is even more delightful. To reach it, drive 2.5 miles (4 km) north of Selinunte on the S115d and turn left (west) at the junction on the unclassified road to Campobello di Mazara. Continue south toward Tre Fontane for just over a mile (2 km); the quarry road is on the right at the Baglio Ingham ruins. Total distance: about 12 miles (20 km). Surrounded by olive and orange groves, the quarries are a mile (1.6 km) long and little more than 100 yards (91 m) wide. Quarrying stopped here abruptly and permanently after the Segestan and Carthaginian sack of the mother city. Everywhere are stone drums, stumps, and partly carved capitals, tossed as if at random by some giant hand.

Especially impressive are the deep cavities created by quarried stone, and the partially cut column fragments that are still part of the ambient rock. Slaves and oxen pulled the finished drums, on iron-strengthened wooden rollers, the 12 miles (20 km) to Selinunte. ■

A pastoral setting and blue sky complement Selinunte's ancient temples.

Agrigento

Below the town of Agrigento lies Sicily's most important archaeological site—the Valle dei Templi, or Valley of the Temples, part of the ancient city of Akragas. Once, this "loveliest of mortal cities," as the Greek writer Pindar described it, was among the wealthiest of Sicily's Greek colonies. Today, its former grandeur is still apparent in the valley's nine temples, a UNESCO World Heritage site and the finest classical remains outside Greece.

Syracuse was the most powerful of Sicily's Greek colonies, but second ranked Akragas (or Acragus) was by far the most decadent: Its people, Pindar famously observed, "built for eternity but lived as if there were no tomorrow."

Founded in about 580 B.C., it eventually had a population of around 200,000 (the figure for the modern town is 55,450), and prospered until 406 B.C., when it was besieged and sacked by the Carthaginians. It rose again under the Romans in the third century B.C., when it was the only city to thrive among Sicily's former Greek colonies. Nemesis came with the Byzantines and early Christian settlers, who probably ravaged the site and many of its "pagan" temples. Earthquakes inflicted further damage. By the eighth century little more than a village remained.

Today, Agrigento presents the dilemma of many celebrated destinations: On one hand the main attraction—in this case, the **Valle dei Templi** *(Piazzale dei Templi, tel 0922 26191, parcovalledei templi.it, open daily 8:30 a.m.–dusk July–early Sept., occasionally open until 9 p.m. Mon.–Fri. & 11:30 p.m. Sat.–Sun., $$$$–ticket also valid for the Museo Archeologico Regionale)* is unmissable, but on the other

its popularity means that it can be uncomfortably crowded during peak times.

In Agrigento, there is the added fact that the contemporary surroundings—namely the present town and its ugly approaches—slightly compromise the splendor of the ancient remains.

Casa Pirandello

Visit the birthplace of Nobel Laureate writer Luigi Pirandello (1867–1936; see pp. 38–39) in Caos, a suburb of Agrigento on the S115 road to Porto Empedocle. The house *(tel 0922 511 826, closed 1 p.m.–2 p.m. daily, $)* **includes his study, editions of his work, photos, films, and the grounds where his ashes were interred.**

The solution is to turn a blind eye to the depredations of the modern age and to visit the pretty, pastoral temple site off-season—January and February, when the almond trees are in bloom (see p. 97), is a lovely time. Failing that, come early in the morning or late in the afternoon. You will need several hours to do the large site and associated museum justice.

Agrigento
🅰 Map p. 88 E2
Visitor information
✉ Via Empedocle 73
☎ 0922 203 91
provincia.agrigento.it
agrigento-sicilia.it

The ancient city was enclosed by a defensive wall, part of which embraced the high ridge to the north, site of the city's acropolis, an area now occupied by the medieval and modern town.

Confusingly, the Valle dei Templi is not really a valley but a second, lower ridge at the southern extent of the old city. The Greeks, wherever possible, built temples where they could be seen against the skyline, particularly from the sea (most famously with the Parthenon in Athens).

Today, this ridge is divided into two sections: an open, eastern zone, and an enclosed western zone. A road, the Via dei Templi, runs from the edge of the modern town to a parking lot between

Tempio della Concordia has 34 columns each 22.5 feet (6.8 m) high

Crepidoma, or stepped base

Tempio della Concordia

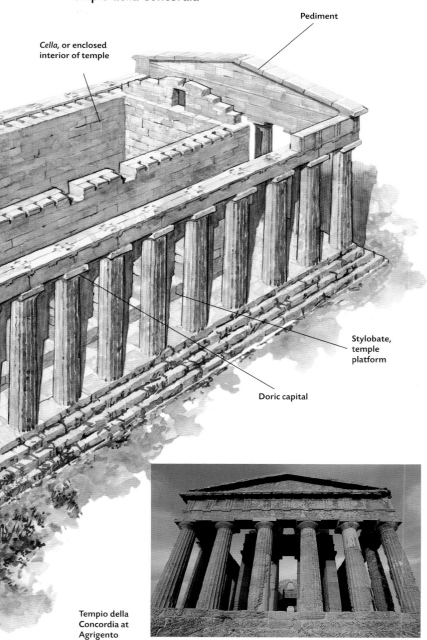

Pediment

Cella, or enclosed
interior of temple

Stylobate,
temple
platform

Doric capital

Tempio della
Concordia at
Agrigento

In Agrigento, the ruins of the ancient Valle dei Templi are a stone's throw from the modern town.

the two zones (the lot also has a café and information kiosk). En route it passes through the Quartiere Ellenistico-Romano (a former residential part of the old city) and the Museo Archeologico Regionale, Agrigento's other key attraction, filled with archaeological finds from the ancient city.

Top Intelligence

Avoid the many unauthorized guides who offer their services in the Valle dei Templi. Instead, book an individual or group tour with one of two excellent, local, English-speaking guides: **Michele Gallo** (tel 360 397 930, sicilytravel.net) or **Luigi Napoli** (tel 1480 252 4325, luiginapoli.tk).

It is possible to make a case for spending a little time in the present town—**Via Atenea.** The shop-lined main street is lively, for example, and churches such as **San Lorenzo, Santo Spirito,** and the **cathedral** have their memorable moments. Without the temples, however, Agrigento would not merit a stop on most travel itineraries.

The Eastern Zone

This is the most intelligible part of the Valle dei Templi, with the most impressive remains and the prettiest open country. Its sights are located mainly on or just off an old lane, the Via Sacra, which heads east from the parking lot. Follow this until you come to a footbridge on the right, which crosses over rock tombs to the first of the temples, the **Tempio di Ercole** (circa 520 B.C.), or Temple of Heracles (Hercules).

This is the oldest and second largest of the temples, and would once have been about the size of the Parthenon in Athens. Nine of its original 38 columns still stand, stranded among a confusion of fallen stones. Many of the columns show the effects of fire, possibly set by the Carthaginians following the siege of 406 B.C. Originally, the fragile golden sandstone of these and other columns would have been protected by a veneer of glazed marble stucco, then painted in bright reds and blues.

Look toward the south and just on the temple side of the S115 road, you can see the vaguely pyramidal **Tomba di Terone,** erroneously described as the tomb of Theron (Terone), the fifth-century B.C. tyrant ruler of Akragas, under whom the city reached its zenith. In truth it is most likely a Roman monument erected to the memory of the Roman soldiers who perished during the Second Punic War (218–201 B.C.) against the Carthaginians.

Returning to the Via Sacra, continue east, passing the **Villa Aurea** on the right. It now houses offices but was once the home of Alexander Hardcastle (died 1933), the Englishman responsible for excavating much of ancient Akragas. A path alongside the villa leads left to the site of a Greek-Roman necropolis and catacombs.

Still farther down the Via Sacra on the right is the site's highlight,

the **Tempio della Concordia** (430 B.C.), or Temple of Concord, Europe's best preserved Greek temple outside the Theseion in Athens. Beautifully situated, with lovely sea views, it owes its fine state of preservation to its conversion to a Christian church in the sixth century (subsequently dismantled).

Just beyond on the left is the **Casa Pace,** a small and only occasionally open antiquarium devoted to the history of three early Christian churches found in and around the site. Should you wish to walk,

EXPERIENCE:
February's Flowers

You'll experience swathes of rural Sicily at their finest in February, when much of the countryside is tinged with the delicate pink of almond blossoms. In Agrigento, the blossom's arrival is celebrated by a festival of food and folk culture, the **Sagra del Mandorlo in Fiore,** on the first Sunday of the month. Be sure to attend the festival's main event, the procession of traditional painted carts (see sidebar p. 73) and groups in folk costume. Get further information from the visitor center (see p. 93).

a small road leads north from here for half a mile (800 m) through olives and orchards to San Nicola and the Museo Archeologico Regionale (see p. 99).

The path of the Via Sacra continues through increasingly peaceful and pretty countryside for about half a mile (800 m) to the picturesque but much ruined hilltop remains of the **Tempio di Giunone Lacinia** (circa 460 B.C.), or Temple of Juno (Hera), goddess of matrimony and childbirth. Just 25 of the original 34 columns survive. Like the Tempio di Ercole, its walls show signs (the reddish patches) of the 406 B.C. fire.

The Western Zone

Walk west from the parking lot, and the first thing you see set back on the right is the **Altare** **Sacrificale,** an altar where as many as a hundred sacrificial oxen could be slaughtered. Beyond it are the jumbled ruins of the **Tempio di Zeus Olimpico,** the largest Doric temple in the Greek world, measuring 373 feet by 118 feet (113 m by 36 m). It was begun in 480 B.C., probably to celebrate Agrigento's sweeping victory over the Carthaginians at the Battle of Himera. Enslaved prisoners provided much of the initial labor.

The now tumbled columns were over 50 feet (15 m) high and large enough to require 20 adults standing in a circle to embrace their girth. Above them, 38 giant figures, or *telamones,* supported the architrave, taking the temple's overall height to more than 100 feet (30 m). One telamone has been reconstructed on site, and another can be seen in the Museo Archeologico Regionale.

The confusion of the site is considerable, earthquakes having felled the temple, though the ruins' scale still hints vividly at the size of the structure. The amount of debris is all the more remarkable given that colossal quantities of stone from the site were removed in the 18th century to build much of nearby Porto Empedocle.

Moving west you come to even more confusing ruins, based around four temples known collectively as the **Santuario delle Divinità Ctonie,** or the Sanctuary of the Chthonic Divinities—namely Persephone (Persefone or Kore), queen of the underworld, and her mother, Demeter (Ceres), goddess of corn, fertility, and agriculture

Artifacts and scale models are displayed in the excellent Museo Archeologico Regionale in Agrigento.

(and one of the most revered goddesses of Sicilian antiquity). All manner of shrines and altars to these and other divinities scatter the area, many from Sikel and prehistoric times, proof that the site was inhabited for centuries before the arrival of the Greeks.

The main monument in this area, the striking **Tempio di Castore e Polluce,** or Temple of Castor and Pollux, is a pastiche that was cobbled together in the 1830s from the ruins of other temples and buildings. Beyond this is the **Giardino della Kolymbetra,** formerly an artificial lake dug by Carthaginian prisoners but now a beautifully restored garden of olive, citrus, and other trees.

Just to its north are the scant ruins of the **Tempio di Efesto** (Temple of Vulcan), the most westerly of the temples built on the imaginary east-west line across the Valle dei Templi.

Museo Archeologico Regionale

This major and well-presented archaeological museum is partly housed in the 13th-century church and monastery of San Nicola.

The museum highlights begin with finds from the early and late Bronze Age, moving quickly to the many outstanding black- and red-figure Attic vases of Room 3 and exhibits devoted to the Temple of Zeus Olimpico in Room 4. The latter includes one of the temple's architectural telamones and three giant heads that represent the three "ethnic types" known in the period: African, Asiatic, and European. The museum's other

---

Mini-Volcanoes

The **Vulcanelli di Macalube** are found in the Riserva Naturale Macalube di Aragona *(tel 0922 699 210, macalife.it),* 2.5 miles (4 km) from Aragona, a village 9.5 miles (15 km) north of Agrigento. *Vulcanelli* are small mud mounds created by an unusual phenomenon in which pressurized natural gas forces itself to the surface, creating eruptions of bubbling mud that then solidify into mounds. The result is a rare and fascinating moonlike landscape.

---

sculptural highlight is the "Ephebus" (circa 480 B.C.), a marble statue of a young man (perhaps a depiction of Apollo or the river god Akragas).

Allow one to two hours to see the museum and the remains of houses and other ruins in the **Quartiere Ellenistico-Romano** across the road. At one time this spread of residential housing would have covered a grid of streets that extended over the entire slope that runs between the temple ridge and what is the present town.

Next, head to **San Biagio,** reached by turning right off Via dei Templi north of the museum on Via Demetra. It is not so much the Norman-era church (built over a Greek temple) that is interesting, as the mysterious **Tempio Rupestre di Demetra** nearby. Probably the most ancient of Agrigento's sacred sites, this cave-shrine was devoted (again) to Demeter and Persephone (and perhaps to earlier water deities), and consists of dank, atmospheric chambers reached by steps cut into the rock. ∎

Museo Archeologico Regionale

🅰 Map p. 89 E2

✉ Via dei Templi

☎ 0922 401 565

🕐 Closed p.m. Sun. & Mon.

💲 $$$ or $$$$, combined ticket that includes admission to the nearby Parco Valle dei Templi

Isole Pelagie

The Isole Pelagie take their name from the Greek word *pelagia,* or sea islands, and consist of three tiny scraps of land—Lampedusa, Linosa, and uninhabited Lampione. Closer in fact and feel to Africa than Europe, they have little to see but are becoming increasingly popular among visitors keen to dive, swim, and snorkel in their pristine waters.

Rocky shores and clear waters attract swimmers to Cala Creta and other beaches on Lampedusa.

Isole Pelagie

🅰 Map p. 88
   B2, C2

Visitor information

✉ Via Vittorio
   Emanuele II 89

☎ 0922 971 390

lampedusa.it
lampedusa35.com

Lampedusa is the largest island, measuring 8 square miles (20.7 sq km). A piece of Africa's continental shelf, it lies a mile closer to Monastir in Tunisia than it does to Porto Empedocle, about 127 miles (205 km) north on Sicily's mainland. Volcanic Linosa belongs to Europe, the last of the line of volcanoes that includes Vesuvius, Etna, and the Pontine islands between Rome and Naples.

Most travelers to the islands visit **Lampedusa,** whose population of just under 6,000 makes a living from fishing, sponges, and, increasingly, tourism. Historically, the island was a plaything of rulers such as Charles II of Spain, who in 1630 awarded Giulio di Tomasi, a Sicilian aristocrat, the title of Prince of Lampedusa. A descendant of Giulio's, Giuseppe Tomasi di Lampedusa, wrote *Il Gattopardo (The Leopard),* one of the great Sicilian novels (see p. 39).

INSIDER TIP:

Environmentalists occasionally release rare loggerhead turtles into the sea here—usually at night. Check with the visitor information office.

—TINO SORIANO
National Geographic photographer

Centuries of agricultural mismanagement and deforestation have left the interior mostly barren, the topsoil scattered by the almost constant wind. It is the coast and its pellucid waters—and largely untouched beaches—that attract visitors.

Lampedusa town is the main settlement, minutes from the small airport and ferry terminal, and the place to stay—possibly in a rented *dammuso,* one of the traditional Arab-style domed houses. It is also the place to rent bikes, scooters, cars, scuba, and other equipment.

The best beaches are all on the southern coast, the northern coast being a series of spectacular cliffs best seen on one of the highly recommended boat tours from town.

Just west of town are **Spiaggia di Guitgia,** a fine sandy crescent, and the less crowded beaches at **Cala Croce. La Tabaccara** is another glorious bay (accessible only by boat), though the island's best beach is the unnamed but well-known strand opposite the small **Isola dei Conigli.** The Isola dei Conigli is known for the loggerhead turtles that lay their eggs here. The increasing numbers of human spectators now threaten this event. You may also see dolphins, or the March migration of the sperm whale, though note that Lampedusa is not at its best in spring or winter.

The same goes for **Linosa,** an hour away by hydrofoil, although it is to be recommended in summer, when it is quieter than Lampedusa and well removed from the Italian mainstream. All the island boasts are pristine waters, three extinct craters, a couple of black-sand beaches, one hotel, a hundred-strong village, and a wealth of peace and quiet.

Be warned, though, that Linosa is hot—very hot—unlike Lampedusa, where a breeze blows just about year-round and even summer nights have a desert chill. ∎

GETTING THERE:
By air: Daily one-hour flights on Meridiana *(tel 892 298 in Italy, meridiania.it)* to Lampedusa from Palermo and Catania. Also, flights from six major Italian cities in summer.
By sea: Overnight ferry with Siremar *(tel 091 749 3315, siremar .it),* daily except Friday, from Porto Empedocle to Linosa and Lampedusa. Hydrofoil service with Ustica Lines *(tel 0923 873 813, usticalines.it)* from Porto Empedocle late June–mid-Sept.

The Black Sands of Linosa

Linosa—an island closer to Africa than to Europe— was created by volcanoes. You can see—and explore—three craters here: Monte Vulcano, Monte Rosse, and Monte Nero. Now extinct, they were responsible for the beautiful, sole-scorching lava sand that lines the turquoise-sea beaches. The high-temperature sand of cliff-backed Cala Pozzolana is favored by local sea turtles at egg-laying time.

Villa Imperiale del Casale

The Villa Imperiale del Casale is an isolated Roman villa in lovely countryside a few miles from the sleepy village of Piazza Armerina. Here are preserved the world's finest Roman mosaics, a vast and almost pristine array of color and narrative drama spread over 50 rooms—an artistic wonder that was declared one of Sicily's five UNESCO World Heritage sites in 1997.

The villa's Roman mosaics depict history and myth.

Mosaics are not to all tastes, but even the most skeptical viewer cannot help but be impressed by the must-see Villa Imperiale. Be advised, though, that the site is extremely popular, especially in spring and summer. Note, too, that the plastic coverings raised to protect the mosaics and suggest the villa's original outlines create a sometimes stifling greenhouse effect in warm weather. The best times to visit are out of season or early or late in the day.

A visit should be combined with a trip to the nearby Greek remains at **Morgantina,** which by contrast receives only a scattering of tourists (see sidebar p. 103). If you wish to stay close to the villa, there are only a handful of local hotels, none of them outstanding; be sure to book well ahead. Enna makes a good alternative base (see p. 153).

Early History

The villa's origins are shadowy, and scholars dispute its precise age and original ownership. The present structure dates from the late third, or early fourth century, but it was built over a more humble second-century dwelling.

Most scholars believe the villa was a hunting lodge because of the mosaics' many hunting-related scenes, and also the building's position, which even today is in wooded country that once would have been rich in game.

The villa's size gives further clues as to its ownership, for only two private buildings in the Roman world of the era rival it for scale or splendor: Hadrian's second-century villa at Tivoli, near Rome, and the contemporary palace of the emperor Diocletian in Split, in present-day Croatia. Only a man of great wealth and standing could have created such a building, which is why most scholars believe it belonged to Diocletian's co-emperor, Maximilian, who ruled between A.D. 286 and 305.

Diocletian realized that the Roman Empire was too unwieldy to be ruled successfully as a single entity, which eventually led to its division into Western and Eastern (Byzantine) empires. A hint of this split is perhaps contained in the villa, which was built far from an increasingly fractious Rome and close to northern Africa, one of Maximilian's spheres of authority in the unraveling empire.

The villa's age is also significant artistically, for within a few years the empire (under the emperor Constantine) would recognize Christianity, and the subjects and imagery available or allowable to art would be largely religious.

Indeed, among the mosaics' many attributes are their exuberant paganism and vivid narrative variety. All the pleasures and events of everyday life are depicted, from dancing, lovemaking, and massage to hunting, sport, and children playing—none of which would have

been sanctioned a few years later, at least not on such a scale. Few mosaics before or since—and little subsequent Italian art of any sort until the advent of Giotto in the 13th century—would show the same intense naturalism combined with such subtlety, intimacy, sensuality, and sheer joie de vivre.

The Villa's Art

The mosaics were probably the work of North African artists. Roman mosaics tended to employ simple black-and-white designs, unlike polychrome panels found in the villa, which were probably based on Greek paintings. At the same time, the mosaics utilize monochrome backgrounds, suggesting a significant and early fusing of two mosaic traditions.

Villa Imperiale del Casale

⚠ Map p. 89 G3

✉ Casale, 3.5 miles (5.5 km) SW of Piazza Armerina

☎ 0935 680 036

🕐 Open daily 8 a.m.–dusk

$ $$$$

villaromanadelcasale.it

Piazza Armerina

⚠ Map p. 89 G3

Visitor information

✉ Viale Generale Muscarà 47a

☎ 0935 680 201

🕐 Closed Sat.–Sun. & p.m. daily except Wed.

comune.piazza armerina.en.it

Morgantina

Seven miles (11 km) northeast of Piazza Armerina in Aidone, the Museo Archeologico (Largo Torres Trupia, tel 0935 87 307, $) **and archaeological site offer a good introduction to Morgantina** (tel 0935 87 955, $), **the fascinating archaeological site and museum 3 miles (5 km) to the east. The site consists of the hilltop Cittadella (Citadel), once inhabited by Sikel and Bronze Age tribes, and a later Greek colony. Teams from Princeton University have been excavating the site since 1955.**

Much Christian and other art vanished in the so-called Dark Ages, the five or so centuries after the sack of Rome by hostile northern invaders in 410. The mosaics were luckier, first because the villa seems to have been respected by its subsequent owners, and second

INSIDER TIP:

Try to arrive at the Villa Imperiale del Casale as early as possible in the morning to avoid lines of people pouring in from tour buses. Besides, later in the day it can become very hot, especially under the awnings set up to protect some of the mosaics.

—SHEILA BUCKMASTER
National Geographic Traveler
magazine editor at large

because they were covered in a landslide in the 12th century. The site remained unknown until 1761, and almost entirely unexcavated until the late 1950s. Areas of the slave and other quarters remain buried under the trees.

The site is large and confusing, the mosaics alone covering 37,600 square feet (about 3,500 sq m) in 40 distinct scenes. However,

a knowledge of the villa's original structure is not required to appreciate its highlight—the mosaics. Nor do you need to know the story behind individual mosaics, as the narratives are often vivid enough for meanings to be clear.

The villa as currently excavated has several basic components, each with many minor rooms and connecting doors, passageways, and courtyards. These are the **Thermae,** or baths (on the left of the lane as you approach the site's modern entrance); the **Peristyle,** or great central courtyard, where visitors would have been met, and in whose upper rooms they would have been housed); the **servants quarters** and **kitchens** (on the left, or north, side of the Peristyle; the main **living quarters,** including the Triclinium (a large dining room) on the south side of the Peristyle; and the **Ambulatorio,** or walkway, which runs the length of the Peristyle's eastern flank.

The Ambulatorio and its majestic mosaic of **"The Great Hunt"** is the villa's highlight and centerpiece, a 200-foot (59 m) carpet of stone depicting the hunt and capture of

Piazza Armerina: Where History Comes Out to Play

Were it not for the Villa Imperiale's world-class mosaics, it is unlikely that many visitors would find their way to nearby Piazza Armerina, yet this old hill town has considerable charm, especially around the cathedral and Piazza Garibaldi.

Every year, the town bursts into life August 13–14 during the **Palio dei Normanni,** the biggest event on its calendar. The medieval pageant celebrates the

Norman count Roger's capture of the town from the Moors in 1087, and begins with a costumed procession and the reenactment of the moment Roger was presented with the keys to the town. On the next day, the highlight of the event is the Quintana, a joust among the four districts of the town—Monte, Canali, Castellina, and Casalotto—in which the winner is presented with a *palio* (banner) depicting the Virgin Mary.

A historic reenactment in the town of Piazza Armerina honors 11th-century Norman king Roger I.

wild animals of land and sea, some destined for Rome's Colosseum for use in gladiatorial games.

Staggering in its detail and animation, the rippling sea of color is crammed with human figures, tigers, elephants, ostriches, antelope, wild boars, panthers, and creatures such as the North African lion that the Romans would eventually hunt to extinction. At the midway point, near the steps, is a red-cloaked figure (flanked by guards) thought to be Maximilian.

Most pleasure in the villa can be had by simply wandering and admiring the mosaics, but there are several works worth tracking down: One is the **Sala della Piccola Caccia,** or Room of the Small Hunt, which depicts key episodes from a hunt, including an outdoor banquet. Others are the **Sala del Circo,** which portrays a Roman "circus," or chariot racetrack (based on Rome's actual Circus

Maximus), and the outstanding mosaics of the Triclinium, which illustrate the **"Labors of Hercules,"** panels that vie with those of the "The Great Hunt."

Also celebrated are the so-called **"Scena Erotica"**—a rather tame mosaic of a kissing couple—and the **Sala delle Dieci Ragazze** (Room of the Ten Girls) in the southeast corner of the Peristyle. The latter features a mosaic of ten women gymnasts apparently wearing bikinis some 1,700 years before they were "invented." In truth the women are probably portrayed in their underwear, which was also worn during gymnastic games.

Be sure to see the "kindergarten" rooms: the **Vestibolo del Piccolo Circo,** where children are shown racing little chariots pulled by birds, and **Cubicolo dei Fanciulli Cacciatori** (Cubicle of the Child Hunters), with children shown chasing—and being chased by—ducks and hare. ∎

More Places to Visit in Southern Sicily

Caltagirone

The town of Caltagirone, 20 miles (32 km) southeast of Piazza Armerina, is famous across Italy for its beautiful ceramics *(ceramichedical tagirone.it)*, the legacy of high-quality local clays that have sustained the craft for more than 1,000 years. Although you cannot tour local factories, you can watch craftspeople at work in some of the 120 or so stores around town. Have a look at **Piazza Municipio**'s 142 steps adorned with hand-painted tiles. The staircase is at its most spectacular during the town's Festa di San Giacomo (July 24–25), when it is lit by more than 4,000 oil lamps. For information, contact the visitor center *(Piazza Municipio 10, Galleria Luigi Sturzo, tel 0933 41 365, closed Sat.–Sun. & p.m. daily)*, which can help you make appointments to visit specific ceramicists.
▲ Map p. 89 H3

Eraclea Minoa

This former Greek colony, founded in the sixth century B.C., occupies one of the loveliest ancient sites in Sicily. Fringed around a headland, it looks to the mouth of the Platini River on one side, and the sea and a crescent of cliff- and pine-backed white sand on the other. The fine **beach** is worth a visit except in crowded July and August. You'll find beaches just as nice 10 miles (16 km) east at **Siculiana Marina.** Only about a third of the archaeological site *(tel 0922 846 005, closed Sun., $)* above Eraclea's beach has been excavated, revealing a theater and traces of tombs, mosaics, and city walls.
▲ Map p. 88 D3 **Visitor information** ✉ Via Empodocle 73, Agrigento ☎ 0922 20 391

Gela

Gela is an appalling prospect, its environs blighted by industry, yet in the fifth century B.C. it was one of Sicily's most important Greek colonies, rivaling even Syracuse. Today, it attracts ancient Greek history enthusiasts, who come for the ruins at **Capo Soprano** *(tel 0933 930*

975, $ includes archaeology museum) west of town, where the fortifications are the best preserved in Europe, and for the fine **Museo Archeologico** *(Corso Vittorio Emanuele II 1, tel 0933 912 626, closed Mon., $)*. Inland, the 12-mile (19 km) scenic drive to the village of **Butera** is highly worthwhile.
▲ Map p. 89 G1

Monti Sicani

The Sicani are wild, empty mountains, rarely visited and barely inhabited, but if you have time, they offer an interesting and scenic route toward Agrigento from the west. A good route (117 miles/189 km) follows the road from Selinunte to Sciacca by way of Menfi, then climbs to Caltabellotta and Villafranca Sicula. From south of Villafranca, minor roads lead east via Bivona to link with the S118. A left turn at Bivona runs to Santo Stefano for the high road to San Giovanni Gemini that passes just north of Monte Cammarata (5,177 feet/1,578 m), the Sicani's highest point. Continue east to the S189 for the drive south to Agrigento or north to Palermo.
▲ Map pp. 88–89 B4–E4

Sciacca

Sciacca's **spa** *(Via Agatocle 2, tel 0925 96 1111, termesciaccaspa.it)*, used since Greek times, is considered the world's oldest. A thriving fishing center, the port is lively rather than pretty, with charm reserved for the old, little-visited upper town, worth a couple of hours of exploration. Sciacca is also known for its ceramics and for the work of Filippo Bentivegna (1888–1967), carver of thousands of heads in a strange, naive style. Many of these are at his estate just west of town *(Via Filippo Bentivegna 16, tel 0925 993 044, closed Mon. & 1 p.m.–4 p.m. daily but hours may vary, $)*. An essential side trip from Sciacca is the scenic 12-mile (19 km) drive northeast into the mountains to **Caltabellotta,** a majestically situated hill town. *prolocosciaccaterme.com*
▲ Map pp. 88 C3 **Visitor information**
✉ Corso Vittorio Emanuele II 84 ☎ 0925 21 182

Magnificence abounds: the island's finest ancient city, Syracuse, and baroque architectural gems Noto and Ragusa

Syracuse & the Southeast

A column decorating the exterior of Syracuse's Duomo is laced with grapes.

Syracuse & the Southeast

Sicily's southeast corner has always been one of the island's most fascinating enclaves, and its principal center, Syracuse (Siracusa), one of its most powerful and fascinating cities. Dotted around the region's rugged hinterland, a remote fastness dominated by the Monti Iblei, are several planned 18th-century towns—notably Ragusa, Noto, and Modica—which contain some of Europe's best baroque architecture.

Wedding guests watch as the bride tosses her bouquet from the steps of San Giorgio in Modica.

The southeast has an ancient past, exemplified by the magnificent necropolis at Pantalica, a vast gorge riddled with prehistoric rock-cut

NOT TO BE MISSED:

tombs. Even this outstanding site, however, pales alongside Syracuse, the area's key historic spot, founded as a Greek colony almost 3,000 years ago, and for centuries the most important city in the Hellenic world. Few places in Sicily are as charming as the city's venerable heart, Ortygia (Ortigia), a beguiling labyrinth with sights and monuments from virtually every age.

Countless other local towns have Greek or older origins, and there are several archaeological sites—notably Megara Hyblaea near Augusta—that under other circumstances might be worth a visit. (Augusta lies close to a vast petrochemical plant that discourages a visit to the coast north of Syracuse.)

This modern desecration echoes an earlier disaster, the earthquake of January 11, 1693, which devastated the entire region. It was "so horrible," reported one eyewitness, "that the

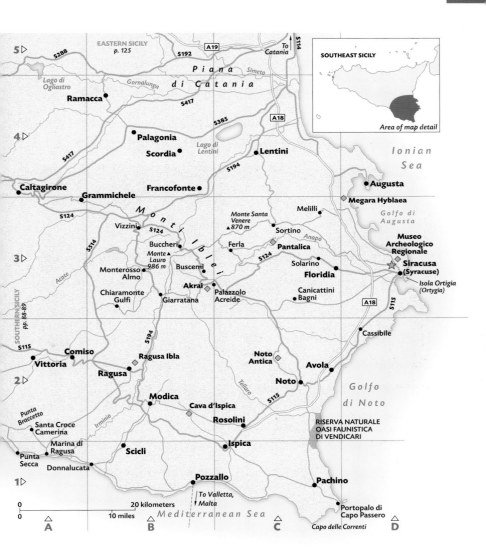

soil undulated like the waves of a stormy sea, and the mountains danced as if drunk."

Unlike other earthquakes in Sicily's long seismic history, the 1693 cataclysm allowed little by way of recovery or rebuilding because the destruction was almost total. But Sicily's quake resulted in some of the most compelling architecture in Europe. Why? Because the disaster occurred when baroque architecture was close to its zenith across Italy, some of the era's best architects were able to create entirely new towns, designing them according to idealized precepts and filling them with magnificent baroque churches, palaces, and civic buildings.

Noto is the most striking of these baroque fantasies, but Ragusa, once vaguely forlorn, now increasingly chic, is ultimately more enticing. It also lies in the foothills of the Monti Iblei, limestone mountains scattered with interesting villages worth a day's exploration by car. ∎

Syracuse

For some two centuries Syracuse was the most powerful city in the known world. This supremacy was challenged only by the Greeks, Etruscans, and Carthaginians, all of whom Syracuse defeated before succumbing to Rome. Today, its old town, Ortygia, and the extensive archaeological zone (Parco Archeologico) are essential stops on any Sicilian itinerary. Only the modern town, largely raised from the ruins of World War II bombing, is a disappointment.

Floodlights on the 18th-century baroque facade of Syracuse's Duomo light up the night.

The Greek historian Thucydides (circa 460–400 B.C.) claimed that emigrants from the Greek colony of Corinth founded Syracuse in 733 B.C. They were prompted, he wrote, by the urgings of Greece's Delphic oracle and attracted by the harbors, fresh springs, fertile hinterland, and the easily defended island redoubt of Ortygia. Before that it had Phoenician connections—its name may derive from Suraka, a Phoenician name for a nearby marsh—and was also inhabited by a native Sikel population.

Within 250 years it had become not only Sicily's most important colony but also one of the most powerful cities in the Mediterranean. In 480 B.C. under Helon, one of its many despotic rulers, it defeated the Carthaginians; in 415 B.C. it annihilated a colossal force dispatched by a jealous Athens, Greece's most powerful mainland colony and its only rival in terms of size and beauty.

For centuries the city enjoyed military, political, and artistic supremacy, producing or attracting some of the leading cultural names of the Greek world. Plato came here in around 397 B.C. to teach philosophy; Syracuse-born

Archimedes (287–212 B.C.) worked as scientist and engineer; lyric poet Pindar (circa 522–438 B.C.) was employed as a court writer; and the great playwright Aeschylus (522–456 B.C.) is believed to have written *Prometheus Bound* and *Prometheus Unbound* here.

Defeat came at the hands of the Romans, who took the colony in 212 B.C. after a two-year siege. Even then, the city's heritage and natural advantages helped it retain some of its importance, and it became capital of the new Roman province of Sicily. It was also prominent during the early days of Christianity, and for a brief period in the sixth century it was capital of the Byzantine Empire.

Today, Syracuse is a delightful place to visit and an excellent base from which to explore southeast Sicily. Even its climate is kindly— the Roman orator Cicero (106– 43 B.C.) noted that the city never knew a day without sun, even in winter. He also called it the most beautiful of the Greek cities. This is not something you could say of the modern city, a mainland grid between Ortygia and the Parco Archeologico. The latter is a pleasing open area ranged across the site of the ancient city's recreational area, Neapolis. Generally, however, the city is best avoided.

Ortygia

The island of Ortygia, linked to the mainland and modern city by two causeways, formed the heart of Syracuse for 2,700 years. Until recently it was a moribund district, full of crumbling monuments and dilapidated streets. Recently,

Syracuse

▲ Map p. 109 D3

Visitor information

✉ Info Point, Via Roma 30, Ortygia

☎ 0931 462 946, or toll-free in Italy 800 055 500

🕐 Closed Sat. p.m. & Sun.

siracusaturismo.net

EXPERIENCE: Cooking With the Locals

Food is a pleasure everywhere in Sicily, but in Syracuse—close to the fertile slopes of Etna, to the Catania plains, and to the sea—the rich medley of regional ingredients makes it especially enticing. The hotels and specialists that offer residential or full- and half-day cooking courses vary from year to year, but most offer similar culinary experiences. You'll likely be based in town; you might walk around the noisy fish market with an expert, learning about the wealth of seafood on display; you might visit a local family to cook regional dishes with sardines, red mullet, shrimp, sea urchins, and more.

You'll almost certainly tour other markets and learn recipes that use the island's wonderful cornucopia of fruits and vegetables, including specialties such as Taracco blood oranges, summer's white eggplants, and nearby Pachino's delicious tiny tomatoes. Syracuse and its environs also offer fun and educational visits to local cheese- and winemakers, as well as wine tastings and trips to vintners on and around Etna.

Consult the Syracuse visitor center for current courses or contact **Sicilian Demo Cooking** (siciliandemocooking.com), which offers two- and seven-day courses with B&B accommodation in Syracuse (with trips to the leading Planeta winery). Father afield, **Love Sicily** (lovesicily.com) currently offers four six-day culinary and gastronomic vacations annually from a base in Modica, a town 17 miles (27 km) southwest of Syracuse. The courses are conducted in English and include a full day in Syracuse and a day visiting a local winery and olive farm.

however, the area has undergone a renaissance, marked by extensive restoration projects and the opening of new hotels, bars, and restaurants. As a result, this is the place you should aim to stay, devoting time to the many sights, but also exploring the pretty flower-hung alleys and tree-lined waterfront promenades.

The Ponte Nuovo leads to Piazza Pancali and Largo XXV Luglio, home to the fragmentary **Tempio di Apollo** (circa 565 B.C.), remains of the first major Doric temple built by the Greeks in Sicily. Just to the north is the covered **Antico Mercato,** the town's

Kids take five on the steps of the city's cathedral.

former 19th-century marketplace, *(Via Trento 2).* A picturesque market *(Via Emanuele de Benedictis, closed Sun. & p.m.)* is held in the surrounding streets, while Largo Graziella nearby is the focus of the old casbah district, a reminder of the ninth- and tenth-century period of Arab domination.

The elegant shop-lined Corso Matteotti leads southeast from Largo XXV Luglio to **Piazza Archimede,** Ortygia's mostly 19th-century main square. Walk south down Via Roma, turn right along Via Minerva, and you come to **Piazza del Duomo,** a far lovelier square (particularly at night when floodlit). Here you'll find the area's most compelling monuments, chiefly the **Duomo** *(tel 0931 65 328, $),* last of a succession of sacred buildings that have occupied the site for more than 2,500 years.

The ancient building's grand decoration is long gone, pillaged or despoiled by the Romans and others, but the basic edifice was saved by its conversion into the city's cathedral in 640. Its present facade (1728–1754), one of Italy's last major baroque works, was added after the 1693 earthquake toppled the Norman frontage.

The baroque interior was largely removed in 1927, revealing the outlines of the original temple, notably its ancient columns on the left (north) side. The first chapel is the baptistry, with a fifth-century B.C. Greek font (a burial urn recovered from the city's catacombs) resting on 13th-century bronze lions. The Cappella del Crocefisso chapel has a 15th-century painting

Ortygia Diversions

The **Biblios Café** and bookstore *(Via del Consiglio Reginale 11, tel 0931 61 627, biblioscafe.it)* offers a range of cultural activities, including trips to vineyards, art courses, and Italian lessons that can be taken hourly or as part of week- or month-long full-immersion courses.

Do as the locals do and take coffee in the **Gran Caffè del Duomo** *(Piazza del Duomo 18–19, tel 0931 21 544, gran caffedelduomo.com)* on Ortygia's main square, which has a restaurant, bar, and shaded terrace. Off Piazza Archimede, **Le Antiche Siracuse** *(Via Roma 21, tel 0931 461 365)*, with its delicious baked goods, is ideal for breakfast. For more great

pastries after a visit to the Parco Archeologico, join the lines of locals at **Leonardi** *(Viale Teocrito 123, tel 0931 61 411, www .pasticcerialeonardi.com).*

Experience historic buildings and hidden coastal nooks and crannies on an exhilarating boat trip round Ortygia's shores. **Compagnia del Selene** *(Via Malta 63, tel 340 055 8769, compagniadelselene .it)* offers 50-minute tours from March to October. Or book a crewed yacht for the day to explore remote beaches and nature reserves with **Sailing Team** *(Via Savoia 14, tel 0931 60 808, sailingteam.biz, $$$$$ for 12 people)*. The company also offers sailing courses.

---

of St. Zosimus attributed to Antonello da Messina, Sicily's foremost Renaissance artist.

Leave Piazza del Duomo to the south on Via Picherale, and you pass **Santa Lucia alla Badia** *(closed Mon.)* on the right, a church dedicated to Syracuse's most venerated saint. Martyred in the city in A.D. 304, she was buried in the local catacombs and is depicted in paintings across Italy, usually holding a saucer containing a pair of eyes. This alludes to the story in which she is said to have torn out her eyes after being complimented on them by an unwanted pagan suitor. Her feast day and procession on December 13 is one of Sicily's most striking.

A Famous Fountain: At the end of Via Picherale is the papyrus-shaded **Fonte Arethusa,** one of the most important springs in the Hellenic world. Celebrated by the poets Pindar, Virgil, and

others, it was supposedly mentioned in Delphi's oracular directions that drove Corinthian exiles to found Syracuse. It also features in the Greek myth of Arethusa, one of the nymphs of Artemis, goddess of virginity. Arethusa, so the story goes, was bathing in the Alpheus River near Olympia when she was propositioned by Alpheus, the river's predatory god. Anxious to preserve her modesty, Arethusa appealed to Artemis for help, who saved her by turning her into a fountain. Thus transformed, she was able to escape under the sea to Sicily, where she emerged as the spring of the Fonte Arethusa. To no avail, however; Alpheus pursued her, mingling his river waters with those of the spring.

Myth aside, a spring of such purity so close to the sea was of great practical use, and its waters sustained Ortygia through centuries of siege and warfare. Earthquakes and new buildings

**Parco
Archeologico**

✉ Viale Augusto-
Via Paradiso 14

☎ 0931 66 206

🕐 Open daily
9 a.m.–one hour
before sunset

💲 $$$$

NOTE: Two-day combination tickets are available for admission to all or any two of the following: Museo Regionale, Parco Archeologico, and Museo Archeologico Regionale.

subsequently compromised the purity, but the spring still flows.

Fonte Arethusa is the focus of the *passeggiata* (evening stroll), along with the **Foro Vittorio Emanuele II,** also known as the Marina, the lovely tree-lined waterfront promenade north of the fountain. To the south rises the **Castello Maniace,** a 13th-century fortress named after George Maniakes, the Byzantine general who recaptured the city from the Arabs in 1038.

Walk east from the fountain on Via Capodieci and you come to the **Museo Regionale** (*Palazzo Bellomo, Via Capodieci 14, tel 0931 69 511, closed Sun. p.m. & Mon., $$$*),

---

Going Underground

Syracuse's catacombs are the most extensive in Italy after those of Rome. Their main entrance is beside the ruined church of San Giovanni, west of the Museo Archeologico Regionale.

Only a small area is currently open to the public—and only via guided tours (*Via Girolamo Savonarola, closed Sun.–Mon. & 12:30 p.m.–2:30 p.m. daily, $$$*).

Ortygia's principal museum. A mixture of artistic, decorative, and archaeological exhibits, highlights include an "Annunciation" (1474) by Antonello da Messina.

Spend some time just wandering the alleys and streets. Some of the best are **Via Roma,** the palace-lined **Via Vittorio Veneto, Via Maestranza,** and **Via della Giudecca,** heart of the old Jewish quarter. Beneath the Alla Giudecca hotel (*Via G. B. Alagona 42, tel

00931 22 255, guided tours daily on the hour 11 a.m.–6 p.m. & Sun. midday, $$) it is possible to visit the fascinating remains of a *miqwe,* an ancient Jewish ritual bathhouse.

Parco Archeologico

The park lies north of the modern city, but the walk from Ortygia is dull; take a cab or bus No. 1 from Ortygia's Piazza della Posta. The park extends over a "new" area of the ancient city, built as a predominantly recreational zone in the third century B.C.

The entrance is marked by a small visitor center and souvenir stands. Beyond these on the left lies the site's first major ruin, the **Ara di Ierone II** (241–217 B.C.), created as a vast sacrificial altar where as many as 350 bulls could be killed in a single day. Though little survives (the Spanish plundered its stone in 1526 to build the city's harbor), the structure's outlines still bear impressive witness to its enormous scale.

Far more remains of the **Teatro Greco,** an amphitheater carved from the rock. One of the grandest theaters in the Greek world, it was begun in the sixth century B.C.; in the third century B.C. it was enlarged to accommodate 15,000 people in nine 59-row sections, of which 42 remain. The Romans made further changes, partly for the staging of gladiatorial combat and mock sea battles.

Concerts and plays are still performed here in May and June (*contact visitor center for details*). Performances are also held in the **Anfiteatro Romano** (*south of main entrance*), the Roman

Syracuse's ancient Roman amphitheater was carved in part from the local stone.

amphitheater built in the third century B.C. to meet the demand for circus and gladiatorial games.

West of the Greek theater stretches the **Latomia del Paradiso,** the largest of at least a dozen local quarries that supplied limestone for the ancient city.

Today, much of its area is given over to gardens, though one gargantuan cavern, the **Orecchio di Dionisio,** still offers a vivid impression of the quarry's scale. These quarries were long used as prisons, and it was in these *latomie* that 8,000 Athenian prisoners captured after Syracuse's victory in 415 B.C. died after eight years of hard labor. Only those able to recite verses from the Greek playwright Euripedes were given their freedom.

Museo Archeologico Regionale

Italy is scattered with archaeological museums, but few are as impressive as Syracuse's Museo Archeologico Regionale, secreted in the gardens of the Villa Landolina about a ten-minute walk east of the Parco Archeologico. With finds from the Parco Archeologico and elsewhere, the museum chronicles the history of Syracuse and eastern Sicily. The modern building is a little faded and the English labeling is limited, but the exhibitions are memorable.

Ironically, the star exhibit—the first-century "Venus Landolina"—is a Roman sculpture in marble, not Greek (though it was copied from a Greek original). It is a piece that is celebrated for the sensual pose of its protagonist.

Also outstanding are the vast seventh-century burial urns; the fourth-century Sarcophagus of Adelfia; the reconstructed Temple of Athena (now Syracuse's cathedral); and "Mother Goddess Nursing Twins," a redoubtable statue from the sixth century B.C. ■

Museo Archeologico Regionale
⊠ Viale Teocrito 66
☎ 0931 489 514
🕐 Closed Mon. & Sun. p.m.
💲 $$$

Noto

Noto is the finest baroque town in Sicily—which is to say the finest baroque town in Italy. Raised from nothing after the earthquake of 1693, it is a gloriously theatrical confection, an architectural ensemble of grace, symmetry, tawny-stoned palaces, opulent piazzas, sweeping vistas, and majestic churches.

Built during the golden age of the baroque, Noto adopted the best of the 18th century's architectural ideals. Streets were laid out on a neat grid, for example, glimpses of countryside were introduced as unexpected features of urban vistas, and hillsides were used to site

Engagingly ornate balconies adorn Noto's baroque Palazzo Nicolaci di Villadorata.

piazzas and staircases that played deliberate tricks of perspective.

The town was also divided in two, with a patrician lower section and another more humble quarter devoted to the accommodation of ordinary people. Most of what you want to see is in the former, an area that consists of three key piazzas and three principal streets.

The main street is **Corso Vittorio Emanuele II,** entered from the gardens at its eastern end via the **Porta Reale,** a gateway modeled on a Roman triumphal arch and built to mark the visit of Ferdinand II in 1838. Then come **Piazza Immacolata** and Vincenzo Sinatra's church of **San Francesco all'Immacolata** (1704–1748) to the right. Beyond is the more extravagant convent of **Santissimo Salvatore,** whose balconies are echoed across the street by Rosario Gagliardi's church of **Santa Chiara** (1730–1748). Venture inside, but know that Noto's interiors tend to be rather plain. You can climb to the roof *(closed 1 p.m.–3 p.m. daily year-round, plus p.m. daily Nov.–Feb., $)* for excellent views of the Duomo.

"Plain" is not a charge that could be leveled at **Piazza Municipio,** perhaps Sicily's most beautiful square. To the right stands

Noto in a Nutshell

The story of Noto can be told twice: The first recounts the genius and good fortune that produced one of Europe's most beautiful towns. The second recounts the battle to ensure the town's survival.

Old Noto—Noto Antica—came to an end on January 11, 1693, when a catastrophic earthquake reduced the town to rubble. Three excellent architects—Rosario Gagliardi, Paolo Labisi, and Vincenzo Sinatra—were hired to create a model town from scratch, which they did, 8 miles (13 km) from the old site, out of the local, soft tufa-limestone that lent itself to intricate baroque carving. The stone's dazzling white intensity weathered to a glorious honey color. Sicilians called the resulting town "a garden of stone." Little could they know that it would be susceptible to the depredations and the pollution of later centuries.

Based on findings that the whole town was inherently fragile, a massive restoration project was launched in the late 1980s, and UNESCO declared Noto a World Heritage site in 1996.

INSIDER TIP:

If you're using public transport to get to Noto from Syracuse, take a bus, not the train. Noto's railroad station isn't close to the town center.

—TIM JEPSON
National Geographic author

the **Duomo** (*cattedraledinoto.it, closed 1 p.m.–3 p.m.*), completed in 1776, and probably the work of Sinatra and Gagliardi. To the left is Sinatra's arcaded town hall, **Municipio** (begun 1743; $), also known as the Palazzo Ducezio, and the more sober 19th-century Palazzo Vescovile (Bishop's Palace) and Palazzo Landolina, former home of prominent aristocrats. At the first junction beyond the square, on the left, stands Gagliardi's 1730 church of **San Carlo** (*closed 12:30 p.m.–4 p.m., $*), whose tower can be climbed for superb views.

Follow the Via Corrado Nicolaci, right off the corso. A little way up and on the left is the **Palazzo Nicolaci di Villadorata** (*tel 338 742 7022, palazzonicolaci.com, closed 12:30 p.m.–3:30 p.m., $*), celebrated for its magnificent exterior. The palace is open for tours, but only one room, the **Salone delle Feste,** captures the former interior splendor.

Return to the corso and the **Piazza XVI Maggio** to take in the **Teatro Comunale,** a lovely 330-seat theater, and the church of **San Domenico** (1737–1756), one of Gagliardi's finest buildings.

The Upper Town

It's the simpler side of Noto (Gagliardi's **Santissimo Crocefisso** on Piazza Mazzini is the key building). Walk the streets parallel to the corso: Via Ducezio, with the churches of the **Carmine** and **Santa Maria dell'Arco,** and Via Cavour, with the 1735 **Palazzo Battaglia.** ∎

Noto

⓰ Map p. 109 C2

Visitor information

✉ Piazza XVI Maggio 12

☎ 0931 573 779

comune.noto.sr.it

✉ Via Gioberti 13

☎ 0931 572 156

pronoto.it

A Drive Through the Rugged Monti Iblei

Wild limestone mountains, the Monti Iblei are famed for their olive oil and sweeping views, and dotted with sleepy villages and major archaeological sites.

Prickly pear cactus and other hardy plants thrive on the upland slopes of the Monti Iblei.

Leave Syracuse west on the minor road toward Belvedere, pausing to visit the ruins of the fourth-century B.C. **Castello Eurialo** *(tel 091 711 773, closed Sun. p.m. Nov.–Feb., $)* ❶, part of Syracuse's outer defenses. Pass under the autostrada (expressway) and turn right and then left after 3 miles (4.8 km) to the Anapo River. At the bridge, Ponte Diddino, turn right on the high, scenic road to Sortino.

From Sortino, take the minor road west toward Buccheri, which dips and climbs toward Monte Santa Venere (2,851 feet/870 m). After 10 miles (16 km), turn left to **Ferla,** where another left turn in the village center takes you 5.5 miles (9 km) above the Anapo Valley to **Pantalica** ❷, Sicily's most important necropolis.

The easily defended site was inhabited by the ancient Sikels between the 13th and 8th centuries B.C. It's a spectacular place, with more

NOT TO BE MISSED:

Pantalica • High scenic road to Buccheri • Casa-Museo di Antonino Uccello • Buscemi and museum

than 5,000 tombs honeycombed into the rock. Many easy paths meander around the area or drop toward the Anapo Valley below, where the trackless line of the old Syracuse to Vizzini railroad (now a trail) can be seen.

Return via Ferla to the Buccheri road, turning left to the mountain hamlet of **Buccheri.** From here, take the S124 ridgetop road northwest to **Vizzini 3,** birthplace of the 19th-century writer Giovanni Verga, who used the village as the setting for several novels, including *La Lupa (The She-Wolf).*

See the churches of San Sebastiano, Santa Maria del Gesù, and Chiesa Madre, and then take the road south to **Monterosso Almo,** with two fine little churches, San Giovanni and Sant'Antonio. From here, continue south to **Giarratana 4,** another hamlet with a medley of churches, and then turn left (east)

toward Palazzolo Acreide. After less than a mile (1.6 km), a minor road veers left back toward Buccheri, a lovely high route with superb views, running 7 miles (9.8 km) almost to the summit of 3,234-foot-high (986 m) **Monte Lauro,** the Iblei's highest point. You can take this route and double back for the views or just go directly to **Palazzolo Acreide 5.** The village, with good baroque buildings and an excellent museum of Sicilian rural life, the **Casa-Museo di Antonino Uccello** (*Via Machiavelli 19, tel 0931 881 499, casamuseo.it, closed Sun. a.m.–2:30 p.m., $*), is best known for the well-kept ruins of **Akrai** (*tel 0931 876 602, or combined ticket with Casa-Museo, closed Sun. p.m. & daily from 3:30 p.m., $$*), immediately to the southwest. This was Greek Syracuse's first inland colony. There's a charming Greek theater and extensive fragments from the seventh-century B.C. settlement.

If time allows, detour north from Palazzolo Acreide to **Buscemi** to see a fascinating ethnological "museum," the **Luoghi del Lavoro Contadino** (*Via Libertà 10, tel 0931 878 528, museobuscemi.org, closed Sun. & p.m. daily, $$*). Exhibits focus on rustic life in the Monti Iblei. Return to Syracuse on the S124 via Solarino.

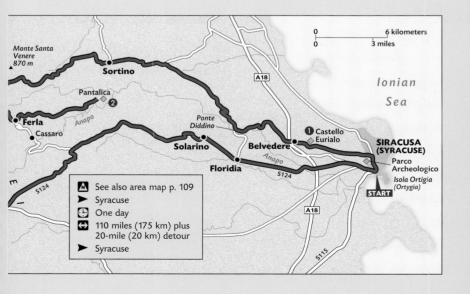

Ragusa

Ragusa is really two towns: the unremarkable 18th-century town created in the wake of the 1693 earthquake and Ragusa Ibla, the older hill town restored by its inhabitants after the quake to its original medieval appearance. Today, the latter has one of the most appealing and atmospheric old quarters in Sicily.

Modern electric lights illuminate the medieval town of Ragusa Ibla.

Ragusa

 Map p. 109 B2

Visitor information

✉ Piazza San
Giovanni,
Palazzo
Ina, Ragusa
Superiore

☎ 0932 684 780

🕐 Closed Sat.–Sun.

comune.ragusa.gov.it

Ragusa Ibla's origins date back to Hybla Heraia, one of the ancient Sikels' principal settlements. It was a Greek and then a Roman colony, and assumed prominence under the Normans when Count Roger created a fiefdom here for his son, Roger II, in 1091. The 1693 earthquake led to a decline that has continued to this day.

Decline in Ragusa Ibla, however, has been picturesque rather than catastrophic, and the town's warren of tiny streets is full of baroque and other buildings of ramshackle and wonderfully faded charm. The pace of life is slow, the views superb, and the opportunities for finding hidden nooks and crannies almost endless.

Both Ragusa Ibla and the newer town occupy a large spur between two valleys, with Ragusa Ibla set lower than its neighbor, which is known simply as Ragusa, or Ragusa Superiore. Buses and cabs run to Ragusa Ibla from Ragusa, but it is better to make for Ragusa's eastern margin and then walk into Ragusa Ibla.

INSIDER TIP:

Nearby Modica [see p. 122] lures chocolate lovers with sweets shops and December's Chocobaroco festival.

—RENEÉ RESTIVO
National Geographic Traveler
magazine writer

Start from the church of **Santa Maria delle Scale** (Corso Mazzini), and either follow the winding Corso Mazzini down to Ragusa Ibla or—a better option—take the steps (333 in all) that make the tortuous but panoramic descent to the old town. The view over the rocky outcrop, the sparse limestone hills, and the sea of weathered roofs is just one of many striking vistas here.

As you descend, look first for the lovely doorway of **Palazzo Nicastro** (1760), the town's old prison (also known as the Vecchia Cancelleria), and (to its left) the 18th-century church of **Santa Maria dell'Itria** (entrance on Corso Mazzini), distinguished by the majolica tiles on its dome. A few steps below the church on the right is the 18th-century **Palazzo Cosentini,** with a series of fine balconies and brackets carved with masks and caricatured figures.

From Piazza della Repubblica, either bear left to panoramic **Via del Mercato** or become happily lost in the labyrinth of alleys, steps, and small squares (take Via Aquila Sveva as a starting point). Either way, you will eventually stumble on **Piazza del Duomo,** the town's focal point and home to the 1744 cathedral of **San Giorgio** *(tel 0932 220 085, closed 12:30 p.m.–4 p.m.).*

San Giorgio was the work of Rosario Gagliardi (circa 1700–1770), the architect responsible for much of Noto (see pp. 116–117), and is one of the masterpieces of Sicilian baroque. Forty years in the making, its beauty is all in the pink-stoned facade—the interior is dull. Then visit the smaller but otherwise similar church of **San Giuseppe** (Piazza Pola), also attributed to Gagliardi, a few steps down Corso XXV Aprile.

Follow the corso farther downhill and you come to the **Giardino Ibleo** (1858), delightful gardens that occupy the town's eastern tip. In and around them is a trio of little churches, though the main distractions here, as so often in the town, are the sweeping views. ■

EXPERIENCE:
The Cheese to Try

The country around Ragusa is noted for its cheese, but there's no need to visit far-flung farms to try it because Ragusa has the most celebrated cheese (and local produce) shop in Sicily, the **Casa del Formaggio Sant'Anna di Dipasquale** *(Corso Italia 387, tel 0932 227 485),* founded in 1959.

In particular, be sure to try the cheese for which the region is most famous, the Cacciocavallo Ragusano DOP, one of Sicily's most ancient—available aged but best eaten fresh. This means between November and May, before the Sicilian sun has scorched the rich, grassy pasture grazed by the cows whose milk goes to make this standout Sicilian specialty. The local name for the cheese is *scaluni* (steps), after the shape of the vast blocks into which it is formed. If you do want to visit small local producers, contact the visitor center.

More Places to Visit in Southeast Sicily

A baroque staircase leads to the entrance of San Pietro in Modica's upper town.

Cava d'Ispica

From Modica, visit the Cava d'Ispica, a deep, 7-mile (12 km) gorge entered 8 miles (13 km) east of the town on the road to Rosolini. You can walk much of the lush gorge, which is riddled with rock tombs, Greek necropolises, cave dwellings, and Christian catacombs.
Map p. 109 B2

The Coast

The coast north of Syracuse has been spoiled, but much to the south remains appealing, whether you want a modern resort—**Marina di Ragusa** is the locals' favorite—or a nature reserve, **Riserva Naturale Oasi Faunistica di Vendicari.** You'll find low-key resorts near Pachino, and all along the southern coast, with undeveloped beaches, especially at **Camerina, Punta Braccetto,** and **Donnalucata.**

Modica

Modica's valley setting 12 miles (20 km) from Ragusa and multitiered old center make it well worth a visit—as do its many chocolate shops. The lower town, **Modica Bassa,** has several baroque churches and a small **Museo Civico**

(Palazzo della Cultura, Corso Umberto I, tel 0932 752 747, closed Mon. & 1 p.m.–4 p.m., $). The upper town, **Modica Alta,** rises in a jumble of houses, churches, and palaces, linked in part by a superb staircase (1818) off the lively Corso Umberto I. This road leads to the 1702–1738 church of **San Giorgio** *(closed 1 p.m.–3:30 p.m.),* the town's architectural highlight, and possibly the work of Rosario Gagliardi.
Map p. 109 B2 **Visitor information**
✉ Corso Umberto I 141 ☎ 0932 759 204
🕐 Closed 1 p.m.–3:30 p.m. & Sun p.m.

Scicli

A lovely road links sleepy Modica to Scicli, 7 miles (9 km) to the south. The market town's center dates from the 1693 earthquake. On Piazza Italia is the 18th-century baroque **Duomo of Sant'Ignazio** and nearby, the **Palazzo Beneventano.** Other monuments, such as **San Giovanni,** lie on or just off the town's Via Mormino Penna. Walk to **San Matteo,** heart of the medieval town, for views of Scicli below and (from the ridge beyond) of the Neolithic tombs and cave dwellings throughout the hills. Map p. 109 B1

The island at its most ancient (the towns) and strange (the other-worldly landscapes of Mount Etna, Europe's crowning volcano)

Eastern Sicily

Hardy plants thrive on Mount Etna's fertile, sun-washed slopes.

Eastern Sicily

Towns in eastern Sicily are thousands of years old, already thriving settlements when the Greeks arrived some five centuries before the birth of Christ. Some have lost their original glory; others, such as Taormina, have preserved their charm. Ancient or modern, however, faded or beguiling, the towns all live in the shadow of Sicily's greatest natural feature—the brooding mass of Mount Etna (Monte Etna).

Vapor issues from the smoldering summit of Mount Etna, Europe's most active volcano.

NOT TO BE MISSED:

Etna is unmissable. Visible from much of Sicily and the Italian mainland, its smoking and often snow-covered summit is an almost constant presence along the Ionian coast between the towns of Messina in the north and Catania to the south. Over the centuries it has been a mixed blessing for those who live on its slopes, frequently wreaking death and destruction but also bequeathing soils of almost untold richness. As a result, Etna's foothills are covered in vines, olives, citrus groves, pistachios, and almonds.

On the upper slopes the story is different, for here the almost barren landscape is an eerie expanse of blackened lava and shifting sands of ash, pumice, and other volcanic debris. The lower slopes and their interesting villages are easily seen by car or train—roads and the Circumetnea railroad almost circle the volcano—and the upper slopes, eruptions allowing, are accessible on foot

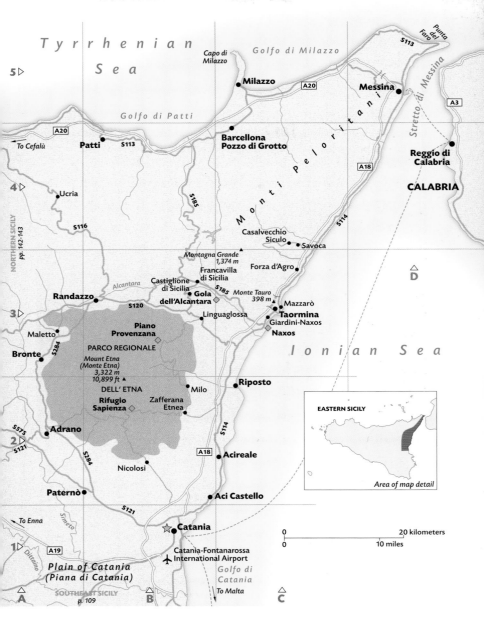

or on organized tours (with off-road vehicles) from two base stations: Piano Provenzana and the Rifugio Sapienza, high up the mountain's northern and southern slopes, respectively.

If Etna makes a virtue of its strange ugliness, the same cannot be said of the towns and coast below. North of the volcano, the Monti Peloritani, some of Sicily's wildest and most intractable mountains, squeeze highways and railroads hard against the sea, creating an almost continuous ribbon of forgettable towns and resorts between Messina and Catania.

Beyond the crumbling, sleepy villages in the Peloritani foothills, Taormina provides a pretty, sophisticated playground that has attracted visitors for more than a hundred years. ■

Etna

Ancient navigators thought it the highest point on Earth. To the Arabs it was *Gibel utlamat*—the mountain of mountains. Pindar (circa 522–438 B.C.), the ancient Greek lyric poet, described it as the column that supports the sky. Today, no trip to Sicily is complete without a visit to Mount Etna, Europe's highest and most spectacular volcano.

Hikers follow vehicle-packed lava up one of Mount Etna's blackened slopes.

Etna

🅰 Maps p. 125 B2
   & p. 131

Visitor information

✉ Etna Park
   Visitor Center,
   Via Manzoni,
   Fornazzo

☎ 095 955 159

⊕ Closed Tues.

parcoetna.it

NOTE: Most local tourist offices can assist in booking Etna excursions.

Etna is the most monumental landform in the Mediterranean, covering an areal larger than London or New York. On clear days the peak is visible from 155 miles (250 km) away. The mountain is about 10,900 feet (3,322 m) high and 20 miles (32 km) in diameter. Eruptions occur about once every five to ten years.

For all its sinister splendor, Etna is a young mountain. Geologists believe it began life around 500,000 years ago, bursting from the seabed of a vanished gulf in what is now the Plain of Catania. Over the millennia, and the last 60,000 years in particular, it has built layer upon layer of ash and

lava to create a colossal peak that casts its shadow over much of eastern Sicily.

The first recorded eruption was in 475 B.C. Since then there have been at least 250 eruptions—90 of them major ones, the last in 2003. The most catastrophic was in 1669, when the mountain was torn apart, leaving a chasm on its southern flank 16 miles (26 km) long. Magma flowed for 122 days, engulfing the town of Catania, while ash was thrown 60 miles. The lava took eight years to cool; local peasants were able to boil water on it long after the eruption.

Today, Etna—whose name derives from a Greek word

meaning "to burn"—is almost always smoldering if not erupting, its distinctive coronet of smoke a familiar sight across much of Sicily. Black smoke is apparently a good sign; white smoke is a more sinister portent.

Etna's volcanic character is marked by its tendency to split at the seams rather than explode from a central point. These ruptures have added 350 secondary craters to the four larger craters near the summit. This quartet has accounted for most of the activity of the past 30 years.

It is this volcanic activity, of course, that most visitors wish to see. Etna is so large and its environs so varied that you will need at least two days to do the region justice. One day should be devoted to getting as close to the summit as conditions allow. This will take you onto the barren, lunar-like upper slopes, where pumice litters the lava fields, and shifting sands and powdered ash drift across macabre hills. If you are lucky you will enjoy not only one of Europe's strangest landscapes but also some of its most remarkable panoramas.

Spend a second day (see pp. 130–32) exploring the volcano's very different lower slopes, best seen as a circular tour, either on the Circumetnea railroad or on the road that parallels its tracks for much of its course. Both routes virtually encircle the volcano, passing through a succession of tiny, often picturesque villages, and offering glimpses of the dulcet, pastoral corners and lush landscapes—forests of larch and beech, vineyards, orange groves, and orchards of pistachio and almond—that have sprung from Etna's fertile soils.

Seeing the Volcano

Visits to Etna's upper reaches can be made from either the north or south side of the volcano, and in particular from two base stations: **Piano Provenzana,** a ski station on the northern slope at about 5,970 feet (1,820 m), with a parking lot and ski lift; and the **Rifugio Sapienza,** an ugly conglomeration of mountain refuge, souvenir stands, parking lot, and restaurants located on the southern slope at 6,262 feet (1,909 m). Both can be reached by road: The 21-mile (34 km) drive from Catania via

**Piano
Provenzana**

⚠ Maps p. 125 B3
& p. 131

Rifugio Sapienza

⚠ Maps p. 125 B2
& p. 131

Visitor information

☎ 095 915 321

rifugiosapienza.com

Toasting the Volcano

Etna has fine conditions for producing great grapes. It boasts high altitude and rich, well-drained volcanic soils. The vast day-to-night temperature range produces a stop-start ripening process that can push back the harvest to the last week of October on the mountain's northern slopes, adding complexity to the wine.

Recently the wines' full potential has begun to be realized. Some critics are calling the region the "Burgundy of the Mediterranean," with some of southern Italy's most exciting new wines. Look for Etna-specific grape varieties, notably red Nerello Mascarese and Nerello Cappuccio, or the white Carricante, and for small producers such as Tenuta di Fessina (tenuta difessina.com). **Or make an appointment for a wider ranging experience with Giuseppe Benanti** (tel 095 789 0928, vinicolabenanti.it), **offering tours in English, lunches, and tastings.**

EXPERIENCE: Active on Etna

Etna is not only Europe's single greatest land form but also one of its largest—and most unusual—recreational areas. You may have hiked in mountains across the world, but have you ever walked, skied, snowboarded, run a team of sled dogs, or ridden a mountain bike on an active volcano? Physical pursuits offer an exciting twist when accomplished amid black moon-scapes, steaming vents, and otherworldly lava fields. And for naturalists, the remarkable scope of flora able to flourish on a volcano's apparently barren slopes becomes evident.

Dogsledding on Mount Etna ranks as a Sicilian surprise.

will also collect you at your Catania hotel for a half-day minibus tour, and **Etna Sicily Touring** (etnasicilytouring .com) offers mountain-bike options with pick-ups and transfers.

Other Activities

You can also mountain bike on numerous trails, some of them demanding. **Etna Touring,** in the main square in Nicolosi (Via Roma 1, tel 095 791 8000, etnatouring .com), rents bikes and offers group tours.

April, May, September, and October are the best hiking months; during the first two, you have the bonus of spring flora. In this high-mountain environment you need proper hiking and bad-weather equipment year-round.

Buy Selca's 1:25,000 Mount Etna map and you can hike alone—visitor and park centers have plenty of safety and other information—but to get the most out of a trip, go with a guide. If you are coming from the north, hire an official guide from the **Gruppo Guide Alpine Etna Nord** (Piazza Attilio Castrogiovanni 19, Linguaglossa, tel 095 777 4502).

For a southern approach, contact **Gruppo Guide Alpine Etna Sud** (Piazza Vittorio Emanuele II 43, Nicolosi, Linguaglossa, etnaguide.eu). They'll tailor a hike to your requirements and take you to the most spectacular viewpoints and places. The **Italian Alpine Club** in Catania (tel 095 715 3515, caicatania.it) is another good source of guides and information. Many companies have group tours. **Etna Experience** (tel 095 873 8756, etna experience.com) offers walking and minibus options, with hotel pickup in Catania. Tours are conducted in English and Italian. **Go Etna** (go-etna.com)

Etna's size and altitude range mean there are plenty of activities away from its upper slopes, not least in the Alcantara gorge (see sidebar p. 140). Contact **Acquaterra** (tel 095 503 020, acquaterra .it) for details on rafting, kayaking, canyoning, climbing, and river trekking.

In winter there's enough snow for five skiing and snowboarding pistes on the northern slopes and three on its southern flank, with skiing December to March (etnasci.it). Other winter activities, including dogsledding, can be arranged through visitor centers or the guide associations.

Nicolosi leads through brooding lava fields, while the similar length route to Piano Provenzana from Taormina via Linguaglossa winds through lovely pinewoods before encountering the lava wastes.

Whichever side you choose—the Rifugio Sapienza is the most popular—trips can be made in one of three ways: The first is to make your way by car or bus to the Rifugio and buy tickets on one of the 20-person, off-road vehicles that transport visitors higher up the mountain to around 8,850 feet (2,697 m). From here, a qualified guide takes you on foot another 650 feet (198 m) with the option—additional fee and conditions allowing—of ascending to safe areas nearer the summit craters. Access to or around the four main crater rims is prohibited after nine visitors were killed here during the eruptions of 1979.

The second option is to join a daylong tour, departing from Catania or Taormina. A tour includes transport to the Rifugio Sapienza, warm clothing and sturdy footwear, and, for an additional fee, the excursion by off-road vehicle.

The third approach is to make your own way to the Rifugio and then hike to the upper slopes, a rather monotonous route that follows the vehicular tracks (allow four hours each way). Or take the Funivia dell'Etna cable car from the refuge (tel 095 914 141, funiviaetna.com, $$$–$$$$$). You can also arrange to take the cable car plus a minibus shuttle from the upper cable car station ($$$–$$$$$) to near the crater rim at Torre del Filosofo, 9,580 feet (2,920 m),

conditions allowing. Food is often overpriced and mediocre; pack a picnic. Note that cable car service is suspended in windy conditions.

Whichever option you choose, views are better in the morning (a dawn hike is recommended). If conditions are misty or visibility looks questionable, do not make the trip. Other organized tours, hikes, and off-road options are available from Piano Provenzana, though here the setup is more pleasantly low-key. Tours and excursions generally operate from about May to September.

INSIDER TIP:

Below Etna, in the town of Castiglione di Sicilia, Alcantara Formaggi [*Via Federico II, tel 0942 984 268*] produces a variety of fine sheep's milk cheese.

—ROS BELFORD
National Geographic Traveler
magazine writer

Organized tours are the best option; everything is done for you, and you can avoid the lines for the off-road-vehicle excursions. Tours can be arranged through local travel agents and information centers. Should you prefer to make your own way, you will need to drive or take one of the daily AST buses (twice daily July–Aug.) from Catania's Stazione Centrale, or main railway station. Buses usually depart around 8:15 a.m. and return about 4:30 p.m. ∎

Getting Around the Volcano

The best way to get a sense of Etna's enormous size and to experience its remarkable scenic diversity is to drive or, from Catania, take the Circumetnea railroad (it leaves from its own private station), either following a clockwise circular tour around the volcano or concluding the excursion at Taormina.

A ride on the Circumetnea railroad comes with views of Mount Etna and its lovely environs.

By Circumetnea Train

The train leaves from a station just north of Catania's city center *(Via Caronda 352/A, tel 095 541 111, circumetnea.it)*—not Stazione Centrale, to which it is linked by metro. It takes about 3.5 hours (with connections required at Randazzo on some of the runs) to reach its terminus at the small coastal village of Riposto.

From here you can pick up connections on the main state (Trenitalia) network north or south to Taormina or Catania, respectively. It's a delightful ride, with many superb views of Mount Etna, but for flexibility and the opportunity to explore more thoroughly, it is better to have a car.

By Car

The following drive can be picked up at several points but is described from Catania and does not mention the many minor roads that

NOT TO BE MISSED:

Adrano and environs • Abbazia di Maniace • Castagno dei Cento Cavalli • minor roads to upper slopes • Randazzo

access Etna's upper slopes. These are all highly recommended, especially those to the Rifugio Sapienza from Adrano (see below) and to **Nicolosi,** home to a museum devoted to Etna *(Via Cesare Battisti 28, closed Mon., $)*, and a focus of the **Parco Regionale dell'Etna** *(Via Etnea 63–65, tel 095 401 4070, turismo.provincia .ct.it)*, which protects much of Etna. Also worthwhile are those roads to Piano Provenzana from Milo and Linguaglossa.

From **Catania ①** *(visitor information, Via Etnea 63–65, tel 095 401 4070, turismo.provincia.ct.it)* take the S121 road west to **Paternò ②,** known for its orange groves and restored Norman castle *(tel 095 621 109, closed Mon. & Sat.–Sun. p.m.)*, and then follow the S284 to **Adrano ③.** Founded in 400 B.C., this village is one of Etna's most ancient settlements. It boasts a castle built in 1070 by the Norman ruler Roger I. Inside you will find a charming archaeological **museum** *(Piazza Umberto I, tel 095 769 2660, closed Mon. & Sun. p.m. & 1 p.m.–4 p.m. Tues.–Sat., $)*. Stop by the adjacent **Chiesa Madre,** a Norman church with 16 basalt columns, possibly from an ancient Greek temple, then leave town northwest on the S121 road.

After 5 miles (8 km) look for signs to the **Ponte dei Saraceni ④,** a graceful bridge of Roman origin over a peaceful stretch of the Simeto River. Two miles (3.2 km) upstream (walk or drive on minor roads from Adrano) is the beautiful **Gola di Simeto,** an 8-mile (13 km) gorge formed by lava flows and protected by the **Riserva Naturale Ingrottato Lavico del Simeto** (nature reserve).

Return to Adrano and pick up the S284 to **Bronte ⑤,** a road that offers some of the drive's best views of the scenic high point: Etna. Bronte is the center of Italy's pistachio industry, responsible for 85 percent of the country's output.

The town of Bronte's rather drab appearance belies its romantic history. In 1799, Ferdinand IV of Naples presented the dukedom of Bronte to Horatio Nelson in gratitude for the British admiral's assistance (he had whisked away the king to Palermo just as the attacking French were about to enter Naples). Nelson died before he could take advantage of his gift, although the title and estate passed through the marriage of his niece to the British Bridport family, which retained the estate until 1981.

The Nelson and Bridport estate, the Abbazia di Maniace, lies just north of Bronte. Take the minor road left (west) off the gloriously

---

- 🄰 See also area map p. 125
- ► Catania
- 🕓 At least one day
- ⬌ 100 miles (160 km) round-trip
- ► Catania or Taormina

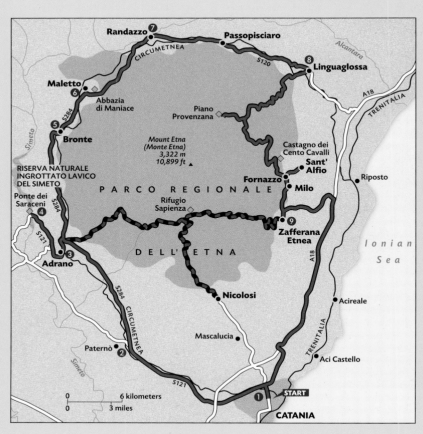

high Bronte-to-Randazzo road at **Maletto** ⑥ (renowned for its strawberries), where you can have a look at the 1823 lava flow that came close to destroying the town.

The **Abbazia di Maniace** *(tel 095 690 018, closed 1 p.m.–2:30 p.m., $)* began life as a convent in 1173, though today the building resembles an English country house, complete with appropriate (and beautiful) furnishings and a pretty English-style garden. Bronte also gave its name to the 19th-century English writers Emily, Charlotte, and Ann Brontë, their father—a passionate devotee of Nelson—having changed his surname from Brunty in honor of his hero.

Randazzo ⑦, the closest settlement to Etna's summit (less than 10 miles/16 km), has

Vegetation continues to reclaim Etna's once barren, blackened slopes.

miraculously escaped destruction, though it was badly damaged by Allied bombing in 1943—the Nazis having made it a defensive redoubt as they sought to hold Sicily. As a result, much in the lava-black village is restored, though the streets retain a brooding medieval air. The 15th-century church of **Santa Maria** is worth a visit for its strange, dark lava columns. So, too, is the private **Museo Archeologico Paolo Vagliasindi** *(Via Castello Suevo 1, tel 095 921 861, closed 1 p.m.–3:30 p.m. & p.m. Mon.–Fri., Nov.–April, $)*, an archaeological collection housed in the town's former castle and prison.

From Randazzo the road and railroad curve eastward, passing through some of the prettiest scenery in the Etna foothills. Just beyond **Passopisciaro** is a colossal lava flow from the 1981 eruption, but note also the olive and other trees and vegetation that flourish in the region's fertile soils.

Farther east, **Linguaglossa** ⑧ *(visitor information, Piazza Annunziata 5–7, tel 095 643 094, prolocolinguaglossa.it)* is the main center for exploring Etna's northern slopes and busy ski resort. From here take the minor road south toward Piano Provenzana to visit the **Castagno dei Cento Cavalli,** or the Chestnut of a Hundred Horses, half a mile (0.8 km) before the hamlets of Fornazzo and Sant'Alfio. More than 2,000 years old, it is one of Italy's largest and most venerable trees. It takes its name from the legend that Queen Joan of Anjou once sheltered beneath its branches with a hundred horsemen. The tale may not be so far-fetched, as the combined circumference of the three linked trunks is a staggering 196 feet (60 m).

From Fornazzo the road runs south to **Zafferana Etnea** ⑨, a passable resort surrounded by vineyards and orange groves (it is renowned nationally for its orange blossom honey). If time and weather allow, you could drive west from here to the **Rifugio Sapienza** on a steep and spectacular road, returning by minor roads, or head to the A18 autostrada to return to Catania or Taormina.

Taormina

Taormina is Sicily's best known and most urbane resort, a beguiling and bucolic hill town that for more than a century has been a favored winter and summer retreat, offering flower-scented piazzas, charming streets, chic boutiques, subtropical gardens, and endless sea views and mountain vistas.

A café beckons at the foot of Taormina's stately church of San Giuseppe.

Taormina's extraordinary site curves around a natural terrace 675 feet (204 m) above the sea, in the shadow of the rocky peak of Monte Tauro. History tells it has been inhabited for at least three millennia.

Taormina's first documented settlement was the Greek colony of Tauromenion, founded in 403 B.C. by refugees from nearby Naxos, a Greek city destroyed by Syracuse. The colony prospered quietly under the Romans and was briefly the capital of Byzantine

Sicily, but it fell to the Arabs in 902 and the Normans in 1078. Thereafter it slumbered for centuries, little more than a pretty, mild-weathered village known only for its superb position and remarkable Greek theater.

Grand tourists, the English and Germans in particular, were the chief visitors during the 18th century. German writer J. W. von Goethe (1749–1832) pronounced the town "a patch of paradise on earth." In 1850, though, English visitor W. H. Bartlett, lamenting

Taormina
- Map p. 125 C3

Visitor information
- Palazzo Corvaia, Piazza Santa Caterina
- 0942 23 243
- Closed Sun. & daily 1:30 p.m.– 4 p.m.

the locals' lack of enterprise, observed that "anywhere but in Sicily a place like Taormina would be a fortune to the innkeepers, but here is not a single place where a traveller can linger to explore the spot."

This would change after 1866, when the village was linked to Messina by rail, improving accessibility, and again after 1874, when Taormina's first hotel, the Timeo, opened (it is still in business). Today, the town boasts more than 60 hotels.

their home, including the British writer D. H. Lawrence (1885–1930), who lived here from 1920 to 1923. The town's lovely east-facing position, he declared, was "the dawn-coast of Europe." Even battle-hardened soldiers were seduced, the German field marshal Kesselring having made the town—not a place of any great strategic importance—his headquarters in 1943.

In the 1950s the village became even more chic as its growing reputation, and the

A motorcyclist roars past the Palazzo Corvaia, site of Sicily's first parliament.

The village became a favored winter resort to rival similar retreats on the French Riviera. The German emperor Kaiser Wilhelm II visited in 1896, and was followed by British king Edward VII in 1906.

After World War I, writers, artists, and other exiles made it

advent of a film festival, drew still more celebrated visitors. Among these were Orson Welles, John Steinbeck, Greta Garbo, Rita Hayworth, Cary Grant, and Salvador Dalí. Truman Capote wrote *Breakfast at Tiffany's* and *In Cold Blood* here, while Tennessee Williams penned *A Streetcar Named Desire* and *Cat on a Hot Tin Roof*. In 2015 the British songwriter Mark Knopfler released an atmospheric ballad called *Lights of Taormina*.

Today Taormina is a victim of its own popularity: Between June and September, when visitors cram the beaches and tiny streets, it is best avoided. April, May, and October are better, but winter and spring reveal the town at its picturesque best, with generally clear skies, carpets of wildflowers, and a chance to enjoy the genuine hill-village charm that originally brought visitors here.

INSIDER TIP:

Have a look at the macabre/whimsical paintings of minor local disasters at the Museo Siciliano d'Arte e Tradizioni Popolari [see p. 136].

—RAPHAEL KADUSHIN
National Geographic Traveler
magazine writer

The Heart of Town

Much of the town center is pedestrianized, and parking spaces are almost impossible to come by. If you arrive by train, take an Interbus *(interbus.it)* from outside the railroad station to the old center.

Most people park in outlying lots (Lumbi is the most convenient) and then make their way to the town center by special shuttle bus, cab, or the small cable car *(funivia)* from Mazzarò, the beach resort below the town (where there is another large

Following in Corleone's Footsteps

Are you a fan of Francis Ford Coppola's *The Godfather*? Do you remember the part where Michael Corleone (Al Pacino) is sent to Sicily, where he marries the ill-fated Apollonia? Much of this sequence was shot in and around Savoca (a village in the Monti Peloritani that's a 20-minute drive northwest of Taormina), not least in the village bar, the Vitelli, where you can still stop for coffee or a lemon *granita* (a local crushed-ice treat).

A visit here—and to other of the region's sleepy villages, such as Forza d'Agro and Casalvecchio Siculo—reveals a fascinating slice of the old Sicily, with landscapes and ways of daily life that have changed little over the centuries.

parking lot). All three options leave you on the upper reaches of Via Luigi Pirandello, the long, curving road that climbs from the coast.

At the end of this road, the **Porta Messina** gateway marks the beginning of Taormina's single main street, the gently climbing **Corso Umberto I,** lined with boutiques, souvenir shops, elegant cafés, flower-filled balconies, antiques stores, several churches, and lots of pretty palaces and other minor historic buildings.

Once through the gateway, the corso opens onto **Piazza Vittorio Emanuele II,** built on the site of the old Roman forum. The **Shaker Bar** here (on the left) was a favorite of Tennessee Williams, whose habit was apparently to buy a single glass of whiskey and replenish it from a bottle bought cheaply elsewhere and kept hidden in a pocket between refills.

Almond Nectar

If you can't be in Taormina in early spring to see the almond blossoms, then at least enjoy the fruits of the tree year-round in the shape of the distinctive sweet and aromatic almond wine. You'll find it on sale across the island, but the version made in and around **Castelmola** is particularly prized.

The square's principal building is the 14th-century **Palazzo Corvaia** (or Corvaja) on the right, with a central Moorish tower from the tenth century, decorated in the vividly contrasting black lava and white pumice characteristic of many local buildings.

The palace houses the town's visitor center and the **Museo Siciliano d'Arte e Tradizioni**

Popolari (tel 0942 610 274, closed Mon. & 1 p.m.–4 p.m. daily, $), an entertaining and occasionally eccentric collection of folk art and artifacts. The exhibits include carts, puppets, costumes, ceramics from across Sicily, handicrafts, and a variety of shepherds' accoutrements—notably some beautifully made sheep's collars in wood and horn. Also interesting are the series of ex-votos—paintings giving thanks for miraculous salvation from a variety of often unlikely fates (attack by cats, falling onto a stove, being blinded while playing tennis).

The palace's main salon, the Norman-era **Sala del Parlamento,** is so called because it was the seat of the Sicilian parliament in 1410, when it met to discuss a successor for the lapsed Aragon royal line. To the left of the palace is the 17th-century church of **Santa Caterina,** partly

Passersby eye the goods at one of the chic boutiques along Corso Umberto I.

built over the remains of the **Odeon,** first-century Roman theater, the rather paltry remains of which can be seen behind the church and built into its nave. On the opposite side of the square, Via Teatro Greco leads to the **Teatro Greco.** This is Taormina's main sight, which deserves an in-depth visit (see p. 139). For now, continue along the corso, passing a tiny side street on the left (Via Naumachie) that leads quickly to the **Naumachie,** the remains of what was a Roman cistern or gymnasium.

The City's Main Square

Rejoining the main street, you come to **Piazza IX Aprile,** a place to see and be seen. Its name refers to the date in 1860 on which Taormina's citizens revolted against Bourbon rule during the battle for Italian unification. The halfway point down the corso is a good place to stop, day or night, for a drink, albeit at a far higher price than you'll probably pay elsewhere in Sicily. Here you can enjoy superb views to Etna and the sea and also take in the square's fascinating human spectacle. The most prestigious spots are Caffè Wunderbar and the Mocambo, now rather more genteel than in the days when they were the scene of many a scandalous imbroglio and the occasional celebrity catfight.

Beyond the square and its clock tower, the corso enters the **Borgo Medioevale,** the oldest part of town, full of medieval palaces and the odd architectural reminder of the town's Arab past.

Church Fountain & Jewish Ghetto

Piazza del Duomo (closed noon–4:30 p.m.) is the site of a lackluster cathedral founded in the 13th century, though the piazza is noteworthy for its **fountain** (1635), topped by a strange female centaur. The corso ends at the **Porta Catania** gateway (1440). On the left is Via del Ghetto, part of the town's Jewish quarter until the

---

EXPERIENCE: Fine Diving

The waters off Taormina are some of the best on the eastern coast—so clean and clear, in fact, that the area around the **Isola Bella,** barely five minutes by boat from the mainland, is a designated marine reserve. As a diver you'll be able to explore subterranean caves and canyons (and tunnels on the north coast of Isola Bella for more accomplished divers) and see rays, lizardfish, and perhaps the rare white scorpionfish. But the real treat is the chance to explore several vast marble columns destined for Roman temples and other buildings, lost when the boat carrying them sank off Cape Taormina some 2,000 years ago. Contact the **Nike Diving Center** (tel 339 196 1559, diveniketaormina .com), which offers day and night dives, for further information.

Jews were expelled from Sicily and other Spanish possessions in 1492. A lane leads to the **Palazzo Duchi di Santo Stefano,** a fine 15th-century palace that hosts art and other exhibitions.

Bear left past the palace and you come to **Piazza San Domenico,** home to the San Domenico Palace hotel, opened in 1894 and

Taormina's Teatro Greco hosts a spectacular performance during the arts festival.

still one of Taormina's top hotels. Much of this part of town was damaged by Allied bombing in July 1943; the hotel was targeted after it had been designated the German headquarters of Field Marshal Kesselring.

On the Outskirts

Via Roma south of the piazza arcs back to Piazza IX Aprile—with panoramic views en route (beware the traffic)—but it is worth returning to Porta Catania and taking one of the lanes right off the corso to the **Badia Vecchia,** home to a tiny archaeological museum *(Via Circonvallazione 30, closed Sun.–Mon., tel 0942 620 112, free)* with displays of finds from in and around the Teatro Greco (see p. 139).

Continue along Via Dionisio (with the Badia on your right)

and it becomes Via Circonvallazione, which runs parallel to the corso below. Some 300 yards (274 m) beyond the Badia, a signposted footpath leads left, winding steeply to the sanctuary of Madonna della Rocca and the ruined **Castello Saraceno** on Monte Tauro (1,306 feet/398 m). The views are tremendous, but the climb is not one for hot days.

The peak can also be accessed from the road (Via Leonardo da Vinci) that runs to **Castelmola,** a rock-top hamlet about 3 miles (5 km) north of Taormina—and a popular excursion (lovely off-season, horribly crowded at other times) thanks to its views and celebrated almond wine.

Winston Churchill used to come here to drink and paint (as did Kesselring), settling down at the Caffè San Giorgio (Piazza Sant'Antonio 1, tel 0942 28 228, closed Tues. in winter), founded in 1907 and still in business. Look at the signatures in the visitors book, including those of John D. Rockefeller and Mr. Rolls and Mr. Royce of luxury automobile fame.

Teatro Greco

Taormina's fourth-century B.C. Greek theater (Via Teatro Greco 40, tel 0942 232 20, open daily 9 a.m.– dusk, $$) is a little smaller than the theater in Syracuse, but its setting is many times more magnificent. It is carved from the surrounding rock and has a panorama that embraces Etna, the highlands of the Sicilian interior, the azure of the Ionian Sea, and the shadowy mountains of the Aspromonte on the Italian mainland. "Never did any audience, in any theater," said the German writer J. W. von Goethe in 1787, "have before it such a spectacle."

Despite its Greek origins, most of the present structure dates from the Roman period, and from alterations between the first and third centuries. This is when, among other things, the still well preserved brick stage buildings (scena) were added and the shape of the auditorium (cavea) was altered to stage gladiatorial games.

Unlike its rival in Syracuse, the theater is not used to stage classical drama, but hosts performances during Taormina's arts festival, **Taormina Arte** (Corso Umberto I 19, tel 0942 21 142, www.taormina -arte.com), held July to September.

Below the theater are the town's delightful public gardens at

INSIDER TIP:

To sample Zafferana Etnea's famous honey, visit Oro d'Etna [Via San Giacomo 135, tel 095 708 1411, orodetna .it]—the chestnut, orange, and lemon blossom honeys are especially delicious.

—TIM JEPSON
National Geographic author

Parco Duca di Cesarò (Via Bagnoli Croce), a site that rivals the theater for beauty—albeit of a quieter and more horticultural kind. An oasis of trees, shrubs, and other plants, many rare or exotic, the gardens were created in 1899 by Lady Florence Trevelyan, a Scotswoman "encouraged" to leave Britain hurriedly after a scandalous affair with the future king Edward VII. ∎

A Day Trip to the South

Sicily provides a springboard to another appealing Mediterranean island with a unique culture and history—**Malta.**

Virtu Ferries (tel 095 703 1211, virtuferries.com) offers a crossing in each direction up to six times weekly from **Catania** (tel 095 535 711) and once or twice daily from **Pozzallo** (tel 0932 811 811), south of **Ragusa.** You can leave from one port and return to the other. Crossings from Pozzallo take 90 minutes; from Catania, three hours. Early morning outbound and evening inbound sailings (June–Oct.) allow you a day's sightseeing in Valletta, the hilly Maltese capital, as well as a quick bus trip to a nearby place of interest.

More Places to Visit in Eastern Sicily

Catania

Sicily's second largest city, Catania lacks the sights commensurate with a place of its size. Natural disasters (earthquakes and Etna's eruptions) are partly to blame for its unappealing appearance, but so are decades of bureaucratic incompetence. Economically, it is doing relatively well, but most of the city's businesses and more affluent residents have relocated to the suburbs, with the result that the inner city (despite recent efforts by more enlightened governing councils) is in a poor state.

If you do find yourself here, make sure it is not in summer, for this is one of Italy's hottest cities, with temperatures often in excess of 104°F (40°C). Devote your time to the **cathedral** *(Piazza del Duomo)*, the masterpiece of Giovanni Battista Vaccarini (1702–1768), who designed much of Catania's baroque center. Also walk down **Via Crociferi,** the city's best baroque street, and **Via Etnea,** Catania's main thoroughfare. For quiet and shade, visit **Villa Bellini** park just north of the center off

Via Santo Euplio and Via Pacini. Catania also offers many theaters, concerts, and festivals. *turismo.provincia.ct.it*
🅰 Map p. 125 B1 **Visitor information**
✉ Via Etnea 63–65 ☎ 095 401 4070
🕐 Closed Sat. p.m. & Sun.

Messina

The large coastal town of Messina, hemmed in by the Peloritani Mountains to the rear, is the first sight of Sicily for visitors approaching from the Italian mainland. As a distant prospect, it is easy to imagine the town as that in which Shakespeare set *Much Ado About Nothing.* Up close, however, Messina reveals itself as a busy and thoroughly modern place, with almost no redeeming visual features.

The fault for this is not Messina's, for the town has had a share of bad luck that is excessive even by Sicilian standards. In 1908, for example, an earthquake killed 80,000 people (out of a population of 120,000), razing the town and causing the coast to sink by 19 inches (50 cm). No sooner had rebuilding been completed than the Allies bombed it almost flat again in World War II—Messina had the unfortunate distinction of being the most heavily bombed of any town in Italy.

Apart from the rebuilt **cathedral** *(Piazza del Duomo)* and its charming bell tower, the only real reason to visit is the **Museo Regionale** *(Via della Libertà 465, tel 090 361 292, closed Wed. & p.m. Sun., $$$).* This rich and varied regional museum is known mainly for the five-panel polyptych of the "Madonna With St. Gregory and St. Benedict" (1473) by Antonello da Messina (1430–1479), Sicily's foremost Renaissance painter. Also outstanding are two paintings by Caravaggio (1573–1610), commissioned by the town during the year he spent here in 1609. *comune.messina.it*
🅰 Map p. 125 D5 **Visitor information**
✉ Via Calabria 301 ☎ 090 672 236
🕐 Closed Sat.–Sun. & p.m. Mon., Wed., & Fri.

Explore a Gorge

The dramatic **Gola dell'Alcantara** gorge lies 10.5 miles (17 km) west of Taormina on the S185 road to Francavilla di Sicilia. It is commercialized but still well worth exploring, with lava monoliths covered with water and showing the effects of water as sculptor. You'll find good walking/running trails. Waders can be rented at the entrance to the park, and an elevator can take you down to river level.

The gorge is not passable in winter or after heavy rain. Much of the area is part of a protected regional park. The park website *(goalealcantara.com)* has details regarding hiking trails, activities—including cooking classes—accommodations, and more.

Sicily's most captivating islands—the Isole Eolie—and the wild Madonie and Nebrodi Mountains, where rural ways of life endure

Northern Sicily

From Lipari in the Isole Eolie comes a god crafted of clay.

Northern Sicily

The area between Palermo and Messina offers a quartet of landscapes: a highly developed coastal strip, where one town and resort, Cefalù, stands out; the glorious offshore Isole Eolie (Lipari Islands); a wall of mountains that comprises the Nebrodi and Madonie ranges; and the rolling hills and plains of Sicily's northern interior.

Just one coastal town, Cefalù, can be unreservedly recommended, thanks to its charming streets, excellent beach, and Sicily's loveliest Norman cathedral after Monreale. Other diversions include the ancient sites at Tindari and Solunto, the Norman castle at Caccamo, and the passable beach resorts of Sant'Agata di Militello, Capo d'Orlando, and Capo Zafferano.

It is still best to direct yourself through the coastal mountains—notably the Nebrodi and Madonie ranges, part of the Apennines, the mountainous spine running down the Italian peninsula. The roads are slow, but the scenic rewards are considerable, and you will discover

rural ways of life vanishing elsewhere in Sicily. The mountain roads are the highest and have more alluring villages.

Driving is not a realistic option on the Isole Eolie—seven tiny islets—so plan on taking a ferry or hydrofoil. Stromboli, with its regular volcanic eruptions, is the Eolies' main draw. All the islands, though, have their charms, not least outstanding black-sand beaches, excellent dessert wines, and delightful scenery (boat trips are highly recommended). Regular ferries link the islands, with the least frequent services running to the most beautiful and most distant islets—the little jewels of Panarea and Alicudi, respectively. ■

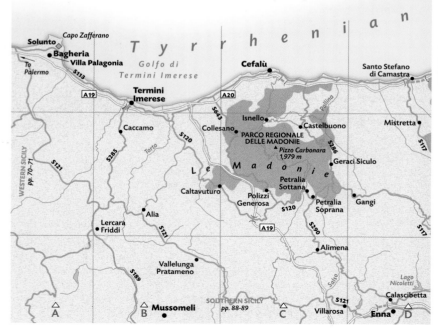

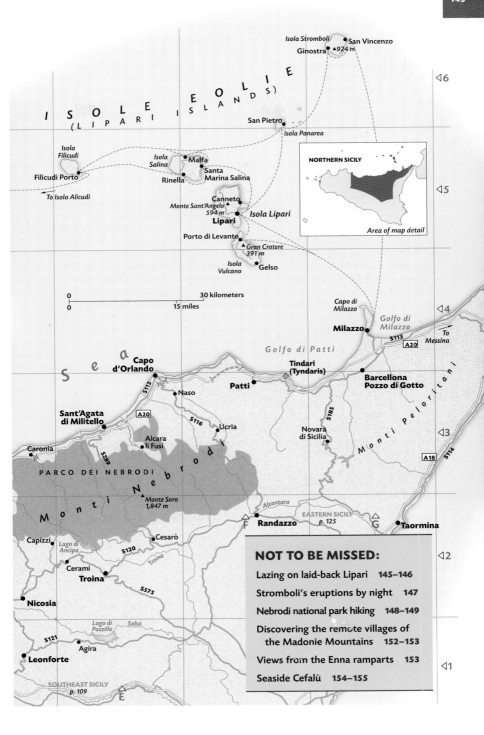

Isola Stromboli · San Vincenzo
Ginostra · ▲924 m.

I S O L E   E O L I E
(L I P A R I   I S L A N D S)

San Pietro
Isola Panarea

Isola
Filicudi
Isola
Salina   Malfa
Santa
Filicudi Porto   Rinella   Marina Salina
To Isola Alicudi

Canneto
Monte Sant'Angelo ▲
594 m   Isola Lipari
Lipari
Porto di Levante
▲ Gran Cratere
391 m
Isola
Vulcano   Gelso

NORTHERN SICILY

Area of map detail

0   30 kilometers
0   15 miles

Capo di
Milazzo

Golfo di
Milazzo

Milazzo   S113   To
Messina
A20

Golfo di Patti

Tindari
(Tyndaris)
Capo
d'Orlando   Patti   Barcellona
Pozzo di Gotto

S113   Naso
Novara
di Sicilia
Sant'Agata
di Militello   A20   S116   Ucria

Caronia   S289   Alcara
li Fusi

PARCO DEI NEBRODI   M o n t i   P e l o r i t a n i

A18   S114

M o n t i   N e b r o d i
Monte Soro
1,847 m

Alcantara
EASTERN SICILY
Capizzi   Cesarò   F   Randazzo   p. 125   G   Taormina

Lago di
Ancipa
Cerami   S120   Troina
Troina   S575

Nicosia

Lago di   Salso
Pozzillo

S121   Agira
Leonforte

SOUTHEAST SICILY
p. 109
E

NOT TO BE MISSED:

Lazing on laid-back Lipari   145–146

Stromboli's eruptions by night   147

Nebrodi national park hiking   148–149

Discovering the remote villages of
the Madonie Mountains   152–153

Views from the Enna ramparts   153

Seaside Cefalù   154–155

Isole Eolie

Sicily has numerous ravishing offshore islands—Pantelleria, Lampedusa, Marettimo, and others—but none are as spectacular as the Isole Eolie (Lipari Islands), the legendary home of Vulcan, god of fire, and Aeolus, god of the winds. The seven islets are the remnants of volcanoes both active and extinct, and visitors come to witness volcanic activity in the raw, and to enjoy the islands' peace and quiet, varied landscapes, and aquamarine seas. The islands could well fill a week's visit to Sicily.

Night falls on lively Lipari town, the main settlement on the archipelago's largest island.

Ferries and hydrofoils run to the Isole Eolie from Naples, Palermo, Cefalù, and Messina, but the most direct access is from Milazzo, a port 16 miles (26 km) away on the north coast of Sicily. Boats also run among the islands, with Lipari—the islands' largest and most developed outpost—the hub for most services. It is also the only island on which a car might be useful; nonetheless, it is advisable to visit without one. Many of the islands have good bus service or are small enough to explore on foot, bike, or scooter.

You can leave your car in a garage in Milazzo, such as Central *(tel 090 928 2472, centralmilazzo.com),* or inquire at the visitor center *(Piazza Caio Duilio 10, tel 090 922 2865 or 090 922 2790, milazzo.info, closed Sun. & p.m. daily except Mon.).*

INSIDER TIP:

Da Alfredo [Piazza Marina Garibaldi, Salina] is famous for its granita (flavored crushed ice), made in the bar's tiny kitchen and served on a piazza above a pebbly beach with heavenly views across the sea to the islands of Lipari, Panarea, and Stromboli. Keep an eye out for dolphins.

—ROS BELFORD
National Geographic Traveler
magazine writer

Hiking and snorkeling are major attractions throughout the Eolie, as are distinctive food and wine, hot pools and volcanic mud baths, fabulous marine and coastal landscapes, and the pleasures of small-town life and the islands' relaxed atmosphere.

You won't have the islands to yourself, however. The big three—Stromboli, Vulcano, and Lipari—are extremely popular, so you need to reserve accommodations in advance, at least for visits in July and August. Outside these months, and other peak periods such as Easter, you should have few problems securing a room.

Lipari is the obvious base, with Salina a less busy alternative. Stromboli is the most popular excursion—a trip on foot to its active crater, especially at night, is an unforgettable experience.

Vulcano has no active crater, but its natural hot springs and volcanic mud baths make it popular with Italians. It also offers superb views and good hiking on strange volcanic landscapes.

Panarea is the smallest, prettiest, and most chic of the islands; undeveloped Filicudi of greatest appeal to divers and island lovers; and Alicudi the wildest, least visited, and most far-flung of the scenic septet. Each of the Eolies now enjoys UNESCO World Heritage status.

Lipari

The largest and most scenically varied island, Lipari makes up for what it lacks in volcanic activity with its beauty—albeit one compromised in places by vacation-home development. Boats dock at busy **Lipari town,** a place cradled between two bays, Marina Corta and Marina Lunga, the latter with a small beach and a busy waterfront of bars, cafés, and restaurants. The town has many charming corners as well as plenty of stylish accommodations, trendy nightlife, and good places to eat.

It also has the outstanding **Museo Archeologico Eoliano** *(Via Castello 2, tel 090 988 0174, closed Sun. p.m., $$),* housed in four separate buildings around the 11th-century cathedral in the town's old citadel. The Eolies have been inhabited for at least 7,000 years, early settlers and traders having been attracted by obsidian, a hard volcanic rock used by Neolithic peoples to make tools and weapons. Lipari's museum has one of the world's best collections of

Isole Eolie

Map p. 143
D5–G6

Visitor information

Via Maurolico 17, Lipari

090 988 0095

Closed Sat.–Sun., p.m. Tues. & Thurs., & daily 2 p.m.– 4 p.m.; possible longer hours in high season

comunelipari.gov.it

eolnet.it

isolasalina.com

isoladistromboli.com

NOTE: For ferry or hydrofoil information from Milazzo, contact NGI *(tel 090 928 4091 or 800 250 000 toll-free in Italy, ngi-spa.it)* or Siremar-Tirrenia *(tel 091 749 3315, tirrenia.it)* or Ustica Lines *(tel 0923 873 813, usticalines.it),* which offers two sailings daily in summer from Naples, Palermo, and Cefalù.

Bathers soak in a thermal volcanic pool near Porto di Levante on the island of Vulcano.

such items, plus other prehistoric art and artifacts.

Elsewhere, the island's highlights are **Canneto,** Lipari's second largest village, which has a drab pebble beach, and the sandy **Spiaggia Bianca,** the best beach, only a half mile (1 km) farther north.

Just north of Canneto, the coastal road passes Monte Pelato (1,416 feet/432 m), which is composed partly of pumice, a light volcanic rock that is still quarried for use in the chemical, construction, and glass industries; Chicago's Sears Tower, for example, contains Lipari pumice.

It's worth taking a boat trip to see the **Cave di Pomice** (old pumice cliffs and quarries) in the lovely bay at Porticello. Also be sure to enjoy the views from the lookout at Puntazze and the still more extraordinary panorama at **Quattrocchi,** 2 miles (3 km)

west of Lipari town. Just south is another fine beach, Valle i Muria, a ten-minute walk from the road. If you wish to hike, consider the climb to **Monte Sant'Angelo** (1,949 feet/594 m), an extinct crater reached from Pianoconte.

Stromboli

Stromboli is the one Eolie not to be missed, primarily because of the spectacular eruptions that take place here around four times an hour. This makes it the busiest of the islands (plan ahead accordingly if you wish to stay overnight), but it is an easy day visit from Lipari (65–90 minutes by hydrofoil), Salina, or elsewhere. Boats dock near San Vincenzo, a melancholy hamlet that along with neighboring Piscità, Ficograndε, and San Bartolo forms **Stromboli Paese,** the island's main settlement.

Vulcano

Vulcano, the closest island to Milazzo, takes its name from the myth that Vulcan, god of fire, kept his forge here. Its last major eruption was in 1890, but constant, low-level activity such as bubbling mud pools and fumaroles (jets of steam above and below sea level) characterizes the 8-square-mile (21 sq km) island.

Boats dock at Porto di Levante beneath the main crater, **Gran Cratere,** or Fossa di Vulcano (1,282 feet, 391 m), easily climbed ($) for sensational views of the crater and the rest of the island. Allow two hours round-trip—go early or late in the day for there is no shade along the way. West of the port, at Porto di Ponente, is the celebrated black-sand beach Spiaggia Sabbia Nero. The single scenic road southwest from the port leads via the hamlet of Piano to Gelso, where you'll find the quieter beaches of **Spiaggia dell'Asina** and **Spiaggia Connitello.**

Panarea, Filicudi, and **Alicudi** are all delightful, unspoiled islets with fine coastlines, verdant interiors, and captivating beaches. Prices are higher than elsewhere, but so are the rewards of island life. ∎

EXPERIENCE: Stromboli by Night

Volcanoes, by their nature, are rarely predictable, so while you can climb and explore smoldering or dormant peaks around the world, it's rare to come across a volcano like Stromboli, where superheated gases throw up an almost constant barrage of magma.

One of Sicily's most memorable experiences is to view these pyrotechnics by night, when the burning orange of the molten rock is dramatically visible against the night sky. There are three ways you can do it.

One strategy is to book a table for dinner at **L'Osservatorio** *(tel 090 986 360),* a restaurant at 1,312 feet (400 m) on the volcano's slopes. The food here may be nothing special (play it safe with pizza), but the views of the eruptions are.

The second way to experience Stromboli is on a boat trip. There are many operators in Porto Scari. Two that are recommended are **Società Navigazione Pippo** *(kiosk by the Beach Bar, tel 090 986 135, cell 338 985 7883)* and **Paola e Giovanni** *(stand opposite Sirenetta hotel,* *Ficogrande, tel 338 431 2803, $$$).* Trips last about 2.5 hours.

The third way to view the volcano is to hike to the summit. Conditions at the crater vary, and areas may sometimes be closed. Access is now regulated, and you need to hire a guide or join an organized trek to climb beyond 1,312 feet (400 m). Two dependable operators are **Magmatrek** *(Via Vittorio Emanuele II, tel 090 986 5768, magmatrek.it, daily Easter–June & Sept.–Nov., $$)* and **Stromboli Guide** *(Agenzia Il Vulcano a Piede, Via Pizzillo, tel 090 986 144, stromboliguide.it).* Both these outfitters can arrange guides for individual ascents.

The summit is 3,031 feet (924 m), and group of hikers are generally led at a fairly brisk pace over the course of five to six hours. Bring a flashlight, proper footwear, a day pack, a wind-resistant jacket, and a handkerchief to protect against dust (don't wear contact lenses). Equipment can be rented from **Totem Trekking** *(Piazza San Vincenzo 4, tel 090 986 5752).*

Monti Nebrodi

The Monti Nebrodi, or Nebrodi Mountains, are one of the few areas to retain the pristine appearance of a centuries-old Sicily. A belt of high, verdant wilderness, they divide the island's northeast coast from the rippling uplands of the interior, an area of thick forest, craggy summits, and upland pasture ideal for hiking or solitary, scenic drives.

Called an "island on an island" by the Arabs, the Nebrodi Mountains remain isolated.

The fawns that gave the Nebrodi their name—*nebros* in Greek— are long gone. So, too, are the elephants, rhinoceroses, and hippopotamuses whose remains have been found fossilized here. The last wolves vanished in the 1920s. More flora and fauna might also have disappeared had not this precious wilderness been embraced in 1993 by the **Parco dei Nebrodi,** a protected area that extends for about 45 miles (70 km) from near Randazzo in the east (on the slopes of Mount Etna) to Mistretta and the foothills of the Madonie Mountains to the west (see pp. 152–153).

This is not a park where you will find marked trails, visitor centers, or interpretive guides. It is still virtually untouched, with few cultural interests outside the insights afforded by agricultural and rural traditions disappearing elsewhere in Sicily. On high pastures, for example, you will find shepherds milking by hand and making ricotta cheese outside.

It is also an area with very few roads—ideal for exploring superb wild landscapes—and be prepared to drive long distances to do so. (Many roads twist and turn, adding miles to what might appear short distances on the map.)

One such road, the S120, runs east-west along the mountains' southern flanks, with the medieval town of **Nicosia** the obvious inland base for the region. Just three roads run through the mountains from north to south: the S116, at its best from Ucria to Randazzo; the grand S289, especially attractive in its high central section; and the S117, a scenic delight for most of its upland run between Mistretta and Nicosia.

INSIDER TIP:

In January and August, Novara di Sicilia hosts a cheese-rolling race. (The *maiorchina* is so strong one wonders if the sheep pastured on chili peppers.)

—ROS BELFORD
National Geographic Traveler
magazine writer

A fourth north-south route on a less good but fabulously scenic road runs from **Caronia** on the coast via Capizzi to meet the S120 between Nicosia and **Troina.** The latter, at 3,090 feet (942 m), is one of the loftiest villages in Sicily. Any of these routes can be combined with the S120 and the main coast road to provide rewarding circular or near-circular routes over the mountains. Side roads add spice to your exploration, such as the 2.5-mile (4 km) route off the S289 leading close to the summit of **Monte Soro** (6,058 feet/1,847 m), the Nebrodi's highest point. Also diverting is the road west from **Cesarò** almost to Cerami.

The mountains reveal ancient tracts of forest and large woods of beech, which flourish on limestone soils at high altitudes. These woods, together with lakes and reservoirs, offer refuge for 150 species of birds, while the high crags provide nesting sites for rare raptors such as golden eagles, griffons, and Egyptian vultures (see sidebar above). Along with hiking, the mountains offer opportunities for riding. Many small farms offer pony-trekking (*equiturismo*)—and there is even a species of horse, the *sanfratellano*, indigenous to the Nebrodi. ◼

EXPERIENCE:
To the Vultures' Lair

If you're a birder or a hiker, choose one of three trails recommended by the Nebrodi park authorities (*parcodeinebrodi.it*) in the **Rocche del Crasto** area of the park between Longhi and Alcara li Fusi. Not only will you enjoy some of the Nebrodi's most spectacular scenery—in the shadow of the great crags and peaks of Rocche del Crasto (4,314 feet/1,315 m)—but there's also a good chance you will witness some of the rare griffon vultures reintroduced here after they were all but wiped out in the 1960s.

Monti Nebrodi
🅰 Map p. 143 D2–F3
Visitor information
parks.it/parco .nebrodi
parcodeinebrodi.it

Nicosia
✉ Municipio, Piazza Garibaldi
☎ 0935 638 139

Randazzo
✉ Corso Umberto I 197
☎ 095 799 1611

Cesarò
✉ Palazzo Zito, Via Bellini 79
☎ 095 773 2061

Alcara li Fusi
✉ Via Ugo Foscolo 1
☎ 0941 793 904/5

Fun in the Great Outdoors

Sicily's mountains, coastline, and islands offer natural playgrounds for outdoor adventures. Facilities, however, are generally poorer than elsewhere in Italy, and the island's environmental agencies face an uphill battle in establishing and maintaining parks, reserves, and other protected areas.

With few marked trails, hiking on Stromboli in the Isole Eolie can be an adventure.

Though it was the first Sicilian park aimed at protecting the environment, the Zingaro reserve was established only in 1981. On a more wide-ranging sustainability note, Sicily's various environmental groups, as well as international bodies such as the World Wildlife Fund (WWF), are slowly fighting back against the developers and vested interests peculiar to Sicily.

Hiking in Sicily is still not as easy as it is elsewhere in Italy. Sicily has many centuries-old mule tracks and paths, but few marked trails, and even fewer good maps to help you find your way. The exceptions are on Etna, the Zingaro reserve, Pantalica, and islands such as Marettimo. Elsewhere, such as the big Nebrodi and Madonie parks, new visitor centers have made the outdoors more user friendly with trail maps and advice.

Italy's excellent official park website *(parks .it)* is a good place to start looking for information on hiking and other activities, as is the site of the Club Alpino Italiano (CAI), or Italian Alpine Club *(cai.it)*. Learn about the excellent WWF reserves in Sicily *(sicilia.wwf .it)*. The website of the environmental group Legambiente *(legambientesicilia.it)* has dependably good general, up-to-date information.

Bird-watchers will find many of these aforementioned websites extremely helpful for planning the day's activities. In addition, there's the LIPU site *(lipu.it)*, run by Italy's foremost body for the protection of birds (Lega Italiana Protezione Uccelli), and the Ente Fauna *(entefaunasiciliana.it)*, which is devoted to the protection of Italy's wildlife. All of these groups put together field trips to their own and other reserves.

Visitor centers can provide information on **horseback riding,** which is possible from many of Sicily's rural centers, especially in the Nebrodi and Madonie Mountains. For information on a variety of equestrian pursuits, contact the Federazione Italiano Turismo Equestre *(tel 06 3265 0231, fitetrec-ante.it or sicilia.filetrec-ante.it)*.

Cycling is also easily possible. Bikes can be rented in many main tourist centers, and several old railroad beds have been converted

The north and west coasts have prime windsurfing.

into bikeways. Siciclando *(tel 800/888-0484 toll-free in the U.S. & Canada, 0203 355 4186 in U.K., siciclando.com)* organizes group and individual cycling tours of the island.

Other activities include **canyoning** in the island's gorges (Associazione Italiana Canyoning, *canyoning.it*) and **caving** (Federazione Speleologica Regionale Siciliana; *federazione speleologicasiciliana.it*).

EXPERIENCE: On the Waters off Sicily

Sicily's extensive coastline and its many islands offer obvious opportunities for just about all types of water-based outdoor activities. Most towns and resorts of any size, especially Mondello (near Palermo), Cefalù, and Giardino Naxos, offer fishing charters, and provide the opportunities for sailing, yacht charters (skippered and unskippered), and sailing lessons.

For information on sailing, contact the **Italian Sailing Federation** *(federvela .it)*. There are several good sources of information for sailing charters and lessons *(navigatio.it, sailadventures.com, & lafugasail.it)*.

Only the largest resorts, including those above, however, offer activities such as Jet Skiing and water-skiing. Offshore, **snorkeling** and **diving** are major activities in these waters, particularly on the islands of Pantelleria, Ustica, Lampedusa, and Marettimo (see p. 81).

Not surprisingly, all the major islands have dive centers. Underwater highlights include wrecks (both ancient and modern), volcanic formations topped with huge sea fans, and a wealth of sea life.

Windsurfing *(aicw.it)* is also a popular pastime, especially in Mondello, Cefalù, Marina di Ragusa, Scaletta, Agrigento, and Puzziteddu.

Le Madonie

The lofty peaks of the Madonie Mountains are second only in Sicily to Mount Etna. Soaring above the northern coast, they offer tremendous hiking and touring possibilities, and command views to the Isole Eolie and across the rippling uplands of the Sicilian interior.

A procession marks the celebration of the Festa dei Pastori—Shepherds' Feast—which takes place every seven years (2018) in Geraci Siculo. The was first held in the mid-17th century.

Le Madonie

⬛ Map p. 142
B2–C3

Park information

✉ Park center,
Corso Paolo
Agliata 16,
Petralia Sottana

☎ 0921 684 011

parks.it

parcodellemadonie.it

Le Madonie are similar to the neighboring Nebrodi Mountains—equally wild, empty, scenically diverse, and protected by a *parco regionale* (regional park). The main differences are that they are higher—the highest point, Pizzo Carbonara, is 6,493 feet (1,979 m)—slightly more accessible, and offer more hiking opportunities.

The Madonie also have more villages of intrinsic interest, most of them easily explored from **Cefalù** (see pp. 154–155), the

best base if you wish to devote only a day's driving to the mountains. Otherwise, the area can be seen en route between Cefalù and Enna, the latter a well-placed stopover at the heart of the island. Thereafter you can use the A19 expressway to return to Cefalù (or Palermo) or head east for Etna, Taormina, or Syracuse. Alternatively, continue to the Villa Imperiale del Casale to the south.

To begin a tour, get on the A20 or coast road east from Cefalù

5 miles (8 km), then follow S286 into the Madonie foothills to **Castelbuono,** 7.5 miles (12 km) south, a pretty town built around a 14th-century castle *(tel 0921 671 211).* It also has an interesting museum, the **Museo Minà Palumbo** *(Via Roma 52, tel 0921 671 895, museominapalumbo.it, closed 1 p.m.–3 p.m., $$),* with exhibits of decorative arts, archaeological finds, and natural history.

Continuing to the south, the road passes **Geraci Siculo,** a hill village where it's worth pausing to climb to the ruins of the castle (1072) for superb views. The road then meets the S120, where a 2.5-mile (4 km) detour southeast leads to **Gangi,** an impressively situated town.

Retrace your steps on the S120 and head west to the appealing

Five Viewpoints

The Madonie Mountains offer fine views from scenic roads and hiking trails. Panoramas often extend as far as the Isole Eolie. Five of the best spots for views:
• The Santuario di Gibilmana, 9 miles/14 km south of Cefalù
• The Madonna dell'Alto, northwest of Petralia Sottana, a popular hike from the village
• The Vallone della Madonna degli Angeli, between Polizzi Generosa and Petralia Sottana
• Either of the scenic roads south of Collesano (via Piano Zucci) or Castelbuono (via Geraci Siculo)

EXPERIENCE: Run a Mountain Marathon

EXPERIENCE: Run a Mountain Marathon

Enjoy a long run and admire the beauty of the mountains at the same time by taking part in the annual **Ecomarathon** *(tel 340 400 3490—English spoken, ecomaratonadellemadonie.it),* usually in late spring. The 27-mile (42 km) run weaves through mountainous Madonie national park, leaving from Polizzi Generosa, which is worth a stroll around.

Petralia Soprana. The views of the Madonie from here are exceptional, and the medieval streets are full of incidental interest. Continuing on, turn north on a side road to see the mountain-ringed village of **Petralia Sottana.**

The same can be said of **Polizzi Generosa,** a delightful village a 7.5-mile (12 km) detour west, distinguished by its many churches and small **Museo Madonita** *(Piazza Castello 7, tel 0921 649 184, mam.pa.it, closed p.m. daily, $$).*

The minor road north from Petralia Sottana via Isnello offers a far more scenic alternative to the S643. This spectacular road leads through the heart of the Madonie, with the best views between Piano Battaglia and Piano Zucchi.

Head south from Petralia Soprana to **Enna.** This fine town sits atop a colossal crag whose sweeping views have earned it the title of the Belvedere di Sicilia (Balcony of Sicily). A combination of good restaurants, reasonable hotels, and interesting sights makes this an excellent base. Visit the **castle** *(tel 0935 40 347, closed Mon.)* and the **Duomo.** ■

Castelbuono
✉ Via Umberto I
☎ 0921 671 124 or 0921 673 467
🕐 Closed 1 p.m.– 3 p.m.

comune.castelbuono .pa.it

prolococastelbuono .it

Enna
✉ Piazza Giovanni Rosso
☎ 0935 40 317 or 338 816 6944
🕐 Closed Sun. & p.m. daily except Wed.

welcometoenna.com

Cefalù

Cefalù has largely escaped the modern building that has done so much to spoil Sicily's coastline. Charming and compact, this immediately likable town, built below an immense crag, has several pleasant beaches, one of Sicily's loveliest main squares, and a Norman cathedral graced with one of the most sublime images of Christ in Western art.

Cefalù
- 🅰 Map p. 142 C3
- **Visitor information**
- ✉ Corso Ruggero 77
- ☎ 0921 421 050
- 🕐 Closed Sun. &
  1 p.m.–3 p.m.

Cefalù was probably founded by the Sikels in the ninth century B.C. but takes its name from the Greek *kephalos* or *kephaloidion* (head), after the shape of the crag that overshadows the town and that formed the heart of the original settlement. The Arabs built a citadel here between 858 and 1063, but the town came into its own only when Roger II, Sicily's 12th-century Norman king, extended the settlement toward the sea.

Today, the town's charm and fine beach mean that it has become increasingly popular, so you will need to reserve accommodations for summer visits. Nightlife, shopping, and eating are also good here, but commercialism has not spoiled the town, whose central medieval streets remain pretty and romantic places to stroll.

Any such stroll quickly leads to **Piazza del Duomo,** as satisfying a spot for a quiet drink as you could wish for. Palms grow in each corner, overlooked by the town's wondrous **cathedral** (1131–1240). Legend has it the building was raised to fulfill a vow by Roger II, who survived a shipwreck nearby and pledged a church to the Madonna in gratitude. The shrine was intended to be Sicily's most important religious building and a pantheon for Roger's Norman descendants, but his successors lost interest in the project, and Roger's body was eventually removed to Palermo's cathedral.

Much of the church's austere interior was stripped of its later baroque decoration in

An inviting waterfront is at the core of Cefalù, a popular resort.

the 1970s, but has otherwise remained unchanged for more than 800 years. Note the impressive wooden ceiling and the old Roman columns in the nave, both of which lead the eye to the exquisite **apse mosaic.** This depicts Christ Pantocrator—Christ in the Act of Blessing—and dates from 1148, making it the earliest Sicilian example of a much repeated image.

In Christ's left hand is a text in Greek and Latin from John 8:12— "I am the light of the world: he who follows me will not walk in darkness." Below Christ are three tiers of figures, including the Virgin flanked by archangels and the Apostles below. The mosaics on the side walls of the choir date from the late 13th century. The marble thrones were intended for Cefalù's bishop and Roger II.

A short distance from the cathedral stands the **Museo Mandralisca** *(Via Mandralisca 13, tel 0921 421 547, fondazionemandralisca.it, closed p.m. daily, Nov.–Feb., $$),* a fine little collection of coins and medals, pottery, Greek and Roman artifacts, and an exceptional painting, the "Portrait of an

Unknown Man" (1465–1472) by Sicily's most eminent Renaissance artist, Antonello da Messina (1430–1479). Baron Enrico di Mandralisca (1809 –1864), a local politician who once lived here, bought the painting from a pharmacy on the Eolie island of Lipari, where it had been used to form part of a cupboard door.

A walk to the crag, or **Rocca,** the site of the old citadel, offers superb views. Allow about 40 minutes, and 20 minutes to reach the so-called **Temple of Diana** en route, a fifth-century B.C.

EXPERIENCE:
Cefalù's Best Beaches

If you want a day on the beach, Cefalù is one of the most popular resorts in Sicily. Visitors colonize the sandy town beach, the **Lungomare,** but locals make for the pebbly **Caldura** beach, east of the town, beyond the harbor. **Capo Playa** stretches for 9 miles (15 km) west of Cefalù to Campofelice di Roccella and is known for its surfing. **Salinelle,** 4.5 miles (7 km) west of Cefalù, is especially popular. Nearby Mazzaforno also has a collection of pretty, small beaches.

building of unknown purpose. To reach the site, take Vicolo Saraceni alongside the bank building on the east side of Piazza Garibaldi, a square at the southern end of Corso Ruggero, Cefalù's main street. Look out for the Osteria Magno on the west side of the street (at the corner of Via Amendola), probably once Roger II's palace, and now used for exhibits. ■

More Places to Visit in Northern Sicily

Caccamo

The ancient little town of Caccamo, probably founded by the Phoenicians, is prettily situated among hills and olive groves. Its **cathedral** (founded in 1090) and several of its **churches** are all worth exploring, but it is the well-preserved **castle** *(Via Termitana, tel 091 814 9252, closed Mon. & 1 p.m.–3 p.m. daily, $)* that provides the town's main draw.

Sicily's largest castle—and one of the largest in Italy—it probably dates from the 11th century, but it acquired numerous additions and underwent many alterations over the centuries. Although the fortress is spectacular from afar, the heavily restored interior is far less interesting, with most of its 130 rooms sitting bare and undecorated. Map p. 142 B2

Solunto

Solunto is the shell of one of only three Punic, or Carthaginian, colonies on Sicily, the other being Motya (Mozia) and Palermo. Founded in the eighth century B.C. by the Phoenicians, North African forerunners of the Carthaginians, it fell to the Romans in 254 B.C. and was abandoned in the third century. Rediscovered in 1825, the site remains largely unexcavated. What has been uncovered is mostly Roman, including baths, a gymnasium, and the remains of houses.

As at many other Sicilian archaeological sites, the setting is as memorable as the ruins, though in this instance you have to cross Palermo's very grim eastern suburbs—and the scrappy town of Bagheria in particular (see Villa Palagonia, this page).

But in recompense, the headland just beyond Solunto, **Capo Zafferano,** is appealing—the first stretch of undeveloped coastline beyond Palermo. Map p. 142 A3 **Visitor information** Via Collegio Romano 338 784 5140 Closed Sun. p.m. $

Tindari

One of Sicily's last Greek colonies, ancient Tyndaris (Tindari) was founded as a garrison outpost of Syracuse in 396 B.C. Later, it became one of the Romans' five principal Sicilian colonies, declining only when a large portion of the site tumbled into the sea in the first century.

Today, the extensive **headland site** *(tel 0941 369 023, $)* is one of the island's more beautiful, scattered with mostly Roman ruins and offering lovely views of the Golfo di Patti (Gulf of Patti) and the sweep of sea, beaches, and small resorts to Capo di Milazzo. There is also a superb panorama from the adjacent **Santuario della Madonna Nera,** a blunt 1960s sanctuary built to house a Byzantine icon of the Madonna attributed with miraculous powers. Many thousands of pilgrims visit the sanctuary. Map p. 143 F3

Villa Palagonia

A visit to Solunto (see this page) can be easily combined with one to the Villa Palagonia *(Piazza Garibaldi 3, Bagheria, tel 091 932 088, villapalagonia.it, closed 1 p.m.–4 p.m. daily, $$)*, one of many large villas in and around Bagheria built in the 18th century by Palermo's patrician class as retreats from the city. Today, virtually all of these are in scandalously poor condition, and even the better preserved examples, of which the Villa Palagonia (1705) is the most notable, are compromised by their ugly surroundings.

In its day, the Palagonia's exterior of fantastic stone creatures, gargoyles, and other grotesques was infamous—the work of Prince Francesco Gravina, who, according to one story, created the statues as an act of revenge, portraying his wife's lovers as cruel caricatures. Despite the fact that only 65 of the original 200 statues survive, there is nothing else quite like them anywhere in Sicily. *comune.bagheria .pa.it* Map p. 142 A3 **Visitor information** Vigili Urbani, Corso Umberto I, Bagheria 091 909 020 Closed Sun.

Travelwise

A vivid mural serves as a perfect back-
drop for this artful motor scooter by
Palermitan painter Franco Bertolino.

TRAVELWISE

PLANNING YOUR TRIP

When to Go

High summer (July–August) in Sicily is hot, busy, and expensive, with a shortage of accommodations. The sea is warm as late as November, and in May, June, and September you can enjoy fine weather without the crowds.

Spring is delightful, especially if you are hiking or relaxing in the countryside. Almond and other trees bloom as early as February, but wildflowers are at their best in April and May. Easter is busy, but also a fine time to visit if you like festivals. Winters are mild (but sometimes wet) along the coast; however, inland and upland areas can be cold, with snow on high ground. The visitor season for island and coastal resorts often runs from only April or May to September. See pp. 182–183 for more details if you wish to plan your trip around one of the many festivals and events that take place across Sicily year-round. Additional trip-planning help is available from Italian state tourist offices (ENIT) outside Italy (see p. 164).

Websites

Websites for visitor centers are provided where appropriate in the text. Other more general sites include

pti.regione.sicilia.it
bestofsicily.com
siciliaonline.it
insicilia.it
festedisicilia.it
siciliano.it
trenitalia.com
enit.it
palermotourism.com
www.beniculturali.it
museionline.info
parks.it

Climate

As a rule, Sicily has mild winters and very hot, dry summers. Temperatures can be especially high (as much as or more than 104°F/40°C) on the southern coast, mostly when the hot sirocco wind blows from North Africa.

Northern and eastern coasts have less extreme climates but are still very hot. Upland areas are cooler, and in winter can be very cold, with temperatures below freezing at high altitudes.

Average daytime temperatures in Palermo are 50.5°F (10.3°C) in January; 65.6°F (18.7°C) in May; 77.5°F (25.3°C) in July; and 68.5°F (19.9°C) in October. Note that temperatures may often exceed these figures.

Italy uses degrees Celsius (°C) as its unit of temperature. To convert degrees Celsius to degrees Fahrenheit, multiply °C by 9, divide by 5, and add 32.

What to Take

You should be able to buy everything you need in Sicily. Pharmacies offer a wide range of drugs, medical supplies, and toiletries, along with expert advice, but bring along any prescription drugs you might need. Many brand-name drugs are different in Italy. A pharmacy (farmacia) is indicated by a green cross outside the store.

It is also useful to bring a second pair of glasses or contact lenses if you wear them. Sunscreen and mosquito repellent products are advisable in summer.

Clothing depends on the time of year and the activities you plan. You will need to dress up only for the grandest restaurants, but don't be too casual, as Italians generally dress more fashionably than most U.S., Canadian, and

northern European visitors. Make some effort for a meal out, and always dress appropriately for visits to churches—no bare shoulders or shorts. Note, too, that dress codes are more conservative in Sicily than in central and northern Italy, especially in rural areas.

Bring a sweater, even in summer, because evenings can be cool. Good rain and cold-weather gear are needed year-round if you intend to hike on Mount Etna or the northern mountains. Come prepared for mostly dry conditions outside the summer months.

Hiking, camping, and other sports equipment can easily be bought or rented as needed.

Electricity in Sicily is 220V, 50 Hz, and plugs have three (sometimes two) round pins. If you bring electrical equipment, you will need a plug adapter plus a transformer for U.S. appliances.

Last, don't forget the essentials: passport, driver's license, traveler's checks, and insurance documents.

Insurance

Make sure you have adequate travel and medical coverage. Keep all receipts for expenses. Report losses or thefts to the police and obtain a signed statement (denuncia) from police stations to help with insurance claims.

Further Reading

Among the books you may want to pack or read before your trip is *The Italians* by Luigi Barzini (Simon & Schuster, 1996). It was first published in 1964, but no writer before or since has produced a more penetrating or better written analysis of Italy (including Sicily).

The best Sicilian or Sicily-set literature available in translation includes *The Leopard* by Giuseppe

Tomasi di Lampedusa; *Conversation in Sicily* by Elio Vittorini; *The Day of the Owl, The Wine-Dark Sea,* and other novels by Leonardo Sciascia; and *The Godfather* by Mario Puzo.

Evocative travelogues—artistic, practical, or cultural analyses—include *In Sicily* and *The Honoured Society* by Norman Lewis; *On Persephone's Island: A Sicilian Journal* by Mary Taylor Simeti; *Mattanza: Love and Death in the Sea of Sicily* by Theresa Maggio; *Walking in Sicily* by Gillian Price; *Midnight in Sicily* by Peter Robb; *Sicilian Odyssey* by Francine Prose; and *The Normans in Sicily* by John Julius Norwich.

HOW TO GET TO SICILY
Passports
U.S. and Canadian citizens must have a passport to enter Italy for stays as long as 90 days; no visa is required. U.K. citizens need a passport but can remain as long as they wish.

Airlines
Several scheduled, charter, and low-cost airlines offer direct flights to Sicily from the U.K. and other European cities. Nonstop flights from the U.S. are more difficult to source. Some airlines schedule summer-only services some years. At the time of writing, Meridiana (see below) offers from Palermo to JFK in New York from April to September.

All major North American airlines have flights to Rome's Leonardo da Vinci airport (also known as Fiumicino) and Milan's Malpensa, where connecting flights with Alitalia, Easyjet, or Meridiana operate to Palermo, Catania, and some smaller Sicilian airports. Rome, the closer and more convenient hub, has a wider and more easily accessible network of internal flights.

Flying time to Italy is 8–9 hours from New York, 10–11 hours from

Chicago, and 12–13 hours from Los Angeles. Flying time from Rome to Sicily is about 1 hour.

Useful Numbers
In Italy
Rome airports, tel 06 65 951, www.adr.it; **Milan airports,** tel 02 232 323; **Alitalia,** tel 892 010, 0871 424 1424 in U.K., alitalia .com; **Meridiana,** tel 0789 52 682 in Italy, 0844 482 2360 in the U.K., +1 718 751 4499 from the U.S., meridiana.it

In the U.S. & Canada
Alitalia (U.S.) tel 800/223-5730
Alitalia (Canada) tel 800/361-8336, alitalia.com
American Airlines, tel 800/433-7300, aa.com
Delta, tel 800/221-1212 or 404/765-4000, delta.com
United, tel 800/864-8331, united.com

When you arrive in Sicily, you will enter at either Palermo's Falcone-Borsellino airport (previously known as Punta Raisi) or Catania's Fontanarossa airport.

Falcone-Borsellino *(tel 091 702 0273 or 091 702 0111, gesap.it)* is at Punta Raisi, 19 miles (31 km) west of the city on the A29 expressway.

Prestia e Comande shuttle buses *(tel 091 586 351 or 091 580 457, prestiaecomande.it)* depart twice hourly from outside the terminal for the 50-minute journey to the city center. There are eight intermediate stops; buses terminate at the Stazione Centrale, Palermo's main railroad station for train connections to many Sicilian destinations (see p. 161).

Catania's **Fontanarossa** airport *(tel 095 723 9111, aeroporto .catania.it)* lies 3 miles (5 km) south of the city and is more convenient for Taormina, Syracuse, and southeastern Sicily.

Alibus *(tel 095 751 9111 or*

toll-free in Italy 800 018 696, amt .ct.it) shuttles run every 20 minutes from 5 a.m. to midnight to Via Etnea and the Stazione Centrale, where you can pick up train connections for Messina and Syracuse.

Direct buses also run from the airport to Agrigento, Enna, Palermo, Ragusa, Syracuse, Taormina, and Milazzo (for the ferry to the Isole Eolie). See airport website for details and links.

Take only authorized white cabs from either airport, and ignore offers from solicitors inside or outside the terminals.

There are other smaller airports around Sicily, notably at Trapani (Birgi) and on the islands of Pantelleria and Lampedusa. These are serviced by connections at Palermo; in summer there are additional flights from other major Italian cities.

If you are beginning your trip in the U.K., you can fly nonstop to Catania from Gatwick airport with British Airways *(tel 0844 493 0787 daily 7:30 a.m.–8 p.m., ba.com).*

You can also fly to Palermo from London Stansted, Dublin, Paris Beauvais, Madrid, Berlin Schönefeld, Memmingen, and Düsseldorf Weeze with Ryanair *(tel 0871 246 0000, ryanair.com)* or to Palermo with Easyjet *(0905 821 0905, easyjet.com)* from London Gatwick, Geneva, Lyon, Nice, Milan Malpensa, and Paris Orly. Travel time from London to Palermo is about 2 hours and 30 minutes. An alternative is to fly to Naples and catch a ferry to Palermo or the Isole Eolie. Charter flights often are available to Catania (and occasionally to Palermo) in summer.

GETTING AROUND
By Airplane
It is worth traveling by plane only if you are bound for Sicily's more distant islands such as Pantelleria or Lampedusa. A variety of small carriers operate out of Palermo,

Catania, and Trapani, notably Air One *(tel +39 06 4888 0069 outside Italy or toll-free 199 207 080 in Italy, flyairone.com).*

By Bus

Buses *(pullman* or *autobus)* are an efficient means of traveling around much of Sicily, especially in rural areas. Express buses also run on highways, serving all major towns. Although buses generally look alike (usually blue), they are operated by a number of companies.

Buses usually depart from a town's main square, outside a railroad station, or from a bus depot *(autostazione).* In general, you must buy your ticket, usually from the depot or the nearest bar or station kiosk, before boarding the bus. Inquire at local visitor centers for details. Note that bus service is generally limited on Sundays.

By Car

Sicilian town centers, and Palermo's in particular, may be congested, but in rural parts of the island you will often have the road to yourself. Routes are generally well marked, from the ordinary thoroughfare, known as a *nazionale* (N) or *statale/strada statale* (S or SS), to the four- or six-lane expressway known as an *autostrada* (A). *autostrade.it*

The latter are toll roads; sometimes you pay a fixed rate, but usually you pick up a ticket where you enter the expressway and pay accordingly at the booth *(stazione)* when you exit.

If you have to travel a substantial distance, it is advisable to take an expressway: Most other roads in Sicily, especially in rural areas and in the mountains, are slow and winding. Always allow extra time to get to your destination when traveling along these routes.

Maps are available at bookstores, online, and other outlets.

The best map for touring by road is the Touring Club of Italy "Sicilia" (sheet D19).

Driving Information

If you break down, put on emergency lights and place a warning triangle behind the car. Call the Automobile Club d'Italia (ACI) emergency number *(tel 803116, aci.it)* and provide your location, make of car, and registration. The car will be towed to the nearest ACI-approved garage. Car rental firms often have their own arrangements for breakdowns and accidents; ask for details.

Peak traffic times in Sicilian cities and larger towns are weekdays and Saturdays from 10 a.m.– 1 p.m. and 4 p.m.–9 p.m., particularly on Friday and Sunday. Also expect heavy traffic before and after major public holidays, and the first and last weekends in August, when many Italians begin and end their vacation.

All distances are shown in kilometers (1 km = 0.62 mile).

Gas *(benzina),* expensive in Italy, is priced by the liter (0.26 U.S. gallon). Gas stations along autostradas are open 24 hours and generally accept credit cards. Elsewhere, gas stations usually close between 1 p.m. and 4 p.m., after 7 p.m., and all day Sunday; many stations accept only cash.

Be sure all pump meters are set to zero before the attendant starts filling your tank. Some stations have machines that accept large-denomination euro notes and dispense gas automatically during closed periods.

Parking is often difficult in Sicilian cities and towns. This is especially true in Palermo, where it is better to visit without a car. In most towns, street parking and parking lots *(parcheggi)* are likely to be filled with local vehicles. Many old centers have areas that are

completely closed to traffic; others may have restrictions at busy times during the day. If in doubt, park in an outlying lot and walk to the center. Metered parking *(parcometro)* is being introduced in some locales.

Car theft and theft from cars can be a problem in some areas. Try to leave your car in a supervised lot, and never leave valuables in the car. Illegally parked cars, especially those in a "removal zone" *(zona di rimozione)* may be ticketed or towed.

U.S. and Canadian drivers in Sicily must hold a national driver's license *(patente)* or an international driver's license. They are also required, by law, to carry a translation of the license in the event that the police ask to see it; this law is rarely enforced, however. For details of current regulations and how to obtain a translation or an international driver's license, contact any branch of the American Automobile Association or Canadian Automobile Association.

Most rules of the road in Sicily and elsewhere in Italy are similar to those in the U.S.: You drive on the right and pass only on the left. Seat belts are compulsory both in the front and back seats, and you must have with you at all times your driver's license, insurance information, registration, and other relevant documents. Note, on main roads it is obligatory to drive with headlights on even during daylight hours. You will be fined if you don't.

The penalties for drunk driving are severe, with heavy fines and the possibility of imprisonment. A red warning triangle for use in case of accidents must be carried by law (all rental cars should be provided with one; check before you leave).

The speed limit in towns and developed areas is 50 km/h (31 mph) and 110 km/h (68 mph) outside cities, unless otherwise indicated. Limits on the autostradas are 130 km/h (80 mph), 150 km/h (93 mph) on certain designated stretches, and 110 km/h (68 mph) for vehicles with engine capacity under 1100cc.

Renting a Car

It is easy to rent a car in Sicily's large towns and cities, and at the two major airports, where most international companies have offices. Costs are high by U.S. standards; it may be worthwhile to make car rental arrangements (through your travel agent or on the Internet) before leaving home.

Less expensive deals in Sicily can often be obtained through small, local companies; see listings under "Autonoleggio" in the Yellow Pages (Pagine Gialle) or online at paginegialle.it. Drivers must be at least 21 years of age and hold a full license in order to rent a car. Most large companies do not charge a drop-off fee as long as both locations are in Sicily. This allows you to pick up a car, for example, in Palermo and drop it off in Catania. Inquire about policy when renting.

By Ferry

Car and passenger ferries (traghetti) and/or hydrofoils (aliscafi) operate among Sicily's main ports and its many islands. Hydrofoils are generally twice as fast and twice as expensive as ferries.

Services include links from Milazzo to the Isole Eolie, which also have connections with Naples and Palermo; to the Isole Egadi and Pantelleria from Trapani; to Ustica from Palermo; and from Porto Empedocle near Agrigento to the Isole Pelagie.

If you plan to take a car, it is essential to book ahead in summer. The main operators are Siremar (siremar.it), SNAV (snav.it), and Tirrenia (tirrenia.it).

By Train

All of Sicily's main centers are connected by rail, but train service is slow and infrequent unless you take the express Inter-City (IC) train (for which you pay a supplementary fare) between Palermo and Messina; otherwise, buses are the quicker way to go.

Trains also link some small rural centers, notably in the east and the villages around Mount Etna. These services are especially slow, but if you have time and patience, can be enjoyable sightseeing excursions.

Before traveling, tickets must be validated in the yellow or gold machines located on train platforms and in station ticket halls. You risk paying the penalty of a heavy fine if you are caught traveling with a nonvalidated ticket.

If you intend to travel extensively by train, it's worthwhile to buy the Pozzo Orario, a cheap biennial schedule available in bookstores and at station kiosks. Or visit the website (trenitalia.com) of the state rail network Trenitalia, still known widely by its former name, Ferrovie dello Stato (FS). Trenitalia train passes are available, but are not a good value if you intend to travel only in Sicily.

Transportation in Towns & Cities

Most historic town and city centers are small enough to explore on foot. Only one or two outlying sights in Palermo, Syracuse, and Agrigento require taking a taxi or public transport. Bicycles are available for rent in several towns. You can also rent motor scooters; use extreme caution.

By Bus

The procedure for using town and city buses is the same across Sicily: You buy your ticket beforehand, usually from designated bars (look for bus company logos or bar-tobacconists (tabacchi) with a white T on a blue background).

You then validate your ticket by stamping it on a machine on the bus. Generally you board a bus through the rear doors and leave through the central doors. A bus stop is una fermata. Inspectors board buses at random; passengers without valid tickets are subject to a fine.

By Cab

Cabs are generally difficult to hail on the street. Most congregate at taxi stands on main piazzas or outside railroad stations. It is legal for drivers to charge extra for luggage placed in the trunk; and for rides early or late in the day, on Sundays and public holidays, and to airports or outside city limits. Always ask before departing and insist that the meter is switched on and reset at the start of a trip.

Take only licensed white cabs with official license numbers. In case of a dispute, note the cab number. You may wish to negotiate a nonmetered price for longer trips. Taxis can usually be reserved by phone. The operator will give you the number and call sign of the cab that has been dispatched. A supplement is charged for reserved cabs. Round up tips to the nearest euro, or tip about 10 percent.

PRACTICAL ADVICE
Communications
Post Offices

You can buy stamps (francobolli) from a post office (ufficio postale) or from most tabacchi, the latter indicated by a blue sign with a white T. Offices are generally open Monday through Friday between 8 a.m. and 9 a.m. to 2 p.m., and on Saturday from 8 a.m. or 8:30 a.m. until noon. Main post offices in towns and cities usually are open Monday–Saturday until 7 p.m. or 8 p.m.

The Italian postal system (poste .it) can be slow. Allow 15 days for letter delivery between Italy and North America, sometimes longer for postcards. Priority post (posta prioritaria) costs more, but delivery is guaranteed—within three days to the U.S. and the next day in Europe. Use e-mail for hotel and other reservations.

Small red mailboxes (blue for priority post) marked "Poste" are found outside post offices and on walls around towns and cities. Red boxes usually have two slots: one marked Per la città (town or local mail), the other Per tutte le altre destinazioni (other destinations).

You can arrange to receive mail at general delivery (fermo posta). Mail should show your name and be addressed to Ufficio Posta Centrale, Fermo Posta plus the name of the town or city. Pick up mail at the town's main post office; you will need to show a passport or photo ID and pay a small fee.

Telephones

Italy's telephone network is operated mainly by Telecom Italia (TI; telecomitalia.it). Public telephone booths can be found on streets, in bars and restaurants, and in TI offices in larger towns. Look for red or yellow signs with a telephone symbol.

Most phones take coins and cards (schede telefoniche), which can be purchased at tabacchi (tobacco shops) and newspaper stands in a range of euro denominations. Cards have a small perforated corner that must be removed before use.

To make a telephone call, pick up the phone, insert the card or money, and then dial the number. (Most booths post instructions in English.) Calls can be made direct, without operator assistance or long-distance connections.

Telephone numbers in Sicily may have between 4 and 11 digits.

Go to 1254.virgilio.it for all telephone numbers and other related information.

Calling rates are lowest on Sundays and between 10 p.m. and 8 a.m. Monday–Friday.

Note that hotels are likely to add a significant surcharge to calls made from guest rooms. Cell-phone network coverage is good in Sicily.

To call anywhere within Sicily or the Italian mainland, dial the number, including the town or city code (for example, 091 in Palermo or 0931 in Syracuse). The code must also be used when calling within a city or code area. Thus in Palermo, for instance, you dial the 091 code when calling another number in the city.

To call Italy from abroad, dial the international calling code (011 from the U.S. and Canada, 00 from the U.K.), the code for Italy (39), the area code (including the initial 0), and the number.

Conversions

1 kilo = 2.2 pounds
1 liter = 0.2642 U.S. gallon
1 kilometer = 0.62 mile
1 meter = 1.093 yards

Women's clothing
U.S.	8	10	12	14	16	18
Italian	40	42	44	46	48	50

Men's clothing
U.S.	36	38	40	42	44	46
Italian	46	48	50	52	54	56

Women's shoes
U.S.	6–6.5	7–7.5	8–8.5	9–9.5
Italian	36	37	38	39	40–41

Men's shoes
U.S.	8	8.5	9.5	10.5	11.5	12
Italian	41	42	43	44	45	46

Etiquette & Local Customs

On the whole, Sicilians are a little more reserved and a little

more conservative than northern Italians in all matters of morals and manners. While Italians on the whole may have a reputation for being passionate and excitable, they are generally polite and considerate in public and in social situations.

Upon meeting someone, or on entering or leaving stores, bars, hotels, and restaurants, use a simple buon giorno (good day) or buona sera (good afternoon/evening). Do not use the informal ciao (hi or good-bye) with strangers.

"Please" is per favore, "thank you" is grazie, and prego means "you're welcome."

Before a meal you might say buon appetito (enjoy your meal), to which the reply is grazie, altrettanto (thank you, and the same to you). The toast before a drink is salute or cin cin.

Say permesso when you wish to pass people, and mi scusi if you wish to apologize, excuse yourself, or stop someone to ask for help.

A woman is addressed as signora, a young woman as signorina, and a man as signore.

For additional vocabulary, see pp. 184–185.

Kissing on both cheeks is a common form of greeting among men and women who know each other well.

Italians dress conservatively for most occasions, and unusual attire will be noticed, particularly in church.

If you visit churches, respect those at worship. Travelers are welcome to explore the interiors and grounds of Sicily's chapels and churches—but only if dressed appropriately and not when services are in progress.

When waiting in line—that is, when they form them at all—Italians are generally fairly assertive. In stores, banks, and other offices you should not expect "fairness" or for people to wait their turn. Feel free to be equally assertive; such behavior generally is not considered rude in Italy.

Smoking is banned in all public indoor spaces such as cafés, bars, restaurants, and railroad stations, but smoking in public is still common in Sicily.

Holidays
Stores, banks, offices, and schools close on the following national holidays:

January 1 (New Year's Day)
January 6 (Epiphany)
Easter Sunday
Easter Monday
April 25 (Liberation Day)
May 1 (Labor Day)
June 2 (Republic Day)
August 15 (Ferragosto or
   Assumption)
November 1 (All Saints' Day)
December 8 (Immaculate
   Conception)
December 25 (Christmas Day)
December 26 (Santo Stefano)

Hours of operation may also be disrupted on either side of public holidays, especially if they fall on a Thursday or Tuesday, when Italians often make what is known as a *ponte* (bridge) and take off the day between the holiday and the weekend.

Roads, as well as planes, trains, buses, and ferries, are busy around public holidays. Local accommodations tend to fill up during major festivals and cultural events.

Media
Most Italian newspapers are sold from newsstands (*edicola*), many of which—in larger towns or resorts such as Palermo, Catania, Taormina, and Cefalù—also stock American, British, and other

foreign-language newspapers and periodicals. In the largest centers, these may be available after about 2 p.m. on the day of issue. Elsewhere, deliveries are likely to be a day or so late.

Airports and railroad stations often have the largest selection of foreign publications.

Among national papers, *Corriere della Sera* is one of the most authoritative, while *La Repubblica* is also widely read. The best-selling publications are sports papers.

Sicily has a strong tradition of regional papers, notably the Palermo-based *Il Giornale di Sicilia,* gds.it, Catania's *La Sicilia,* lasicilia.it, and Messina's *La Gazzetta del Sud,* gazzettadelsud.it. These are often a good source of information on local events, museum hours, and so forth.

Money Matters
The official currency of Italy is the euro. Euro notes come in denominations of 5, 10, 20, 50, 100, 200, and 500 euros. There are 100 cents to the euro. Coins come in denominations of 1 and 2 euros, and 1, 2, 5, 10, 20, and 50 cents.

Most major banks, airports, rail stations, and tourist areas have automatic teller machines (ATMs— *Bancomat* in Italian) for money cards and international credit cards *(carta di credito),* with instructions in various languages. Before leaving home, ask your credit card company for a four-digit number (PIN) to enable you to withdraw money.

Currency and traveler's checks— best bought in euros before you leave—can be exchanged in most banks and exchange offices *(cambio),* but lines are often long and the process slow.

In rural areas, small towns, and throughout much of the south, ATMs and cambio facilities are rarer—and sometimes nonexistent.

Credit cards are accepted in hotels and restaurants in most major towns and cities. Look for Visa, MasterCard, and American Express symbols (Diners Card is less well known), or the Italian *Carta Sì* (literally, "yes to cards") sign.

Many businesses still prefer cash, however, and smaller stores, hotels, and similar establishments, especially in rural areas, may not take cards. Always ask before ordering a meal or reserving a room.

American Express: american express.com, or www.american express.it. In Catania, c/o La Duca Viaggi, Piazza Europa, tel 095 722 2295, ldv.it.

Opening Times
Hours of operation present a problem in Sicily. For the most part, there are no firm schedules and you can't rely on assumptions. Opening times of museums and churches in particular can change with little or no notice.

Stores, banks, and other institutions in big cities are increasingly shifting to northern European hours (with no lunch and afternoon closing, indicated by the phrase *orario continuato*).

Use the following as a general guide only:

Banks are open Monday through Friday 8:30 a.m.–1:30 p.m. Major banks may also open for an hour in the afternoon and on Saturday morning. Hours are becoming longer and more flexible.

Churches are usually open 8 a.m. or 9 a.m.–noon and 3 p.m. or 4 p.m.–6 or 8 p.m., not including services. Many churches close on Sunday afternoon.

Gas stations are open 24 hours a day on the autostradas. Elsewhere, they tend to follow store hours (see below).

National (state-operated) museums usually close Sunday afternoon and Monday. Most close for lunch

(1 p.m.–3 or 4 p.m.), although it is becoming more common for major museums to stay open 9 a.m.–7 p.m. Winter hours are shorter.

Post offices are open Monday–Saturday 8 a.m. or 9 a.m.–2 p.m. Major locations are open 8 a.m. or 9 a.m.–6 p.m. or 8 p.m.

Many restaurants close on Sunday evening and on Monday or another weekday (la chiusura settimanale). Many establishments close in January and for vacation in July or August.

Store hours are generally 8:30 or 9 a.m.–1 p.m. and 3:30 p.m. or 4 p.m.–8 p.m. Monday–Saturday. Many stores close on Monday morning and another half day during the week. Department stores and major city stores may be open seven days a week 9 a.m.–8 p.m.; a few stay open until 10 p.m., but late and Sunday hours are still unusual.

Restrooms
Few public buildings have restrooms. Generally you will have to resort to facilities in bars, railroad stations, and gas stations where standards are generally low. Ask for il bagno (pronounced eel bahn-yo), take a few tissues, and don't confuse Signori (men) with Signore (women). Tip any attendant about half a euro.

Time
Sicily is on CET (central European time), 1 hour ahead of Greenwich mean time and 6 hours ahead of eastern standard time. Noon in Italy is 6 a.m. in New York.

Clocks change for daylight saving in late April (1 hour forward) and early October (1 hour back). Italy uses the 24-hour clock.

Tipping
In restaurants where a service charge (servizio) is not included, leave 10–15 percent; even if the charge is included, you may wish to leave 5–10 percent. In bars, tip a few cents for drinks if you're standing at the bar and 25–50 cents for waiter service. In hotel bars, be slightly more generous.

Service is included in hotel rates, but tip chambermaids and doormen about 50 cents (1 euro for calling a cab), the bellhop 1–3 euros for carrying your bags, and the concierge or porter 3–7 euros if he has been helpful. Double these figures in the most expensive hotels.

Tip checkroom attendants 25 to 50 cents. Porters at airports and railroad stations generally work for fixed wages, but tip up to 2 euros at your discretion. Cab drivers expect around 10 percent. Barbers get around 2 euros, a hairdresser's assistant 2–4 euros, depending on the level service. Tip church or other custodians 1–2 euros.

Travelers With Disabilities
Except for a very small minority of better hotels and major museums with appropriate facilities, Sicily is a very difficult place to visit for those with disabilities.

Busy streets with badly parked vehicles in Palermo, for instance, present obvious problems, and uneven streets in rural villages are unwelcoming to wheelchairs. Towns such as Taormina, with its steep grades, are especially challenging.

Museums, galleries, and public offices in bigger towns and newly built public buildings are making progress in providing wheelchair access, but much remains to be done.

Sicilians, including hoteliers and restaurateurs, will always try to be accommodating, but only the larger luxury hotels are equipped to deal with wheelchairs.

Contact the Italian embassy or consulate for information about bringing a guide dog into Italy.

Useful contacts in Italy include Rome-based COIN (coinsociale.it), which provides information and a guidebook. In North America, Access-Able (access-able.com) specializes in online advice. Other agencies that provide advice for travelers with disabilities include SATH (tel 212/447-7284, sath.org) and Mobility International (tel 541/343-1284, miusa.org).

Visitor Information
Italian State Tourist Offices
italiantourism.com and enit.it

United States
686 Park Ave., 3rd Floor
New York, NY 10065
Tel 212/245-5618
(general inquiries)
Fax 212/586-9249

500 N. Michigan Ave., Suite 506
Chicago, IL 60611
Tel 312/644-0996
Fax 312/644-3019

10850 Wilshire Blvd., Suite 575
Los Angeles, CA 90025
Tel 310/820-1898
Fax 310/470-7788

Canada
110 Yonge St., Suite 503
Toronto, ON M5C IT4
Tel 416/925-4882
Fax 416/925-4799

United Kingdom
1 Princes St.
London W1R 8AY
Tel 020 7408 1254
Fax 020 7493 6695

EMERGENCIES
Embassies & Consulates in Italy
U.S. Embassy
Via Vittorio Veneto 121, Rome
Tel 06 46 741

U.S. Consulate
Via Vaccarini 1, Palermo
Tel 091 305 857
italy.usembassy.gov

Canadian Embassy

Via Salaria 243 (Consular and visa
section: Via Zara 30), Rome
Tel 06 854 441
canadainternational.gc.ca

U.K. Embassy

Via XX Settembre 80a, Rome
Tel 06 4220 0001
gov.uk

Emergency Phone Numbers

Police, tel 112
Emergency, tel 112
Fire, tel 112
Car breakdown, tel 083116
Ambulance, tel 112

For legal assistance in an emergency, contact your embassy or
consulate (see above) to request
a list of English-speaking lawyers.
For general help in English, get
in touch with the Rome-based
English Yellow Pages *(paginegialle
.it* or *englishyellowpages.it).*

What to Do in a Traffic Accident

Put on hazard lights and place a
warning triangle 165 feet (50 m)
behind the car. (Car rental companies are required to provide
these; check to see that there's
one in the car before you leave.)
Call the police *(tel 112 or 113).*
  At the scene of the accident, do
not admit liability or make poten-
tially incriminating statements
to police or onlookers. Ask any
witnesses to remain, make a police
statement, and exchange insurance
and other relevant details with the
other driver(s).
  Call the car rental agency, if
necessary, to inform them of the
incident.

Health

Check that your health insurance
covers you while you are visiting
Italy and that any travel insurance
also includes sufficient medical
coverage.
  For minor complaints, first
visit a drugstore or pharmacy *(una
farmacia),* indicated by a green
cross outside the store. Staff is well
trained and will be able to offer
advice as well as help you find a
doctor *(un medico),* if necessary.
Also consult your hotel, the Yellow Pages, or a visitor center for
assistance in choosing a doctor
or dentist *(un dentista).* Bring an
ample supply of any prescription
drugs *(medicina)* you require.
Should you need to refill a prescription, pharmacies will direct
you to a doctor.
  Visit a hospital *(un ospedale)*
for serious complaints. Emergency
treatment is provided at the Pronto
Soccorso. Italian hospitals often
look run-down, but the treatment
standards are generally good.
  Before leaving for Sicily,
consider contacting the International Association for Medical
Assistance to Travelers (IAMAT;
*tel 716/754-4883 in the U.S. &
416/652-0137 in Canada, iamat
.org),* a nonprofit organization that
anyone can join free of charge.
Members get a directory of English-
speaking IAMAT doctors on call
24 hours a day, and are entitled to
services at set rates.
  Common minor complaints
include overexposure to the sun
and insect bites. Italy does have poi-
sonous snakes *(vipere),* though bites
are usually not fatal unless you have
an allergic reaction.
  Tap water is generally safe in
Sicily. Do not drink water, however,
if marked *acqua non potabile,* and
never drink from streams in the
mountains or elsewhere. Milk is
pasteurized and safe.

Hospitals

Palermo
Palermo Policlinico
Via del Vespro 129
Tel 091 655 1111
policlinico.pa.it

Ospedale Civico
Piazza Leotta
Tel 091 666 1111
arnascivico.it

Lost Property

If you lose property, go first to
the local visitor center and ask
for assistance. Bus, tram, train,
and metro systems in cities usually have special offices to deal
with lost property, but they can
be hard to find and are usually
open only a few hours a day. Ask
for directions at visitor centers,
and also try bus depots and rail
stations. Hotels should be able to
provide assistance as well.
  To report a more serious loss or
theft such as that of a passport, go
to the local police station or *Questura.* In Palermo the main Questura
is at Piazza della Vittoria 8 *(tel 091
210 111, questure.poliziadistato.it/
palermo, closed Sat.–Sun. & p.m. daily
except Wed.).* Many police stations
have English-speaking staff to deal
with visitors' problems. You will be
asked to complete and sign a form
(una denuncia) reporting any crime.
Keep your copy for relevant insurance claims.

Hotels & Restaurants

Sicily offers a variety of accommodations to suit all tastes and budgets. Choose from fine hotels in centuries-old buildings to intimate, family-run establishments or from charming bed-and-breakfasts to luxurious island resorts. Italy boasts one of the world's great cuisines—and the pleasures of Italian/Sicilian food and wine are as much a part of your visit as museums and galleries. Restaurants of various type and quality, from humble pizzerias to venerable classics, are found in every town and village. Below is a selection of some of the most interesting places to sleep and eat in Sicily.

HOTELS

In general, accommodations that provide the best central locations within a town or city have been recommended. Noise can be a problem in urban areas, so when possible, quiet, out-of-town alternatives are provided as well. Hotels and other accommodations were also selected for their character, charm, or historical associations.

Note that even in the finest hotels, bathrooms may have only a shower (*doccia*) and no tub (*vasca*). Rooms are often small by U.S. standards, even in the most upscale establishments. Always request to see a selection of rooms before you register.

All-day room service and air-conditioning are also comparatively rare in Sicily.

Grading System

Hotels are officially graded from one star (the simplest accommodations) to five star (luxury). There are new levels of four- and five-star accommodations: *****L and ***** a level down; and ****S (*superiore*) and less elevated ****.

Grading criteria are complex in Italy, but in a three-star establishment and above, all rooms should have private bath/shower, a telephone, and a television. Most two-star hotels will also have private bathrooms.

B&Bs, a historic residence (Residenza d'Epoca), and most villa and other complexes are not given an official star rating.

Reservations

It is advisable to reserve accommodations in advance, especially in major tourist areas, and particularly during high season (June–August). Unless the hotel has a website or e-mail address for reserving online. It is always a good idea to reconfirm reservations a couple of days before arrival.

Hoteliers are obliged to register every guest, so when checking in you will be asked for your passport. It will be returned within a few hours or on the day of departure.

Checkout times range from around 10 a.m. to noon, but you should be able to leave luggage at the hotel reception and pick it up later in the day.

Many hotels, especially on the coast, close in winter (typically November to April or May).

Prices

All prices are officially set, and room rates must be displayed by law at reception and in each room. Prices for different rooms can vary within a hotel, but all taxes and services should be included in the rate.

Hotels often levy additional charges for air-conditioning and garage facilities, while laundry, drinks, minibars, and phone calls made from rooms invariably carry large surcharges.

Price categories given in the following entries are for double (*una matrimoniale*) or twin (*una camera doppia*) rooms and are provided for guidance only. Seasonal variations often apply, especially in coastal resorts, where high-season (summer) rates, especially in resort areas, are usually higher.

At busy times, there may also be a two- or three-day minimum stay policy, and you may be obliged to take full- or half-board packages. Half-board (*mezza pensione*) includes breakfast and lunch, while full-board (*pensione completa*) includes all meals. Such packages are always priced on a per person basis.

Credit Cards

Many large hotels accept major credit cards. Smaller ones may accept only some, as shown in their entries. Abbreviations used are AE (American Express), DC (Diners Club), MC (MasterCard), and V (Visa). Look for card symbols outside establishments, or the Italian "Carta Sì" sign. As a general rule, AE and DC are less widely accepted than V and MC.

Smoking

Smoking is common in Italy, but recent changes in the law have enforced a total ban on smoking in public places, including bars, cafés, and restaurants (indoors). Smoking rooms in hotels need to be requested.

RESTAURANTS

The following selection of restaurants reflects the best of Sicily's regional cooking. Don't be afraid to experiment, especially in small towns and rural areas. If in doubt, see where the locals choose to eat and follow their lead.

PRICES

HOTELS

An indication of the cost of a double room in the high season is given by **$** signs.

$$$$$	Over $250
$$$$	$180–$250
$$$	$140–$180
$$	$100–$140
$	Under $100

RESTAURANTS

An indication of the cost of a three-course meal without drinks is given by **$** signs.

$$$$$	Over $65
$$$$	$45–$65
$$$	$35–$45
$$	$25–$35
$	Under $25

Dining Hours

Breakfast (colazione) usually consists of a cappuccino and bread roll or sweet pastry (una brioche) taken standing in a bar anytime between 7 a.m. and 9 a.m.

Lunch (pranzo) starts around 12:30 p.m. and ends sometime around 2 p.m.—the infamous long lunch and siesta are increasingly a thing of the past in the urban areas.

Dinner (cena) begins about 8 p.m., with last orders taken at around 10 p.m., although dinner hours may be earlier in rural areas and small towns.

Most restaurants close once a week, and many take long vacation breaks (ferie) in January, February, and July or August.

Paying

The check (il conto) must be presented as a formal receipt. A price scrawled on a piece of paper is illegal, and you are within your rights to demand an itemized ricevuta.

Bills once included a cover charge (pane e coperto), a practice the authorities are trying to ban. Many restaurants get around the law by charging for bread brought to your table whether you want it or not.

Smaller, simpler restaurants and those in rural areas are less likely to accept credit cards. It can be worth checking if your card is acceptable, even in places where window signs are displayed.

Meals

Meals traditionally begin with appetizers or hors d'oeuvres (antipasto—literally "before the meal"); a first course (il primo) of soup, pasta, or rice; and a main course (il secondo) of meat or fish. Vegetables (contorni) or salads (insalata) are often served with or after il secondo.

Desserts (dolci) may include or be followed by fruit (frutta) and cheese (formaggio). Italians often round off a meal with an espresso and brandy, grappa (a clear, powerful, brandylike spirit), or an amaro (a bitter digestif).

You don't need to order every course—a primo and salad is acceptable in all but the grandest restaurants. Many Italians choose to go to an ice-cream parlor (gelateria) as part of an after-dinner stroll instead of dessert.

Set Menus

The menu in Italian is il menù or la lista. Fixed-price menus are available in many restaurants in tourist areas. The menù turistico usually includes two courses, a simple dessert, and half a bottle of wine and water per person. Quantity and quality of food are invariably poor in these establishments. Of better value in more upscale restaurants is the menù gastronomico, where you pay a fixed price to sample a selection of the special dishes.

Bars, Cafés, & Snacks

Bars and cafés, perfect for breakfast, often provide snacks such as filled rolls (panini) and sandwiches (tramezzini) throughout the day. A few may offer a light meal at lunch. Stands or small stores selling slices of pizza (pizza al taglio) with various toppings are common. It always costs less to stand at the bar.

Tipping & Dress

Tip between 10 and 15 percent where service has been good and where a service charge (servizio) is not included.

As a rule, Italians dress well but informally to eat out, especially in better restaurants. A relaxed casual style is a good rule of thumb. Jacket and tie for men are rarely necessary, but often the better dressed you are, the better service you receive.

Listings

The hotels and restaurants listed here have been grouped first according to their region, then listed alphabetically by price category. For access by those with disabilities, it is recommended that they check with the establishment to verify the extent of its facilities.

L = lunch   D = dinner

■ PALERMO

CENTRALE PALACE HOTEL

$$$$$ **

CORSO VITTORIO EMANUELE II 327

TEL 091 8539

FAX 091 334 881

E-MAIL reservations@central palacehotel.com

centralepalacehotel.com

Palermo's best city-center hotel occupies a 19th-century building two blocks west of the Quattro Canti, a busy and central location. The rooms are well furnished, the service is excellent, and there is a fine roof garden with restaurant.

🛜 Free ⓘ 102 (plus 2 suites) 🅿️ 🔁 ⚙️ 🛗 🛇 All major cards

🏨 GRAND HOTEL ET DES PALMES
$$$$ ★★★★S
VIA ROMA 398
TEL 091 602 8111
grandhotel-et-des-palmes.com
This historic hotel's fame stems partly from its reputation as an alleged favorite among Mafia dons (including Lucky Luciano) in the 1950s and '60s, but it has always been a good, traditional hotel of belle epoque elegance. Extensive renovations greatly improved its rooms and common areas. Its slightly outlying location (four blocks north of the Museo Archeologico Regionale) is not as convenient as some of the other options.

🛜 Charge ⓘ 172
🅿️ 🔁 ⚙️ 🛇 All major cards

🏨 MASSIMO PLAZA
$$$$ ★★★★
VIA MAQUEDA 437
TEL 091 325 657
FAX 091 325 711
E-MAIL booking@massimo plazahotel.com
massimoplazahotel.com
The Massimo Plaza is an excellent and intimate mid-range choice in the north of the city center opposite the Teatro Massimo. The renovated art nouveau palazzo has spacious soundproofed rooms and restrained and tasteful reception and public areas.

🛜 Free ⓘ 15 🅿️ 🔁 ⚙️ 🛇 All major cards

🏨 PRINCIPE DI VILLAFRANCA
$$$$ ★★★★
VIA G. TURRISI COLONNA 4
TEL 091 611 8523
E-MAIL info@principedi villafranca.it

principedivillafranca.it
A good choice for business travelers or those who wish to be away from the center, this is a recently built, polished, and professionally run hotel. It is in the "new" town district, half a mile (1 km) northwest of the Teatro Massimo.

🛜 Charge ⓘ 32 (plus 2 suites) 🅿️ 🔁 ⚙️ 🛗 🛇 All major cards

🏨 HOTEL GARIBALDI
$$$ ★★★★
VIA EMERICO AMARI 146
TEL 091 601 7111, 800 893344,
TOLL-FREE IN U.S. +1-866/332-3590, U.K. +44 203 564 2773
ghshotels.it/garibaldi/
The Garibaldi has earned deserved plaudits since it opened in 2008, thanks to its bright, modern rooms, polished service, and reasonable prices. It is, though, a little way north of the historic center, opposite the Teatro Politeama. Breakfast is served, but there is no restaurant.

🛜 Charge ⓘ 63 (plus 8 suites) 🅿️ ⚙️ 🛇 All major cards

🏨 POSTA
$$ ★★★
VIA ANTONELLO GAGINI 77
TEL 091 587 338
FAX 091 587 347
E-MAIL info@hotelposta palermo.it
hotelpostapalermo.it
A city institution close to San Domenico, the Posta has been run by the same family for more than 90 years and was traditionally the choice of actors, artists, and bohemians. Recently renovated, it offers good-size rooms and represents excellent value given its central location.

🛜 Free ⓘ 30 🅿️ 🔁 ⚙️ 🛇 All major cards

🏨 QUINTOCANTO HOTEL 🍴 & SPA
$$ ★★★★

CORSO VITTORIO EMANUELE II 310
TEL 091 584 913
FAX 091 757 4117
E-MAIL info@quintocanto hotel.com
quintocantohotel.com
This recently revamped hotel offers a location as central as the Centrale Palace (see pp. 167–168) but at generally lower prices. The decor is contemporary, if slightly bland, but the spa is a bonus, and food in the hotel's **Locanda del Gusto** restaurant is a good mixture of Sicilian and international cuisine; open for breakfast, lunch, and dinner.

ⓘ 21 🅿️ 🔁 ⚙️
🛇 All major cards

🏨 GARDENIA
$$ ★★
VIA MARIANO STABILE 136
TEL 091 333 732
E-MAIL gardeniahotel @gardeniahotel.com
gardeniahotel.com
The Gardenia is an intimate, welcoming, and recently renovated central hotel (on the street that leads from Piazza Politeama to the port). Many rooms have balconies with views, and the facilities and furnishings are better than most hotels in the two-star range.

🛜 Free ⓘ 16 🅿️ ⚙️ 🛇 All major cards

🏨 LA VIA DELLE BICICLETTE
$
VIA DIVISI 74
TEL 091 616 6009
OR 334 383 0969
laviadellebiciclette.com
A small B&B rather than a hotel, but with the advantages of welcoming and helpful owners, clean, simple, and comfortable rooms, and, above all, a convenient location on a narrow side street in the heart of the old city.

ⓘ 2 ⚙️ 🛇 Cash or Paypal

OSTERIA DEI VESPRI
$$$$$
PIAZZA CROCE DEI VESPRI 6
TEL 091 617 1631
osteriadeivespri.it
This restaurant just south of San Francesco was once used to house the carriages of the Palazzo Gangi above the palace in which Luchino Visconti filmed the ballroom scene in his movie *The Leopard.* Today, it offers some of Palermo's most creative and accomplished cooking, including modern reinterpretations of traditional Sicilian meat and fish dishes. Good wine list. During the warmer months outdoor seating is available.
🔲 35 (inside), 40 (outside) 🕐 Closed Sun.; parts of Jan., Feb., & Aug. 🅰 🅰 All major cards

SANTANDREA
$$$$
PIAZZA SANT'ANDREA 4
TEL 091 334 999
ristorantesantandrea.eu
Close to the Vucciria market and San Domenico, Santandrea is a delightful, well-located restaurant with a long-standing good reputation, though service can be uneven. The food features many creative twists but never strays far from its Palermitan roots. Good wine list.
🔲 80 (inside), 80 (outside) 🕐 Closed L daily, Sun., & parts of Aug. 🅰 🅰 AE, MC, V

DAL MAESTRO DEL BRODO
$$$
VIA PANNIERI 7
TEL 091 329 523
Market-fresh ingredients from the Vucciria go into traditional dishes such as *pasta con le sarde* (pasta with sardines) and *pesce spada e menta* (swordfish with mint) at this welcoming, family-run trattoria conveniently situated near

the corner of Via Roma and Corso Vittorio Emanuele II.
🔲 60 🕐 Closed Mon. year-round, D except Fri.–Sat. Oct–June; also 2 weeks in Aug., Sun. in summer 🅰 🅰 AE, MC, V

PICCOLO NAPOLI
$$$
PIAZZETTA MULINO A VENTO 4
TEL 091 320 431
The lively and perennially popular Piccolo Napoli has been a touchstone for the freshest fish and seafood at the heart of the Borgo Vecchio market district since 1951. Start with a buffet of seafood and try local specialties such as pasta with *ricci* (sea urchin) or stick to simply grilled or roasted fish.
🔲 52 🕐 Closed Sun., L July–Sept., L Mon.–Thurs., & parts of Aug. 🅰 🅰 All major cards

VILLA SAN GIOVANNI DEGLI EREMITI
$$$
VICOLO SAN MERCURIO 26/32, OFF VIA DEI BENEDETTINI
TEL 329 867 7551
villasangiovannideglieremiti.it
Recommended for its proximity to the Palazzo dei Normanni or Eremiti church. While the interior is not especially cozy, the menu offers a range of well-prepared pastas, meat dishes, fish, seafood, and pizzas. The service is welcoming and English is spoken.
🔲 20 (70 outside) 🅰 🅰 MC, V

KURSAAL KALHESA
$$–$$$
FORO UMBERTO I 21
TEL 091 616 2282
kursaalkalhesa.it
A pleasant if slightly outlying place near the corner of Via Lincoln and Foro Italico southwest of the Galleria Regionale di Sicilia. It is a combination of a restaurant and a spacious arched bar, jazz venue, coffeehouse, and even a bookstore.

There is also a garden on the premises. The cooking takes its inspiration from a variety of Mediterranean sources.
🔲 50 (inside), 70 (outside) 🕐 Closed Mon. & part of Aug. 🅰 AE, MC, V

CASA DEL BRODO
$$
CORSO VITTORIO EMANUELE II 175
TEL 091 321 655
casadelbrodo.it
This Palermitan favorite, founded in 1890, offers good value for the money, especially if you go for the *brodo* (broth or soup), several different choices of which are available each day. Or choose from the *antipasti* buffet laid out between the two dining rooms.
🔲 60 🕐 Closed Tues. Oct.–May & Sun. June–Sept. 🅰 All major cards

RISTORANTE PIZZERIA PRIMAVERA
$$
VIA PRINCIPI DI GRANATELLI 33B
TEL 091 329 408
The same family has run the Primavera, now in a smart new home in the historic center of the city, for almost four decades. The restaurant offers fair prices and a nice mix of comforting Palermitan classics such as *polpette di sarde al sugo* (sardine "meatballs" with sauce). You can eat à la carte or try the set menu, which starts with a selection of *antipasti* (appetizers) that is a meal in itself.
🔲 50 (inside), 35 (outside) 🕐 Closed Mon. 🅰 V, MC

ANTICA FOCACCERIA
$
VIA ALESSANDRO PATERNOSTRO 59
TEL 091 320 264
anticafocacceria.it
An atmospheric, family-run tavern founded in 1834, with

marble tables (plus outdoor tables on the square), old mirrors, wrought iron, and wood paneling. It offers a handful of hot dishes and snacks such as *panelle* (chickpea fritters) and *purpa* (boiled octopus). More conventional snacks and sandwiches are also available.

200 (indoor), 100 (outdoor) Closed most Tues. All major cards

■ WESTERN SICILY

ERICE

BAGLIO SANTA CROCE
$$ ★★★

CONTRADA RAGOSIA VALDERICE, OFF SS187 ROAD
TEL 0923 891 111
FAX 0923 891 192
E-MAIL info@bagliosanta croce.it
bagliosantacroce.it

Escape the crowds in this delightful rural retreat on Mount Erice. It is located among the olives and citrus groves, 5.5 miles (9 km) east of Erice on the SS187 road. The converted farmhouse dates from 1637, and the 25 simple but appealing rooms and common areas retain old wooden beams and terracotta floors. There are also 42 newer rooms, opened in 2006, in the annex. The gardens offer lovely views, and the restaurant serves wholesome country cooking.

Free in lobby and "Wi-Fi zone" 67 All major cards

MODERNO
$$ ★★★

VIA VITTORIO EMANUELE II 67
TEL 0923 869 300
FAX 0923 869 139
E-MAIL info@hotelmoderno erice.it
hotelmodernoerice.it

A renovated 19th-century building, this centrally located, well-run hotel (with an annex boasting larger rooms across the street) has a roof terrace and restaurant that is worth visiting whether or not you are staying as a guest. Ask for a room with terrace or balcony.

40 100 Restaurant closed Mon. Sept.–March
All major cards

MONTE SAN GIULIANO
$$$

VICOLO SAN ROCCO 7
TEL 0923 869 595
montesangiuliano.it

Enjoy eating in this rustic eatery in one of three dining rooms or, weather permitting, under an arbor in a pleasant courtyard. Be sure to try he classic regional specialties, such as *sarde a beccafico* (sardines), *pesce alla griglia* (grilled fish), and *involtini di melanzane* (rolled, stuffed eggplant).

80 (inside), 100 (outside) Closed Mon. & parts of Jan. & Nov. All major cards

ISOLE EGADI

AEGUSA
$$$ ★★★

VIA GARIBALDI 11–17, FAVIGNANA
TEL 0923 921 638
E-MAIL info@aegusahotel.it
aegusahotel.it

Rooms in this 19th-century palazzo are bright, spacious, and simply furnished, and the restaurant has a small courtyard.

Free in rooms 28
Hotel & restaurant closed Oct.–March All major cards

ALBERGO EGADI
$$$ ★★★

VIA CRISTOFORO COLOMBO 17–19, FAVIGNANA
TEL 0923 921 232
E-MAIL info@albergoegadi.it
albergoegadi.it

PRICES

HOTELS

An indication of the cost of a double room in the high season is given by $ signs.

$$$$$	Over $250
$$$$	$180–$250
$$$	$140–$180
$$	$100–$140
$	Under $100

RESTAURANTS

An indication of the cost of a three-course meal without drinks is given by $ signs.

$$$$$	Over $65
$$$$	$45–$65
$$$	$35–$45
$$	$25–$35
$	Under $25

Bright, well-kept, and refurbished rooms provide a simple and intimate base. The restaurant, although plain in appearance, is highly regarded.

Free 11 80 Closed from Oct.–Easter All major cards

IL VELIERO
$$$

CORSO UMBERTO I 22, MARETTIMO
TEL 0923 923 274

The Bevilacqua family runs this trattoria, where you can fill up on home cooking, including *busiati*, a plump pasta typical of western Sicily, or fish and seafood selected by Peppe Bevilacqua, a former fisherman. Vincenzina and her two sons run a similar hotel-restaurant, **Paradiso**, on the island of Levanzo (*Via Lungomare 8, tel 0923 924 080, closed mid-Nov.–mid-March, albergo paradiso.eu*), with a terrace overlooking the port for summer dining. Some rooms for rent are also available.

⊞ 50 (inside), 80 (outside)
✦ All major cards

PANTELLERIA

⊞ MONASTERO
$$$$$ ★★★★
CONTRADA KASSÀ, SCAURI ALTA
TEL 349 559 5589
E-MAIL info@monastero
pantelleria.com
monasteropantelleria.com
Several traditional houses (dammusi) have been converted into this private villa hotel, a favored retreat of celebrities such as Sting and Madonna. The similar but less expensive and exclusive **Zubebi** (tel 0923 913 653, zubebi.com, closed Nov.–March) opened with eight converted dammusi in 2011 (there's a seven-night minimum stay during the high season).

☎ Free ⓘ 6 villas ✦
✦ All major cards

⊞ MURSIA
$$ ★★★
LOCALITÀ MURSIA 20
TEL 0923 911 217
E-MAIL info@mursiahotel.it
mursiahotel.it
Just 2.5 miles (4 km) from Pantelleria town (to which there is a free hotel boat shuttle), this striking resort offers a pool, private beach, diving center, windsurfing school, tennis courts, and other outdoor facilities. Its **Le Lampare** restaurant offers Sicilian, classic Italian, and Arab-influenced dishes. The 1970s-vintage 100-room **Cossyra** (tel 0923 911 154) nearby—and under the same management—offers similar facilities and prices.

☎ Charge ⓘ 74 Ⓟ Closed Nov.–March
✦ All major cards

⊞ LA NICCHIA
$$$
CONTRADA SCAURI BASSO
TEL 0923 916 342
Dining here is in two rooms in a converted dammuso or in the pretty garden. While the setting is superb, the food can be uneven, but might include innovative dishes such as ravioli di ricotta e menta (pasta stuffed with cheese and mint) or gamberoni all'uva zibibbo (king prawns with local grapes). Pizzas are also available. Also recommended are **La Vela** (Contrada Scauri Scalo, tel 0923 916 566, closed mid-Nov.–Easter), close to the sea; and the inexpensive **Zinedi** (Contrada Zinedi, tel 0923 914 023, agritu rismozinedi.com, closed L & Nov.–April), part of an agriturismo farm-stay accommodations program.

⊞ 40 (inside), 60 (outside)
Ⓒ Closed Nov.–Easter & L year-round ✦ All major cards

SAN VITO LO CAPO

⊞ CAPO SAN VITO
$$$$ ★★★★
VIA SAN VITO I
TEL 0923 972 122
E-MAIL hotel@caposanvito.it
caposanvito.it
The most comfortable location for visiting the Zingaro reserve and the resort of San Vito lo Capo, this charming small (four floors) hotel comes with panoramic views of the sea (most rooms have a terrace), garden, and a private beach. There's also a small café (the **Caruso**) as well as a restaurant (the **Jacaranda**), both offering outdoor tables for warmer-weather dining.

☎ Free ⓘ 35 Ⓒ Hotel closed Jan.–Feb. ✦ All major cards

⊞ GIARDINO DI COSTANZA
$$$$$ ★★★★★
VIA SALEMI (4 MILES/7 KM FROM MAZARA DEL VOLLO)
TEL 0923 675 000
FAX 0923 675 876
E-MAIL bookingcostanza@
bluhotels.it
giardinodicostanza.it
This is one of two large resorts to have opened recently in Sicily (the other is the Rocco Forte Verdura Golf Resort & Spa). It is not convenient for sightseeing, but it has all the trappings of a self-contained, American-style resort, complete with spa, tennis courts, and other sports and recreational facilities (but not golf). It is also set on extensive grounds in very appealing countryside.

ⓘ 96 Ⓒ Closed Dec.–Feb.
✦ Ⓟ ✦ ✦ ✦ All major cards

■ SOUTHERN SICILY

AGRIGENTO

⊞ VILLA ATHENA
$$$$$ ★★★★★
VIA PASSEGGIATA ARCHEO-
LOGICA 33
TEL 0922 59 6288
E-MAIL info@hotelvilla
athena.it
hotelvillaathena.it
Agrigento's finest hotel, the Villa Athena, a converted 18th-century villa, has been recently updated and upgraded. It may remain a little overpriced, but it is still the only place to stay in the Valle dei Templi. It also has a garden and pool, an above-average restaurant (with outdoor dining in the warmer months), and tremendous views of the Tempio della Concordia. Ask for a room with terrace and temple views.

☎ Free ⓘ 40 ✦ ✦
✦ All major cards

✦ Air-conditioning ⬛ Indoor Pool ✦ Outdoor Pool ✦ Health Club ✦ Credit Cards

BAGLIO DELLA LUNA
$$$$ ★★★★
VIA SERAFINA AMABILE
GUASTELLA I/C, CONTRADA
MADDALUSA
TEL 0922 511 061
E-MAIL info@bagliodellaluna
.com
bagliodellaluna.com
About 2.5 miles (4 km) from
Agrigento (off the SS640
road), this beautifully restored
13th- and 15th-century
castle–country house is ringed
by handsome gardens and
has elegant rooms and stylish
common areas furnished with
antiques. **Il Dèhors** (closed L
on Mon.) boasts the region's
best (if expensive) menu and a
good wine list.
🛜 Free 🚪 21 (plus 4 suites)
🛏 100 🅿 🔄 ⚡
🃏 All major cards

COLLEVERDE PARK
$$$–$$$$ ★★★★
STRADA PANORAMICA DEI
TEMPLI
TEL 0922 29 555
FAX 0922 29 012
E-MAIL mail@colleverdehotel
.it
colleverdehotel.it
This hotel is in the archaeo-
logical zone, within an easy
walk of the temples (the gar-
den overlooks them). Rooms
(some with temple views) are
modern and quietly elegant,
the staff charming, and there is
access to a private beach.
🛜 Free 🚪 52
🅿 🔄 ⚡ 🏊 🃏 All major
cards

TRATTORIA DEI TEMPLI
$$$
VIA PANORAMICA DEI
TEMPLI 15
TEL 0922 403 110
trattoriadeitempli.com
Vaulted ceilings, stone arches,
and terra-cotta floors provide
a rustic atmosphere in a busy
but friendly restaurant near the
temples. The menu is mainly
fish and seafood based.

🛏 100 (inside), 20 (outside)
🅿 🕐 Closed parts of July–
Aug., Sun. July–Aug., & Fri. rest
of year 🔄 🃏 All major cards

ISOLE PELAGIE

IL FARO DELLA GUITGIA
TOMMASINO
$$$$$ ★★★
VIA LIDO AZZURRO 13,
LAMPEDUSA
TEL 0922 970 962
FAX 0922 970 316
E-MAIL info@ilfarodella
guitgia.it
ilfarodellaguitgia.it
Two Mediterranean-style
buildings comprise this hotel
on the beach. Request a room
with a balcony and sea views.
In summer, dine on the terrace
of the hotel's **Da Tommasino**
restaurant, which offers a vari-
ety of fish dishes.
🛜 Free 🚪 16 🅿 🔄 🕐 Closed
Nov.–Feb. 🃏 All major cards

GEMELLI
$$$$$
VIA CALA PISANA 2, LAMPEDUSA
TEL 0922 970 699
The Moorish theme in this
highly professional, three-room
restaurant is continued in the
cooking, which blends Arab
influences with traditional
Sicilian cuisine. Standout dishes
include the homemade ravioli
stuffed with prawns. There is
a terrace for warm-weather
dining. Less expensive options
are the small **Da Bernardo**
(Via Terranova 3, tel 0922 971
925, closed L) and **Delfino Blu**
(Via Sbarcatoio 21, tel 0922 622,
closed L & Jan.–April).
🛏 40 (indoor), 40 (outdoor)
🔄 🕐 Closed L & Nov.–Easter
🃏 AE, DC, V

VILLA IMPERIALE
DEL CASALE

OSTELLO DEL BORGO
$
LARGO SAN GIOVANNI 6,

PIAZZA ARMERINA
TEL 0935 687 019
FAX 0935 686 943
ostellodelborgo.it
Some dormitory beds but
also simple double rooms in
the monks' quarters in the
former St. John's monastery
that have been converted into
comfortable guest quarters
with bathrooms.
🚪 16 🃏 MC, V

VILLA CLEMENTINE
$
VIA NINO MARTOGLIO, STRADA
FONTANELLE
TEL 0935 685 622
OR 328 833 1323
villaclementine.com
Piazza Armerina serves mainly
as a base for the Roman mosaics at the Villa Imperiale (which
has few lodgings), so unless
you want to be right in the
center of town this charming
villa on the verdant southern
outskirts is the best place to
stay locally, thanks to its peaceful setting and lovely garden
with pool. There is a choice of
double or triple rooms plus
an apartment for four with
kitchenette. A second equally
pleasant, but more modern
B&B on the town outskirts
with rooms at the same price
is **La Casa sulla Collina d'Oro**
(Via Mattarella, tel 0935 89 680
or 333 466 8829, lacasasulla
collinadoro.it, $).
🛜 Free 🚪 4 🔄 🅿 🏊
🕐 Closed Jan.–Feb.
🃏 No credit cards

AL FOGHER
$$$$
CONTRADA BELLIA 1,
PIAZZA ARMERINA
TEL 0935 684 123
Two intimate rooms in a former railway building are the
stage for a mixture of regional
cooking infused with inventive
touches. The wine list is excellent, and there is a garden
for summer meals alfresco.
Al Fogher is located 2 miles

(3 km) outside Piazza Armerina on the SS117 bis road.
🔲 55 (inside), 30 (outside) 🅿
⊕ Closed parts of Jan. & July,
Sun. D, & Mon. 🖾 AE, M, V

SELINUNTE

🏢 🍴 ALCESTE
$ ★★★
VIA ALCESTE 21
TEL 0924 46184
FAX 0924 46143
E-MAIL info@hotelalceste.it
hotelalceste.it
A simple, family-run hotel built
in the 1980s in the old part of
Marinella, half a mile (1 km)
from Selinunte. Its terrace has
a sea view, and the restaurant
serves traditional Sicilian food.
Under the same management
is the stark, contemporary
Hotel Admeto *(Via Palinuro 3,
tel 0924 46796, hoteladmeto.it)*
with town and sea views.
☎ Charge 🛈 30 🅿 ⊕ Closed
mid-Nov. & mid-Jan.–mid-Feb.
🔁 🆂 🖾 All major cards

🍴 PIERROT
$$$
VIA MARCO POLO 108
TEL 0924 46205
ristorantepierrot.it
Marinella has several good
restaurants with sea and/or
Acropolis views—and this is
one of the best. It serves meat
and fish dishes, as well as piz-
zas. In town, also try the sea-
food at **Fresomare Selinunte**
*(Via Persefone I, tel 347 162
6205, closed L & Nov.–March)*.
🔲 170 (inside), 8 (outside)
🅿 ⊕ Closed Tues. Nov.–
March 🖾 All major cards

■ SYRACUSE & THE SOUTHEAST

SYRACUSE

🏢 ALGILÀ ORTIGIA CHARME HOTEL
$$$$ ★★★★S

VIA VITTORIO VENETO 93
TEL 0931 465 148
FAX 0931 463 889
E-MAIL info@algila.it
algila.it
Opened in 2008, the intimate
Algilà is a beautifully restored
palazzo that dates back to the
14th century. Its decorative
style owes something to North
Africa. There are bright Tuni-
sian tiles in some bathrooms
and kilims on the floors.
📶 Free 🛈 30
🅿 🆂 🔁 ⊕ Closed Jan. &
part of Feb. 🖾 All major cards

🏢 DES ÈTRANGERS HOTEL & SPA
$$$$ ★★★★★
PASSEGGIO ADORNO 10–12
TEL 0931 319 100
FAX 0931 319 000
desetrangers.com
Syracuse's highest rated hotel
is a recently converted 19th-
century palace at the heart of
the old town on the island of
Ortygia. Rooms have numer-
ous high-tech offerings and
other facilities, and there is
access to a private beach, as
well as a health club and sauna.
📶 Charge 🛈 65 (plus
11 suites) 🅿 🔁 🆂 🏊 🎽
🖾 All major cards

🏢 🍴 GRAND HOTEL ORTIGIA
$$$$$ ★★★★★
VIALE MAZZINI 12
TEL 0931 464 600
FAX 0931 464 611
E-MAIL info@grandhotel
ortigia.it
grandhotelortigia.it
A comfortable and pleasing
hotel with a harmonious mix
of modern and Old World
style on the northwest tip of
Ortygia. The hotel's **La Ter-
razza Sul Mare** restaurant has
a roof terrace with fine sea
and harbor views. Hotel
shuttles transport guests to
and from a nearby private
beach. If you prefer to be in

the countryside out of town,
try **Borgo Pantano** *(Traversa
Fontana Mortella 13, tel 0931
721 993, borgo
pantano.it)*, a four-star with
fine gardens and a large pool.
🛈 41 (plus 17 suites) 🆂 🎽
🖾 All major cards

🏢 GRAN BRETAGNA
$$ ★★★
VIA SAVOIA 21
TEL 0931 68765
FAX 0931 449 078
E-MAIL info@hotelgran
bretagna.it
hotelgranbretagna.it
A welcoming and well-run
hotel that has been an Ortygia
travel fixture for many years.
Some of the spacious rooms
in this 18th-century building
feature preserved frescoed
ceilings. Another fine historic
Ortygia hotel is **Charme Hotel
Henry's House** *(Via del Castello
Maniace 68, tel 0931 2361,
hotelhenryshouse.com)*, a more
costly four-star with some
beautiful period touches.
🛈 19 🅿 🆂 🖾 All major cards

🏢 GUTKOWSKI
$$ ★★★
VIA LUNGOMARE VITTORINI
18/26
TEL 0931 465 861
FAX 0931 480 505
E-MAIL info@guthotel.it
guthotel.it
This is the perfect budget
choice in eastern Ortygia: not
luxurious, but simple, modern,
and comfortable, with sea
views from some rooms.
📶 Free 🛈 26 🔁 🆂 🖾 All
major cards

🍴 DON CAMILLO
$$$$$
VIA MAESTRANZA 92–100
TEL 0931 67 133
ristorantedoncamillo
siracusa.it
Relatively expensive, this
restaurant is the top choice
in Syracuse. This beautiful

two-salon establishment occupies a converted 15th-century palazzo (complete with vaulted ceilings) on the eastern side of Ortygia, close to the church of San Francesco. Food is mostly fish based with many elegant and creative touches.

🍴 100 ⬛ 🕐 Closed Sun. & parts of Jan. & July
💳 All major cards

🍴 ARCHIMEDE
$$$
VIA GEMMELLARO 8
TEL 0931 69 701
trattoriaarchimede.it

A Syracusan institution, Archimede has been in business in Ortygia, just south of Santa Maria dei Miracoli, since 1938. Its three large dining rooms are adorned with historic photographs of the town. The fish and seafood cuisine is fairly straightforward, but there is a particularly good antipasti buffet. A pizzeria (under the same management) is right across the street.

🍴 150 ⬛ 🕐 Closed Sun. except July–Aug. 💳 All major cards

🍴 DA MARIANO
$$
VICOLO ZUCCOLÀ 9
TEL 0931 67 444
osteriadamariano.it

This informal restaurant is close to the Fonte Aretusa in the west of Ortygia. It consists of three simply decorated rooms. Service is warm and friendly, and the cooking draws almost entirely on local culinary traditions. Two equally good, low-cost, and intimate trattorias in Ortygia are **Al Mazarì** (*Via G. Torres 7, tel 0931 4836 90, almazari .com*) and the Slow Food–recommended **Vite e Vitello** (*Piazza Corpaci 1, tel 0931 464 269, closed Sun. except July & Aug. plus periods in Feb. & July*). For snack food to go visit **Caseificio Borderi** in Ortygia's

market (*Via Emanuele de Benedictis 6*).

🍴 75 (inside), 40 (outside) ⬛ 🕐 Closed Tues. & July
💳 All major cards

NOTO

🏨 TERRE DI VENDICARI
$$$$
CONTRADA VADDEDDI
TEL 346 359 3845
info@terredivendicari.it
terredivendicari.it

A beautiful and stylishly refurbished old house and a glorious, private setting amid almond and olive groves in the Vendicari nature reserve make this one of the best bases for exploring this part of Sicily.

📶 Free 🚪 9 🅿 🐕 📺 ❄ 🕐 Closed Sun. & parts of Jan. & July 💳 All major cards

🏨 LA CORTE DEL SOLE
$$$ ★★★★
ELORO-PIZZUTA, CONTRADA BUCACHEMI, LIDO DI NOTO
TEL 0931 820 210
FAX 0931 812 913
E-MAIL info@lacortedelsole.it
lacortedelsole.it

The delightful Courtyard of the Sun occupies a traditional 19th-century Sicilian *masseria* (fortified farmhouse) in a pretty, isolated hilltop setting in the Vendicari nature reserve outside Noto, with fine views to the sea (a shuttle bus will take you to the beach). A range of activities is available, including cookery courses and spring trips to study the 80 varieties of orchids and other flora in the reserve.

📶 Free 🚪 34 (plus 10 in a new wing) 🅿 🐕 📺 ❄ 🕐 Closed mid-Jan.–March 💳 All major cards

🏨 VILLA CANISELLO
$ ★★
VIA PAVESE 1
TEL 0931 835 793
FAX 0931 837 700

PRICES

HOTELS
An indication of the cost of a double room in the high season is given by **$** signs.

$$$$$	Over $250
$$$$	$180–$250
$$$	$140–$180
$$	$100–$140
$	Under $100

RESTAURANTS
An indication of the cost of a three-course meal without drinks is given by **$** signs.

$$$$$	Over $65
$$$$	$45–$65
$$$	$35–$45
$$	$25–$35
$	Under $25

E-MAIL info@villacanisello.it
villacanisello.it

The restored, 19th-century farmhouse, with a large garden, is just a ten-minute walk from central Noto. The walls are thick and whitewashed, the decor simple but elegant, and the atmosphere pleasantly old-fashioned.

🚪 6 🅿 ⬛ 🕐 Closed Nov.– March 💳 All major cards

🍴 CROCIFISSO
$$
VIA PRINCIPE UMBERTO 46–48
TEL 0931 571 151
ristorantecrocifisso.it

A taste of old Sicily, this simple, family-run trattoria is located in the upper town. Also good is the similar **Carmine,** with full meals, snacks, and pizzas (*Via Ducezio 1a, tel 0931 838 705, closed Mon. & Nov.– mid-March*). On the same street is **Mandolfiore** (*Via Ducezio 2, tel 0931 836 615*), the best place in town for cakes and pastries.

🔲 48 🕐 Closed Wed., after Easter, & Sept.
🆑 All major cards

RAGUSA

🏨 EREMO DELLA
🍴 GIUBILIANA
$$$$$ ★★★★★
CONTRADA GIUBILIANA
TEL 0932 669 119
FAX 0932 669 129
eremodellagiubiliana.it
This converted 15th-century monastery sits 4.3 miles (7 km) south of Ragusa, off the SP25. Don't be put off by the barren landscape nearby; inside this exclusive complex the grounds are verdant and the rooms wonderful. There is a fine restaurant ($$$$), a hotel beach, and a private boat and airstrip for special excursions.

📶 Free 🅣 15 (plus 3 suites)
🔲 130 (inside), 70 (outside)
🅿 🆑 🆑 🆑 All major cards

🏨 LOCANDA DON
SERAFINO
$$$$ ★★★★
VIA XI FEBBRAIO 15
TEL 0932 220 065
locandadonserafino.it
This charming and intimate boutique-style hotel occupies part of an 18th-century palace at the heart of old Ragusa Ibla. Some rooms are small, so opt for a suite, and don't miss the co-owned restaurant of the same name nearby (Via Avvocato Ottaviano 39, tel 0932 248 778, closed Tues. & parts of Feb. & Nov.). Sophisticated cooking earned it a Michelin star in 2011 and a second in 2014–15.

📶 Free 🅣 10 🆑 🆑 All major cards

🍴 DUOMO
$$$$$
VIA CAPITANO BOCCHIERI 31
TEL 0932 651 265
cicciosultano.it
The Duomo is one of Sicily's best restaurants: elegant, intimate, sophisticated, and beautifully situated in front of the cathedral in old Ragusa. It earned two Michelin stars in 2011, retained in 2015. The wine list is excellent and the cooking assured and based on the best of the old and new.

🔲 50 🆑 🕐 Closed parts of Jan., July, & Nov.; L Sun. & Mon. from May–Sept. (except Aug. when closed L Mon., Thurs. & Sun. only); D on Sun. & Mon. rest of the year
🆑 V, MC

🍴 VINI E CUCINA
$$–$$$
VIA ORFANOTROFIO 91
TEL 0932 686 447
An informal alternative to old Ragusa's expensive dining options, family-run Vini e Cucina has a pretty vaulted interior (and outdoor tables in summer) and meat and fish menus that offer local specialties you'll find nowhere else. On the same street is Il Barocco (Via Orfanotrofio 29, tel 0932 652 397, closed Wed.), less expensive and with the option of pizza from a wood-fired oven. Orfeo (Via Sant'Anna 117, tel 0932 621 035, closed Sun.), in business since 1935, is the best dining option in the "new" town.

🅣 40 (inside), 45 (outside)
🆑 🕐 Closed Wed. & parts of Feb. 🆑 All major cards

SCICLI

🏨 CLUB BAIA SAMUELE
🍴 **$$$$ ★★★★**
LOCALITÀ PUNTA SAMPIERI
TEL 0932 848 111
FAX 0932 939 725
hotelbaiasamuele.it
On a cypress-dotted hillside a half mile (1 km) from Scicli and close to the sea, this large village-style resort will not appeal to all tastes, but the tennis courts, private beach,

and many other facilities are perfect for an activity-oriented or beach-based interlude. **Novecento** (Via Dupré 11, tel 0932 843 817, hotel900 .it) offers a four-star, 9-room alternative in the town's historic center.

📶 Free 🅣 244 🆑 🅿 🆑 🆑
🆑 All major cards

MODICA

🏨 PALAZZO FAILLA
🍴 **$$$$ ★★★★**
VIA BLANDINI 5
TEL 0932 941 059
FAX 0932 941 059
E-MAIL info@palazzofailla.it
OR direzione@palazzofailla.it
palazzofailla.it
Antiques and frescoes adorn this beautifully restored palazzo, which dates from 1780, with a plainer restaurant, **La Gazza Ladro** (Via Blandini 11, tel 0932 755 655, closed Nov.–mid-March, except Aug., Mon., & L Tues.–Fri.), which has earned a Michelin star. The hotel also owns a smaller, less expensive, but no less tempting trattoria, **La Locanda del Colonnello** (Vico Biscari 6, tel 0932 752 423, locandadel colonnello.it, closed Wed. & Nov.– early March).

📶 Free 🅣 10 🅿 🆑 🆑 All major cards

🍴 FATTORIA DELLE TORRI
$$$$
VICO NAPOLITANO 14
TEL 0932 751 286
fattoriadelletorri.it
An old structure in the historic center whose single dining room has been tastefully reworked in a modern idiom. Cooking is traditionally based but can be elaborate, namely in dishes such as tortelli pasta stuffed with swordfish. Excellent wine list.

🔲 40 (inside), 20 (outside)
🆑 🕐 Closed Mon. Sept.–June
🆑 All major cards

🍴 TAVERNA NICASTRO
$–$$
VIA SANT'ANTONINO 30
TEL 0932 945 884
This restaurant in the lower town has been run by the Nicastro family in Modica Alta since 1948, with a tradition of simple country meat and other dishes, many unique to the Modica region. Up in the old town, tiny simple **Basilico** *(Corso Mazzini 2, tel 349 356 5057)* also offers good, inexpensive meals. **Bonajuto** *(Corso Umberto I 159, bonajuto.it),* a confectioner founded in 1880 is also worth a visit; one of the specialties is *'mpanatigghi,* candy made from minced meat and chocolate.
🪑 80 (inside), 40 (outside)
🕐 Closed L, Sun.–Mon., & a week in mid-Aug. 🏵 All major cards

▬ EASTERN SICILY

TAORMINA

🏨 🍴 BELMOND GRAND HOTEL TIMEO
$$$$$ *****L
VIA TEATRO GRECO 59
TEL 0942 627 0200
TOLL-FREE IN U.S. & CANADA
TEL 800 237 1236
FAX 0942 627 0606
E-MAIL frontdeskght@belmond.com
belmond.com/grand-hotel-timeo-taormina
Better value than the famous San Domenico (see this page), the Timeo has a superb terrace setting in its own peaceful park, close to the Greek theater. Rooms in the elegant and sophisticated 1873 villa are spacious and bright, and all have balconies and views of Mount Etna or the sea. **The Restaurant** has earned a good reputation and, like **The Literary Terrace & Bar,** has a panoramic terrace.

📶 Free ⓘ 70
🅿 ⊟ 🏵 ⊠ 📺 🕐 Closed mid-Nov.–late March 🏵 All major cards

🏨 🍴 SAN DOMENICO PALACE
$$$$$ *****L
PIAZZA SAN DOMENICO 5
TEL 0942 613 111
FAX 0942 625 506
E-MAIL res.sandomenico@amthotels.it
san-domenico-palace.com
The great and the good, the famous and infamous, have all stayed at the San Domenico, a converted 15th-century monastery and one of Italy's most celebrated hotels. Its reputation may be overstated, but the vast public spaces, gardens, wonderful rooms, Old World patina, and sense of history and decorum are above reproach. Its main restaurant, **Principe Cerami** *(closed L & Mon. April–Oct.)* had two Michelin stars as of 2014–15.
ⓘ 97 (plus 8 suites) 🅿 ⊟ 🏵 ⊠ 📺 🏵 All major cards

🏨 VILLA BELVEDERE
$$$$ ****
VIA BAGNOLI CROCE 79
TEL 0942 23 791
FAX 0942 625 830
E-MAIL info@villabelvedere.it
villabelvedere.it
Panoramic views distinguish this comfortable and pleasant hotel, situated amid palms and olives a little east of the town center near the public gardens.
📶 Free ⓘ 49
🅿 ⊟ 🏵 ⊠ 🕐 Closed mid-Nov.–mid-March except around Christmas
🏵 All major cards

🏨 VILLA DUCALE
$$$$ ****
VIA LEONARDO DA VINCI 60
TEL 0942 28 153
FAX 0942 28 710
E-MAIL info@villaducale.com
villaducale.com
As pleasing as the Villa Schuler (see this page) but more pricey, the Villa Ducale is a romantic hotel, with period furnishings, rooms with balconies and views, and congenial service. It is a ten-minute (uphill) walk from the town center.
📶 Free ⓘ 11 (plus 6 suites)
🕐 Closed mid-Jan.–mid-Feb.
🅿 🏵 🏵 All major cards

🏨 BEL SOGGIORNO
$$ ***
VIA PIRANDELLO 60
TEL 0942 23 342
FAX 0942 626 298
E-MAIL info@belsoggiorno.com
belsoggiorno.com
This garden-ringed hotel is situated in a peaceful and scenic corner, just east of the center off the town's main approach road.
📶 Free ⓘ 30 🅿 ⊟ 🏵 🏵 All major cards

🏨 VILLA SCHULER
$$–$$$ ***
PIAZZETTA BASTIONE-VIA ROMA
TEL 0942 23 481
FAX 0942 23 522
E-MAIL info@hotelvillaschuler.com
hotelvillaschuler.com
First choice among the less expensive hotels, this is a small, family-run gem of a place to stay. Just a two-minute walk from Piazza Umberto I, it offers lovely views, fine service, and comfortable rooms, many with small balconies.
📶 Free ⓘ 27
🅿 ⊟ 🏵 🕐 Closed mid-Nov.–early March 🏵 All major cards

🍴 CASA GRUGNO
$$$$$
VIA SANTA MARIA DEI GRECI
TEL 0942 21 208
This one-Michelin-star restaurant occupies a lovely historic building, and offers a sophisticated menu of classic Italian and international dishes. There is just one intimate dining

room, so make reservations.
🍴 35 (inside), 40 (outside)
🕐 Closed L, Sun., & early
Jan.–early March 🅂
🅂 All major cards

🍴 LA GIARA
$$$$$
VICO LA FLORESTA 1
TEL 0942 23 360
lagiarataormina.com
Expensive, large, and decidedly
upscale, with elaborate food
and service. In addition, the
draws here are the panoramic
terrace and the restaurant's
historical associations: Ava
Gardner and other stars dined
and partied here in the 1950s.
🍴 200 (inside), 80 (outside)
🕐 Closed Jan., Sun., & L Aug.
🅂 🅂 All major cards

🍴 AL DUOMO
$$$$
VICO EBREI 11
TEL 0942 625 656
ristorantealduomo.it
A lively restaurant in a small
alley just off the cathedral
square (with outdoor dining
options in summer). Marble
tables and homey atmosphere,
good service, and well-prepared
local meats, fish, and seafood.
🍴 40 (inside), 35 (outside)
🕐 Closed Dec.–Jan. & Mon.
🅂 🅂 All major cards

🍴 'A ZAMMÀRA
$$$$
VIA FRATELLI
BANDIERA 15
TEL 0942 24 408
zammara.it
The attraction here is summer
dining in a lovely garden of
orange and mandarin trees.
Regional Sicilian cuisine and a
particularly good wine list.
🍴 90 (inside), 60 (outside)
🕐 Closed Wed. except
Aug. 🅂 🅂 DC, MC, V

🍴 IL CICLOPE
$$$
CORSO UMBERTO I 201
TEL 0942 23 263

This central, family-run eatery
has maintained fair prices and
basic regional cooking since
1970. Another central, reliable,
low-cost option is family-run
La Piazzetta *(Vico Paladini 5–7,
tel 00942 626 317, ristorante
lapiazzettataormina.it, closed
Mon., Oct.–June, & periods in
Nov., Jan.–Feb.).* Even better
is **Malvasia,** just north of the
Duomo *(Via Apollo Arcageta 8,
tel 340 347 7032).* **Vecchia
Taormina** *(Vico Ebrei 3, tel
0942 625 589)* is the place for
pizza, or nearby **Da Cristina**
*(by the Duomo at Via Strabone
2),* for pizza to go.
🍴 50 (inside), 50 (outside)
🕐 Closed Wed. Nov.–March
& mid-Jan.–Feb. 🅂 🅂 All
major cards

ETNA

🏨 BIANCANEVE
$$ ****
VIA ETNEA 163, NICOLOSI
TEL 095 911 176
FAX 095 911 194
E-MAIL sales@hotel
-biancaneve.com
hotel-biancaneve.com
A large, modern hotel 10 miles
(15 km) from Etna and the
sea, with a pool, sports facili-
ties, and views of the volcano.
Much smaller is the simple,
clean, comfortable, nearby
ten-room **Hotel alle Pendici**
*(Viale delle Regione 18, tel 095
791 4310, hotelallependici.com,
$$).* Out of town, the fine
Corsaro *(Piazza Cantoniera,
Etna Sud, tel 095 914 122, hotel
corsaro.it)* is the highest hotel
on Etna and a perfect base.
🕐 Business Center
🛈 83 🅿 🅂 ⊜ ⊠
🅂 All major cards

🏨 IL NIDO DELL'ETNA
$$ ***
VIA MATTEOTTI, LINGUAGLOSSA
TEL 095 643 404
FAX 095 643 242
E-MAIL info@ilnidodelletna.it
ilnidodelletna.it

Il Nido's stylish, contemporary
design raises it above the
mostly functional, modern
hotels on Etna's slopes. It is
in the town center and has a
family-run charm and a pretty
garden, and some rooms enjoy
views of the volcano.
🕐 Charge 🛈 18 🕐 Closed
part of Nov., restaurant L daily
except Sun. 🅿 🅂 ⊜ 🅂 All
major cards

🏨 SCRIVANO
$ ***
VIA BONAVENTURA 2,
RANDAZZO
TEL 095 921 126
FAX 095 921 433
E-MAIL info@hotelscrivano
.com
hotelscrivano.com
This serviceable hotel-
restaurant at the edge of
Randazzo on the volcano's
northern slopes offers simple,
convenient accommodations.
🛈 30 🅿 ⊜ 🅂 🅂 All major
cards

🏨 PARCO DELL'ETNA
$ **
CONTRADA BORGONOVO,
VIA GENERALE DALLA
CHIESA 1, BRONTE
TEL/FAX 095 691 907
hotelparcodelletna.it
A modest hotel with a pool,
built in 1990 on the western
slopes of Mount Etna. Out
of town, a few minutes' drive
north on the SS284, the three-
star **Fucina di Vulcano** *(tel 095
693 730, www.hotelristorantetna
.it)* offers more comforts and
an attractive, rural setting.
🛈 20 🅿 🅂 ⊠ 🅂 All major
cards

🍴 VENEZIANO
$$
VIA DEI ROMANO 8/A,
RANDAZZO
TEL 095 799 1353
ristoranteveneziano.it
This is a typical family-run
trattoria on the edge of

Randazzo with hearty country dishes such as *agnello al forno* (roast lamb) and *zuppa di funghi* (mushroom soup). In the old center, **San Giorgio e Il Drago** (*Piazza San Giorgio 28, tel 095 923 972, closed Tues. & part of Jan.*) is a first-rate trattoria, with outside dining in summer.

100 Closed Mon. All major cards

■ NORTHERN SICILY

ISOLE EOLIE

LIPARI

A' PINNATA
$$$$$ ★★★★
BAIA PIGNATARO
TEL 090 981 1697
FAX 090 981 4782
E-MAIL **pinnata@pinnata.it**
pinnata.it
Room terraces in this smart and intimate hotel offer views along much of Lipari's eastern coast.

Charge 12
Closed Nov.–March
 All major cards

HOTEL RESIDENCE
ACQUACALDA
$$$
VIA LUNGOMARE DI
ACQUACALDA
TEL 090 988 0201
OR 331 424 2602
residenceacquacalda.it
This charming seafront hotel is located in a quiet village just 15 minutes' drive from Lipari town and the ferry terminal (free transfers can be arranged through the hotel). Most of the bright, clean rooms have terraces and fine sea views (ground-floor rooms look onto a garden, with the sea beyond), and the apartment suites have kitchens or kitch-enettes. Scooter and car hire

are available and the hotel is linked to the well-priced **Al Tramonto** (*Via Mazzini, tel 090 982 1094*) restaurant nearby, which has a panoramic terrace; half-board arrangements are possible here; otherwise the hotel offers breakfast only.

Free in common areas
20 All major cards

ORIENTE
$$ ★★★
VIA MARCONI 35
TEL 090 981 1493
FAX 090 988 0198
E-MAIL **info@hoteloriente lipari.com**
hotelorientelipari.it
A modern hotel in a quiet area just five minutes from the port. Rooms are bright, the lobby eccentric, and there is a shady garden terrace.

Free 32 Closed Nov.–Easter All major cards

E' PULERA
$$$$
VILLA ISABELLA CONTI
TEL 090 981 1158
FAX 090 981 2878
eolieexperience.it
E' Pulera offers often exceptional Eolian cooking, with two dining rooms, and garden and pergola for summer dining. The same owners run the larger but similarly priced **Filippino** (*Piazza Mazzini, tel 090 981 1002, closed parts of Nov. & Dec. & Mon. except April–Sept.*), a well-known, informal eatery, opened in 1910, where the cooking is just as good.

80 Closed L & Feb.–April or May DC, MC, V

LA NASSA
$$$$
VIA G FRANZA 36
TEL 090 981 1319
FAX 090 981 2257
lanassa.it
Another reliable restaurant,

also known for Eolian special-ties, with a fine terrace for alfresco dining. For snacks in town, visit **Gilberto e Vera** (*Via Garibaldi 22*).

45 (inside), 70 (outside)
 Closed Nov.–May & L except July–Aug. All major cards

PANAREA

LA PIAZZA
$$$–$$$$$ ★★★
VIA SAN PIETRO
TEL 090 983 154
FAX 090 983 649
E-MAIL **info@hotelpiazza.it**
hotelpiazza.it
This comfortable 1970s hotel near the sea has been recently renovated. Each simple room has a private terrace or bal-cony, and the pool and garden are superb. As with many Eolian hotels, you may have to take half- or full-board in summer—hence the pricey rating. The nearby **Cincotta** (*tel 090 983 014, hotelcincotta .it*) is similar and has a good restaurant.

Free 31
 Closed mid-Oct.–March All major cards

SALINA

SIGNUM
$$$–$$$$$ ★★★★
VIA SCALO 8, MALFA
TEL 090 984 4222
FAX 090 984 4102
E-MAIL **info@hotelsignum.it**
hotelsignum.it
A lovely and quiet hotel, the Eolian-styled Signum has a divine pool and garden, lots of antiques, and rooms with balconies or terraces.

Free 30 Closed mid-Nov.–mid-March
 All major cards

VULCANO

LES SABLES NOIRS
$$$$$ ★★★★

 Hotel   Restaurant   Wi-Fi   No. of Guest Rooms   No. of Seats   Parking   Closed   Elevator

PORTO DI PONENTE
TEL 090 9850
FAX 090 985 2454
E-MAIL info@
hotelvulcanosicily.com
hotelvulcanosicily.com
Vulcano's oldest and best hotel is a typical two-story Mediterranean building by a black-sand beach, from which it takes its name.
🛏 45 (plus 3 suites)
🕐 Closed Nov.–March
🅿 🍽 ❄ ⛱ 🞉 All major cards

LE MADONIE

🏨 POMIERI
$$ ★★
CONTRADA POMIERI, POLIZZI GENEROSA
TEL 0921 649 998
FAX 0921 649 855
hotelpomieri.jimdo.com
The Pomieri offers simple lodgings high in the mountains. Its dining room makes a good stop for lunch if you are touring the area.
🛏 40 🕐 Closed 3 weeks in Sept. 🞉 No credit cards

🏨 BERGI
🍽 $
CONTRADA BERGI, CASTELBUONO (OFF SS286)
TEL 0921 672 045
FAX 0921 676 877
E-MAIL info@agriturismo bergi.com
agriturismobergi.com
This peaceful, rural retreat *(agriturismo)* lies amid orchards and olive groves 11 miles (18 km) south of Castelbuono, toward Geraci Siculo. Rooms are simply designed but pleasing, and much of the food served here is organic and homegrown.
📶 Free 16 🅿 ❄ 🞉 No credit cards

🏨 PIANO TORRE PARK
🍽 $ ★★★
PIANO TORRE, NEAR ISNELLO

TEL 0921 662 671
FAX 0921 662 672
E-MAIL pianotorre@libero .it
pianotorreparkhotel.com
In an area with few accommodations, this is a reliable, country retreat 5 miles (8 km) from Isnello, a small Madonie village that is also convenient to Cefalù. The garden and large restaurant (worth a visit in its own right) are good, and there are tennis courts and other sports and outdoor facilities. The **Relais Santa Anastasia** *(tel 0921 672 233, abbaziasantanastasia.com)*, in a converted 12th-century abbey 5 miles (8 km) from Castelbuono, offers another good but more expensive base.
🛏 27 🛏 350 (inside), 50 (outside) 🅿 🍽 ❄ ⛱ 🞉 All major cards

🍽 NANGALARRUNI
$$$$
VIA DELLE CONFRATERNITE 10, CASTELBUONO
TEL 0921 671 428
hostarianangalarruni.it
The Sicilian cuisine served at this attractive beamed and exposed-brick restaurant is some of the very best in the Madonie—as well as beyond. There's also a very good wine list. A less expensive and more basic option in the village is **Vecchio Palmento** *(Via Failla 4, tel 0921 672 099, closed Mon. & part of Sept.)*, which also is a good place to enjoy pizza.
🛏 100 (inside), 20 (outside)
❄ 🕐 Closed Wed. except in Aug. 🞉 All major cards

🍽 ITRIA
$$
VIA BEATO GNOFFI 8, POLIZZI GENEROSA
TEL 0921 688 790
This traditional trattoria serves robust mountain food (the village sits above 3,300 feet/1,000 m) that capitalizes on regional ingredients such as

cinghiale (wild boar) and *funghi* (mushrooms). Close to the eastern edge of the village, the simple, rustic **U Bagghiu** *(Via Gagliardo 3, tel 0921 55 1111, ristoranteubagghiu.it)* is a good place to eat.
🛏 50 (inside), 30 (outside)
🕐 Closed Wed. & for a break in the fall 🞉 V

CEFALÙ

🏨 KALURA
$$ ★★★
VIA VINCENZO CAVALLARO 13
TEL 0921 421 354
FAX 0921 423 122
hotel-kalura.com
About a mile (1.5 km) east of central Cefalù, this hotel occupies a superb position above the sea (with its own beach), and offers gracious rooms, tennis, and other sports facilities. For something more intimate in a green setting on the edge of town, there is the pretty B&B **Ai Mulini Resort** *(Via dei Mulini 22, tel 320 749 8564)*.
📶 Business Center 🛏 75
🅿 🍽 ❄ ⛱ 🞉 All major cards

🍽 LA BRACE
$$$
VIA XXV NOVEMBRE 10
TEL 0921 423 570
ristorantelabrace.com
Classic Sicilian cooking has been honed here for more than 20 years. Try the *bruschette di pesce* (toasts with fish), *spaghetti all'aglio* (pasta with garlic and chili), and cannoli for dessert. The **Osteria del Duomo** *(Via Seminario 5, tel 0921 421 838, osteriadelduomo .it, closed Mon.)*, in the shadow of the Duomo, is another safe bet.
🛏 50 ❄ 🕐 Closed Mon., L Tues., & mid-Dec.–mid-Jan.
🞉 All major cards

Shopping

Shopping is one of the great pleasures of visiting Sicily. From the smallest village in the mountains to the grandest streets of Palermo, the island's stores offer superb foods and wines, wonderful clothes, precious art and antiques, fine shoes and other leather goods, and a distinctive and colorful array of quality craft products.

Stores

Many Sicilian stores are small, family-run affairs, even in Palermo. Most neighborhoods have their own baker (panificio), fruit seller (fruttivendolo), butcher (macellaio), and food shop (alimentari). Shops for pastry and homemade candy (pasticceria) are plentiful. Department stores and supermarkets are found only in the largest centers.

Markets

Most towns and cities have at least one street market (mercato), usually open every day but Sunday from early a.m. to early p.m. Smaller towns may have a market operating on a similar schedule.

What to Buy

Wine is an emerging specialty (see pp. 20–21). Many of the island's regions and towns also have outstanding local foods, notably cheeses, oils, dried or candied fruits, cakes, sun-dried tomatoes, capers, and artichokes.

Sicily's antiques shops are full of treasures large and small, while ceramics top the list of crafts made here. Coral and turquoise jewelry are good buys on the west coast, and lace and embroidery can be found in Palermo and smaller inland towns. Rugs are a specialty of Erice, and straw and cane goods are made in Monreale. Most larger city stores will handle packing and shipping.

In general, the more fashionable shopping districts of Palermo, Taormina, and other resorts offer the high-quality clothes, lingerie, fabrics, jewelry, kitchenware, and design objects for which Italy is known.

Opening Hours

Most small shops open 8 a.m. or 9 a.m.–1 p.m. and 3:30 p.m.– 8 p.m. Shops in city centers and tourist areas may stay open all day. Virtually all stores close on Sunday, and most have a closing day. Some may also close for a half day, usually Monday a.m., or, in the case of many food stores, Wednesday p.m.

Payment

Supermarkets and department stores usually accept credit cards and traveler's checks, as do larger clothing and shoe stores. But cash is required at virtually all small food and other shops.

Exports

Many products include a value-added tax known as IVA. Non–European Union residents can claim an IVA refund for purchases over 155 euros made in one establishment and on any single day. Inform the store you hope to reclaim IVA. Have your passport and ask for invoices showing individual articles and tax amounts. Keep all receipts and invoices and have them stamped at the customs office at your airport of departure or at the point of exit from EU territory if you are going beyond Italy. You have 90 days to mail the invoice to the store, though it is easier to make the claim at the Tax Free Office in the last EU airport of your trip.

Forms, receipts—and sometimes the goods—must be shown. Refunds are given on the spot as cash or credits to your credit card account. Stores belonging to the Tax-Free Shopping

System can issue a "tax-free check" for the amount of the rebate, which can be cashed at the Tax Free Office.

AGRIGENTO

Caffè Concordia, Piazza Pirandello 36–37, tel 0922 25 894. Visit for cakes and pastries. **Salumeria del Buon Sapore,** Via dei Cappuccini 20, tel 0925 26 562. Excellent for food and wine.

CEFALÙ

A Lumera, Corso Ruggero 180, tel 0921 921 801. You'll find an excellent selection of ceramics from across Sicily. **Sapori di Sicilia,** Via Vittorio Emanuele II 93, tel 0921 422 871, and **Capriccio Siciliano,** Via Umberto I 22, tel 0921 42 0550. Fine gourmet food and wine.

ENNA

Sicilia Outlet Village, just off the A19 autostrada, 20 minutes from Enna, tel 0935 95 0040. An outlet village with about 100 Italian-label fashion and other stores.

ERICE

Crafts are the best buy in Erice. **Altieri,** Via Antonio Cordici 14, tel 0923 869 431. In business since 1881, Altieri offers fine gold, coral, and ceramics. **Laboratorio Ceramiche d'Arte,** Via Tommaso Guarrasi 18, tel 0923 869 383. Excellent ceramics. **Pasticceria Grammatico Maria,** Via Vittorio Emanuele II 4 and 14, Via Guarnotta 1, tel 0923 869 390. Traditional cakes and candies.

FAVIGNANA

La Casa del Tonno, Via Roma 12, tel 0923 922 227. Tuna products on an island known for tuna.

LIPARI

Laise Delizie, Corso Vittorio Emanuele II 118, 090 981 2731. A wide selection of wine, honey, herbs, and items from the Isole Eolie. **Subba,** Corso Vittorio Emanuele II 92, tel 090 981 2731. Great spot for cakes and pastries.

PALERMO

Palermo has Sicily's largest selection of stores. Tiny Via Bara all'Olivella is the street for arts and crafts, along with Via Calderai. Designer Italian names line Via della Libertà and nearby streets such as Via Enrico Parisi. Via Roma, Via Maqueda, Via Ruggero Settimo, and pedestrians-only Via Principe di Belmonte are also major shopping streets.

Arts & Crafts
Angela Tripi
Corso Vittorio Emanuele II 450–52, tel 091 651 2787. Excellent source for terra-cotta figurines.

Gramuglia
Via Roma 412, tel 091 583 262. Palermo's most sumptuous fabrics, fringes, tassels, and other home accessories are found here.

Vincenzo Argento
Corso Vittorio Emanuele II 445, tel 091 611 3680. The Argento family has been making Palermo's puppets for more than 160 years.

Food & Wine
Bar Costa
Via Gabriele d'Annunzio 15, tel 091 345 652. Worth a visit for the fabulous cakes and pastries, as

is **Alba,** Piazza Don Bosco 7c/d, tel 091 309 016, also known for its fine coffee.

Bottega della Salute
Via Goethe 15, tel 091 334 690. A tempting store that sells a wide range of natural foods, cosmetics made from natural ingredients, and healthy and organic products.

Enoteca Picone
Via G. Marconi 36, tel 091 331 300. A family business since 1946, with more than 4,000 Sicilian and international wines.

I Peccatucci di Mamma Andrea
Via Principe di Scordia 67, tel 091 334 835. High-quality, homemade jams, cakes, honeys, and other gourmet foods, beautifully displayed and packaged.

Jewelers
Di Bella
Via Carini 22, tel 091 328 031. Along with the top names in watches, they offer fine rings, necklaces, and other jewelry.

Piazza Meli
This square near the Cala has several silversmiths and jewelers.

Hats
La Coppola Storta
Via Bara all'Olivella 74, tel 091 324 4428. Produces and sells Sicilian caps once associated with the Mafia. Now a unique and fashionable Sicilian souvenir.

Markets
Ballarò
Fruit, vegetables, fabrics, and household items sold in streets around Piazza del Carmine.

Del Capo
This famous market near Via Porta

Carini and Sant'Agostino features clothes, shoes, and fabrics.

I Lattarini
The name comes from the Arabic words for grocery market, but this is now a place for clothing and household goods, near Via Calderai.

Mercato delle Pulci
This flea market is located behind the cathedral and between Piazza Peranni and Corso Amedeo.

Vucciria
Palermo's oldest food and general market fills the streets around Piazza Caracciolo.

SCIACCA

Sciacca is known for its ceramics and in particular the work of ceramicist Gaspare Gatti, whose pieces can be seen around town. **Gaspare Patti,** Corso Vittorio Emanuele II 95, tel 0925 993 298, and **Cascio,** Corso Vittorio Emanuele II 115, tel 0925 82 829, sells a variety of local ceramics.

SYRACUSE

Massimo Izzo, Piazza Archimede 25, tel 0931 223 301. Dramatic jewelry, some made from local coral. A **market** *(closed Sun.)* is held in Ortygia near the Tempio di Apollo.

TAORMINA

Narcisse, Umberto I 33, tel 0942 23 915. Beautiful perfumer and herbalist. **La Torinese,** Corso Umberto I 59, tel 0942 23 321. A first-rate delicatessen—around since 1936. **Il Quadrifoglio,** Corso Umberto I 153, tel 0942 23 545, and **Stroscio,** Corso Umberto I 18 and 169, tel 0942 24 865, both offer beautiful, expensive antique and other jewelry and objets d'art.

Entertainment & Activities

Sicily has numerous fascinating and colorful festivals, religious ceremonies, historical pageants, fairs, markets, and local events. Holy Week celebrations in particular are some of the most striking in Europe, and there are several arts and cultural festivals of international renown. Most celebrations, though, are small, local affairs, restricted to a town or village, and often held in honor of a saint, a historic event, or a local product.

If you wish to plan your trip around a major event, be sure to reserve accommodations and make travel arrangements well in advance or you may find that everything is booked. Should that happen, don't worry; you will likely stumble on a *festa,* or small festival, somewhere on the island, especially around Easter time or during the summer.

Most smaller religious and other festivals follow a pattern similar to the large events, beginning with processions, in which participants often dress in traditional costume, followed by church services, traditional songs and dances, fireworks, and lots of eating and drinking.

Watch for flyers advertising a festa or *sagra* (a food or wine fair). You can also consult local visitor information centers or their websites for details of upcoming events. Also visit festedisicilia.it.

Easter & Carnival

Holy Week celebrations held throughout Sicily are truly extraordinary events well worth witnessing. Most towns and villages hold dramatic processions and *misteri* (scenes from Christ's Passion), often with robed and hooded penitents and confraternities in torch-lit parade.

The most famous and striking of these celebrations are at **Agrigento, Alcamo, Caltanissetta, Enna** (the Good Friday procession here is quite remarkable), **Erice, Marsala, Messina, Noto, Piana degli Albanesi, Ragusa, Scicli,** and **Trapani.** Most events take place on Good Friday.

Carnival celebrations (pre-Lent festivities usually held in late Feb.) are especially colorful at **Acireale, Sciacca,** and **Palazzolo Acreide.**

Art & Music

Concerts and performances of classical drama as well as ballet are held at the Greek theater in **Syracuse** *(May–June, box office tel 800 542 644 toll-free in Italy; information tel 0931 487 200 or 0931 487 201, indafondazione.org)* and at the ancient theaters in **Segesta** and **Taormina** *(June–August).*

Taormina's premier cultural events are part of an important, summerlong arts festival, Taormina Arte *(Corso Umberto I 19, tel 0942 21 142, taormina-arte.com).* The town also hosts a prestigious international film festival in June or July *(taorminafilmfest.it).*

Other summer arts, theater, and music festivals take place annually in **Catania, Enna, Erice** (medieval and Renaissance music festival during 2nd week of July), **Gibellina** (Orestiadi festival), **Noto,** and **Trapani** (Estate Musicale Trapanese; *lugliomusicale.it).*

Marsala hosts many cultural events throughout the summer, and **Monreale** has a music festival in the cathedral during November *(festivalmusicaeartesacra.net).* December sees a festival of music played on traditional instruments at **Erice.**

There is also—usually—an annual festival of plays (in Italian), written by Luigi Pirandello and performed at his birthplace at **Caos,** near Agrigento (see sidebar p. 93).

Calendar of Events

January
Epiphany
Byzantine-Orthodox Festa della Teofana celebrations in Piana degli Albanesi (Jan. 6)

San Sebastiano
Saint's day celebrations in Syracuse, Acireale, and Mistretta (Jan. 20)

February
Sagra della Mandorla
Festival of the Almond Blossom with folklore and cultural events in Agrigento (late Jan.–early Feb.)

Sant'Agata
Major procession and saint's day celebrations in Catania (Feb. 3–5)

Carnevale
Carnival events and celebrations across Sicily (the week before Ash Wed.)

San Corrado
Saint's day celebrations in Noto (Feb. 19)

March
Cavalcata di San Giuseppe
Saint's day celebrations and procession in Scicli. Celebrations also held in Salemi and Santa Croce Camertina (March 18–19)

April
Easter
Events, processions, and services in towns and villages across Sicily (see Easter & Carnival, this page)

Maundy Thursday
Processions in Marsala and
Caltanissetta (Thurs. before
Easter)

San Giorgio
Parades in Ragusa and Piana degli
Albanesi (April 23)

May
Santissimo Crocifisso
Celebrations in Isnello in the
Madonie Mountains (April 31–
May 1)

Santa Lucia
Feast of St. Lucy celebrations
in Syracuse (1st & 2nd Sun.)

Infiorata
Flower festival in Noto (3rd Sun.)

Battaglia delle Milizie
Procession in period costume in
Scicli (end of the month)

Corpus Domini
Festa della Frottola in Cefalù
(May or early June)

San Giorgio
St. George celebrations in Ragusa
Ibla (last Sun.)

Sfilata del Carretto Siciliano
Traditional painted carts and
puppet shows in Taormina (last
3 days of the month)

June
La Mattanza
Monthlong ritual killing of tuna in
Favignana (see pp. 82–83)

Madonna della Lettera
Religious celebrations in Messina
(June 3)

Festa del Mare
Festival of the Sea in Sciacca
(June 27–29)

SS. Pietro e Paolo
Celebrations honoring St. Peter

and St. Paul in Modica, Palazzolo
Acreide, and Pantelleria (June 29)

July
Santa Venera
Weeklong saint's festival in
Acireale (from 1st Sun.)

San Calogero
Folklore and religious festival in
Agrigento (1st Sun.)

Madonna della Visitazione
Religious festival in Enna
(July 2)

U Fistinu
Spectacular festival to honor
St. Rosalia in Palermo
(July 14–15)

Festa di Giacomo Celebrations
and illuminations in Caltagirone
(July 24–25)

August
Palio del Mare
Boat procession and races in
Syracuse (1st Sun.)

Festa di San Salvatore
Religious celebration in Cefalù
(Aug. 2–6)

Festa della Spiga
Corn festival with music, theater,
and dance in Gangi (2nd week)

Madonna della Luce
Procession of boats in Cefalù
(Aug. 14)

Palio dei Normanni
Major festival with jousting
in medieval costume in Piazza
Armerina (Aug. 13–14)

Festa di San Bartolomeo
Saint's festival with offshore
fireworks in Lipari (Aug. 21–24)

San Giovanni Battista
Celebration honoring St. John the
Baptist in Ragusa, the culmination

of a monthlong festival of folklore
in the Iblei region (Aug. 29)

San Corrado
Religious festival in Noto (last
Sun. of Aug. and 1st Sun. of Sept.)

September
Madonna delle Lacrime
Religious festival and pilgrimage
in Syracuse (Aug. 29–Sept. 3)

La Madonna di Porto Salvo
Religious festival and procession
in Lampedusa (Sept. 22)

Festival del Cuscus
Celebration of Sicilian food, plus
workshops and music (six days
in Sept.)

October
Festa di Sant'Angelo
Religious festival in Vulcano
(Oct. 2)

Festa del Pistacchio
Festival celebrating pistachio
harvest in Bronte (early Oct.)

Ottobrata Zafferanese
Autumn food festival in Zafferana
Etnea (each Sun. of the month)

November
Festa dei Morti
All Souls toy fair and children's
festival in Palermo (Nov. 1–2)

December
Festival di Morgana International
puppet festival in Palermo (end of
Nov.–mid-Dec.)

Immacolata
Religious festival in Syracuse
(Dec. 8)

Santa Lucia
St. Lucy saint's day festival and
procession in Syracuse (Dec. 13)

Language Guide

Italians respond well to foreigners who make an effort to speak their language. Many Italians speak at least some English, and more upscale hotels and restaurants have multilingual staff. All Italian words are pronounced as written with each vowel and consonant sounded. The letter c is hard, as in the English "car," except when followed by i or e, when it becomes the soft ch of "children," as in the toast cin cin. The same applies to g when followed by i or e—soft in buon giorno (as in the English "giant"); hard in grazie as in "gate."

Useful Words & Phrases

Yes Sì
No No
Okay/that's fine/sure Va bene
I don't understand Non capisco
Do you speak English? Parla inglese?
I don't know Non lo so
I would like...Vorrei...
Do you have...? Avete...?
How much is it? Quant'è?
What is it? Che cos'è?
Who? Chi?
What? Quale?
Why? Perchè?
When? Quando?
Where? Dove?
What's the time? Che ore sono?
Good morning Buon giorno
Good afternoon/good evening Buona sera
Good night Buona notte
Hello/good-bye (informal) Ciao
Good-bye Arrivederci
Please Per favore
Thank you Grazie
You're welcome Prego
What's your name? Come si chiama?
My name is... Mi chiamo...
I'm American (man/woman) Sono Americano/ Americana
How are you? (polite/informal) Come sta/stai?
Fine, thanks Bene, grazie
And you? E lei?
I'm sorry Mi dispiace
Excuse me/I beg your pardon Mi scusi
Excuse me (in a crowd) Permesso
good buono
bad cattivo
big grande
small piccolo
with con

cell phone cellulare
without senza
more più
less meno
enough basta
near vicino
far lontano
left sinistra
right destra
straight ahead sempre dritto
hot caldo
cold freddo
early presto
late ritardo
here qui
there là
today oggi
tomorrow domani
yesterday ieri
morning la mattina
afternoon il pomeriggio
evening la sera
entrance entrata
exit uscita
open aperto
closed chiuso
bathroom il bagno
toilet il gabinetto/il bagno
Let's go Andiamo

Emergencies

Help! Aiuto!
Can you help me? Mi puo aiutare?
I'm not well Sto male
Call a doctor Chiamate un medico
Where is the police station? Dov'è la polizia/la questura?
first aid pronto soccorso
hospital l'ospedale

Sightseeing

art gallery la pinacoteca
castle il castello/la fortezza
church la chiesa
garden il giardino
museum il museo

postcard la cartolina
website sito internet or sito web
stamp il francobollo
visitor center l'ufficio di turismo

In the Hotel

hotel un albergo
room una camera
single room una camera singola
double room una camera doppia
e-mail un email
room with private bathroom una camera con bagno
I have a reservation Ho una prenotazione

Shopping

shop/store il negozio
market il mercato
Do you have some...? Avete un po' di...?
this one questo
that one quello
a little poco
a lot tanto
enough abbastanza
too much troppo
Do you accept credit cards? Accetate carte di credito?
expensive caro
cheap a buon prezzo

Stores & Shops

bakery il forno/il panificio
bookstore la libreria
butcher la macelleria/il macellaio
cake store la pasticceria
delicatessen la salumeria/la norcineria
drugstore/pharmacy la farmacia
food store l'alimentari
ice-cream parlor la gelateria
post office l'ufficio postale
supermarket il supermercato
tobacconist il tabaccaio

MENU READER

General

Breakfast **la colazione**
Lunch **il pranzo**
Dinner **la cena**
Waiter **il cameriere**
I'd like to reserve a table **Vorrei riservare una tavola**
Have you a table for two? **Avete una tavola per due?**
I'd like to order **Vorrei ordinare**
I'm a vegetarian **Sono vegetariano/a**
The check, please **Il conto, per favore**
Cover charge **il coperto**
Is service included? **Il servizio è incluso?**

The Menu

l'antipasto appetizer
il primo first course
la zuppa soup
il secondo main course
il contorno vegetable, side dish
insalata salad
la frutta fruit
il formaggio cheese
i dolci sweets/desserts
la lista dei vini wine list

Menu Terms

affumicato smoked
ai ferri, alla griglia grilled
alla Milanese in breadcrumbs
arrosto roasted
bollito boiled
costoletta chop
fritto fried
in umido stewed
ripieno stuffed/filled
stracotto braised, stewed
sugo sauce

Pasta & Sauces

agnolotti large, filled pasta parcels
al pomodoro tomato sauce
amatriciana tomato and bacon sauce
arrabbiata spicy tomato sauce
bolognese veal or beef sauce
cannelloni filled pasta tubes
carbonara cream, ham, and egg sauce
farfalle butterfly-shaped pasta
fettucine flat, thick pasta ribbons

gnocchi potato and dough cubes
lasagne layers of meat, cheese, and pasta
pasta e fagioli pasta and beans
penne tubular pasta
peperoncino oil, garlic, and chili peppers
pesto pine nuts, basil, and cheese
puttanesca tomato, anchovy, oil, and oregano sauce
ragù any meat sauce
ravioli filled pasta parcels
rigatoni large pasta tubes
spaghetti long, thin pasta strands
tagliatelle long, flat pasta ribbons
tagliolini thin pasta ribbons
tortellini filled pasta twists
vongole wine, clams, and parsley

Meats

agnello lamb
anatra duck
bistecca beef steak
cinghiale wild boar
coniglio rabbit
fritto misto mixed grill
maiale pork
manzo beef
ossobuco cut of veal
pancetta pork belly/bacon
pollo chicken
prosciutto cotto cooked ham
salsiccia sausage
saltimbocca veal with ham and sage
trippa tripe
vitello veal

Fish & Seafood

acciughe anchovies
aragosta lobster
baccalà dried salt cod
calamari squid
cappesante scallops
cozze mussels
gamberi prawns
granchio crab
merluzzo cod
ostriche oysters
pesce spada swordfish
polpo octopus
rospo monkfish
salmone salmon
sarde sardines
seppie cuttlefish
sgombro mackerel

sogliola sole
tonno tuna
triglie red mullet
trota trout
vongole clams

Vegetables

aglio garlic
asparagi asparagus
capperi capers
carciofi artichokes
carotte carrots
cavolo cabbage
cipolle onions
fagioli beans
funghi mushrooms
funghi porcini ceps, boletus mushrooms
insalata mista mixed salad
insalata verde green salad
melanzane eggplant
patate potatoes
patate fritte French fries
peperoni peppers
pomodoro tomato
radicchio red salad leaf
rucolo/rughetta rocket arugula
tartufo truffle

Fruit

albicocca apricot
ananas pineapple
arance oranges
banane bananas
ciliegie cherries
ficchi figs
fragole strawberries
limone lemon
mele apples
melone melon
pere pears
pesca peach
pompelmo grapefruit
prugna plum

Drinking

acqua water
una birra beer
una bottiglia bottle
una mezza bottiglia half bottle
caffè coffee
caffè Hag/caffè decaffeinato decaffeinated coffee
latte milk
tè tea
vino wine

INDEX

ILLUSTRATIONS CREDITS

All photographs by Tino Soriano unless otherwise noted below.

National Geographic
TRAVELER
Sicily

Published by the National Geographic Society
Gary E. Knell, *President and Chief Executive Officer*
John M. Fahey, *Chairman of the Board*
Declan Moore, *Chief Media Officer*
Chris Johns, *Chief Content Officer*

Prepared by the Book Division
Hector Sierra, *Senior Vice President and General Manager*
Lisa Thomas, *Senior Vice President and Editorial Director*
Jonathan Halling, *Creative Director*
Marianne R. Koszorus, *Design Director*
Barbara A. Noe, *Senior Editor, Travel Books*
R. Gary Colbert, *Production Director*
Jennifer A. Thornton, *Director of Managing Editorial*
Susan S. Blair, *Director of Photography*
Meredith C. Wilcox, *Director, Administration and Rights Clearance*

Staff for This Book
Justin Kavanagh, *Editor*
Elisa Gibbons, *Art Director*
Ruth Ann Thompson, *Designer*
Moira Haney, *Senior Photo Editor*
Michael McNey and Mapping Specialists Limited, *Map Research and Production*
Marshall Kiker, *Associate Managing Editor*
Mike O'Connor, *Production Editor*
Rock Wheeler, *Rights Clearance Specialist*
Nicole Miller, *Design Production Assistant*
Bobby Barr, *Manager, Production Services*

Area map illustrations drawn by Chris Orr Associates, Southampton, England
Cutaway illustrations drawn by Maltings Partnership, Derby, England

The information in this book has been carefully checked and to the best of our knowledge is accurate. However, details are subject to change, and the National Geographic Society cannot be responsible for such changes, or for errors or omissions. Assessments of sites, hotels, and restaurants are based on the author's subjective opinions, which do not necessarily reflect the publisher's opinion.

The National Geographic Society is one of the world's largest nonprofit scientific and educational organizations. Founded in 1888 to "increase and diffuse geographic knowledge," the member-supported Society works to inspire people to care about the planet. Through its online community, members can get closer to explorers and photographers, connect with other members around the world, and help make a difference. National Geographic reflects the world through its magazines, television programs, films, music and radio, books, DVDs, maps, exhibitions, live events, school publishing programs, interactive media, and merchandise. *National Geographic* magazine, the Society's official journal, published in English and 38 local-language editions, is read by more than 60 million people each month. The National Geographic Channel reaches 440 million households in 171 countries in 38 languages. National Geographic Digital Media receives more than 25 million visitors a month. National Geographic has funded more than 10,000 scientific research, conservation, and exploration projects and supports an education program promoting geography literacy. For more information, visit nationalgeographic.com.

For more information, please call 1-800-NGS LINE (647-5463) or write to the following address:

National Geographic Society
1145 17th Street NW
Washington, D.C. 20036-4688 U.S.A.

For information about special discounts for bulk purchases, please contact National Geographic Books Special Sales: ngspecsales@ngs.org

For rights or permissions inquiries, please contact National Geographic Books Subsidiary Rights: ngbookrights@ngs.org

National Geographic Traveler: Sicily (Fourth Edition)
ISBN: 978-1-4262-1646-6

Printed in Hong Kong
15/THK/1